Deep Learning and XAI Techniques for Anomaly Detection

Integrate the theory and practice of deep anomaly explainability

Cher Simon

<packt>

BIRMINGHAM—MUMBAI

Deep Learning and XAI Techniques for Anomaly Detection

Copyright © 2023 Packt Publishing

All rights reserved. No part of this book may be reproduced, stored in a retrieval system, or transmitted in any form or by any means, without the prior written permission of the publisher, except in the case of brief quotations embedded in critical articles or reviews.

Every effort has been made in the preparation of this book to ensure the accuracy of the information presented. However, the information contained in this book is sold without warranty, either express or implied. Neither the author, nor Packt Publishing or its dealers and distributors, will be held liable for any damages caused or alleged to have been caused directly or indirectly by this book.

Packt Publishing has endeavored to provide trademark information about all of the companies and products mentioned in this book by the appropriate use of capitals. However, Packt Publishing cannot guarantee the accuracy of this information.

Publishing Product Manager: Dhruv Jagdish Kataria
Senior Editor: Tazeen Shaikh
Technical Editor: Devanshi Ayare
Copy Editor: Safis Editing
Project Coordinator: Farheen Fathima
Proofreader: Safis Editing
Indexer: Pratik Shirodkar
Production Designer: Arunkumar Govinda Bhat
Marketing Coordinators: Shifa Ansari and Vinishka Kalra

First published: January 2023
Production reference: 1310123

Published by Packt Publishing Ltd.
Livery Place
35 Livery Street
Birmingham
B3 2PB, UK.

ISBN 978-1-80461-775-5

www.packtpub.com

To my family, for your unconditional love and support. To my readers, thank you for the inspiration and for taking the time to read this book.

– Cher Simon

Foreword

I was delighted to be asked to write the foreword for this interesting and helpful book. In my role as Chief Evangelist for **Amazon Web Services** (**AWS**), I can see that our customers are eager to use machine learning to solve many different types of real-world problems at scale. With access to vast amounts of storage and compute power in the cloud, they are able to take on challenges today that would have been impractical or even impossible just a decade ago.

This book addresses one of those challenges in detail: using all of that storage and compute power to create **machine learning** (**ML**) models that can accurately and efficiently detect anomalies hidden in vast amounts of data.

When I think about anomaly detection, I immediately think of my own intuition, my Spidey-sense that something is not quite right. You know that feeling, that early warning deep inside, where your subconscious seemingly knows something before you do, right? That's your internal anomaly detector at work, using rules and patterns that you might not even realize you have set up.

To me, ML-powered anomaly detection is the scientific, mathematically sound, and scalable version of my inexplicable Spidey-sense. This book will show you how to build anomaly detectors that you can apply to all sorts of mission-critical use cases – fraud detection, predictive machine maintenance, and much more. While it will give you a strong grounding in the theory, it will also show you how to put the theory to work right away. In fact, you will learn how to set up Amazon SageMaker Studio Lab before the end of the fourth page!

Early ML models were black boxes and provided no insights into how they made their predictions. As ML moved from the lab to production, forward-thinking people raised very valid concerns and asked hard questions – how did the model make decisions, is the model biased, and why should we trust it to make mission-critical decisions?

To that end, this book will also bring you up to speed on the important topic of **explainable artificial intelligence**, or **XAI** for short. With millions of parameters and millions of weights, sophisticated models might seem to be beyond human comprehension at first glance. Fortunately, that is not actually the case, and as you work through the examples in each chapter, you will learn how you can use explanations to earn trust with your users, ensure compliance with your objectives, and ensure that your models accurately reflect your business needs.

I hope that you will learn a lot from this book (I know that I did!) and that you will be able to put those lessons to use within days.

Good luck, and let me know how it goes!

Jeff Barr

VP and Chief Evangelist, Amazon Web Services

Contributors

About the author

Cher Simon is a principal solutions architect specializing in artificial intelligence, machine learning, and data analytics at AWS. Cher has 20 years of experience in architecting enterprise-scale, data-driven, and AI-powered industry solutions. Besides building cloud-native solutions in her day-to-day role with customers, Cher is also an avid writer and a frequent speaker at AWS conferences.

About the reviewers

Austen Groener is an applied scientist at AWS living in the greater Boston area. His research and work are focused on developing computer vision and artificial intelligence capabilities for the Amazon Dash Cart. Previously, he was a research scientist at Lockheed Martin Space Systems where he worked within the field of remote sensing and anomaly detection. Austen holds a Ph.D. in physics from Drexel University.

Samet Akcay is an AI research engineer/scientist. His primary research interests are real-time image classification, detection, anomaly detection, and unsupervised feature learning via deep or machine learning algorithms. He recently co-authored and open sourced *anomalib*, one of the largest anomaly detection libraries in the field. Samet holds a Ph.D. degree from the department of computer science at Durham University, UK, and received his M.Sc. degree from the Robust Machine Intelligence Lab at the department of electrical engineering at Penn State University, USA. He has over 30 academic papers published in top-tier computer vision and machine/deep learning conferences and journals.

Aditya Jain is a trained computational scientist from the University of Texas at Austin and IIT Roorkee. He has experience in deploying large-scale machine learning models at organizations such as Meta Platforms, SparkCognition, and Ola Cabs for billions of users. He loves demystifying the workings of machine learning models and answering the question, "What is model learning?" thus making models more interpretable. Aditya Jain is a technologist at heart with an avid interest in solving society's biggest problems using deep learning and artificial intelligence. When he is not researching the latest advances in machine learning, he can be found running a marathon, dancing, or scuba diving. Follow his work at `https://adityajain.in/`.

Table of Contents

Preface   xi

Part 1 – Introduction to Explainable Deep Learning Anomaly Detection

1

Understanding Deep Learning Anomaly Detection   3

Technical Requirements	4	Reducing environmental impact	23
Exploring types of anomalies	4	Recommending financial strategies	23
Discovering real-world use cases	12	Considering when to use deep learning and what for	23
Detecting fraud	13		
Predicting industrial maintenance	21	Understanding challenges and opportunities	25
Diagnosing medical conditions	22		
Monitoring cybersecurity threats	22	Summary	26

2

Understanding Explainable AI   27

Understanding the basics of XAI	28	Reviewing XAI significance	36
Differentiating explainability versus interpretability	31	Considering the right to explanation	36
		Driving inclusion with XAI	37
Contextualizing stakeholder needs	32	Mitigating business risks	39
Implementing XAI	33	Choosing XAI techniques	39
		Summary	40

Part 2 – Building an Explainable Deep Learning Anomaly Detector

3

Natural Language Processing Anomaly Explainability   43

Technical requirements	44	Problem	56
Understanding natural language processing	45	Solution walk-through	57
		Exercise	72
Reviewing AutoGluon	45		

4

Time Series Anomaly Explainability   77

Understanding time series	78	The problem	81
Understanding explainable deep anomaly detection for time series	79	Solution walkthrough	81
		Exercise	96
Technical requirements	80	Summary	97

5

Computer Vision Anomaly Explainability   99

Reviewing visual anomaly detection	100	Integrating deep visual anomaly detection with XAI	102
Reviewing image-level visual anomaly detection	100	Technical requirements	103
Reviewing pixel-level visual anomaly detection	101	Problem	104
		Solution walkthrough	104
		Exercise	120
		Summary	120

Part 3 – Evaluating an Explainable Deep Learning Anomaly Detector

6

Differentiating Intrinsic and Post Hoc Explainability — 123

Technical requirements	124	Understanding post hoc explainability	126
Understanding intrinsic explainability	125	Post hoc global explainability	126
Intrinsic global explainability	125	Post hoc local explainability	126
Intrinsic local explainability	125	Considering intrinsic versus post hoc explainability	133
		Summary	134

7

Backpropagation versus Perturbation Explainability — 135

Reviewing backpropagation explainability	136	Reviewing perturbation explainability	141
Saliency maps	137	LIME	141
		Comparing backpropagation and perturbation XAI	151
		Summary	152

8

Model-Agnostic versus Model-Specific Explainability — 153

Technical requirements	154	Reviewing model-specific explainability	172
Reviewing model-agnostic explainability	154	Interpreting saliency with Guided IG	172
Explaining AutoGluon with Kernel SHAP	155	Choosing an XAI method	178
		Summary	180

9
Explainability Evaluation Schemes 181

Reviewing the System Causability Scale (SCS)	182	Understanding faithfulness and monotonicity	185
Exploring Benchmarking Attribution Methods (BAM)	183	Human-grounded evaluation framework	188
		Summary	189

Index 191

Other Books You May Enjoy 198

Preface

Despite promising advances, the opaque nature of deep learning models makes it difficult to interpret them, which is a drawback for practical deployment and regulatory compliance.

Deep Learning and XAI Techniques for Anomaly Detection shows you state-of-the-art methods that'll help you to understand and address these challenges. By leveraging the **Explainable AI** (**XAI**) and deep learning techniques described in this book, you'll discover how to extract business-critical insights while ensuring fair and ethical analysis.

This practical guide will provide tools and best practices to achieve transparency and interpretability with deep learning models, ultimately establishing trust in your anomaly detection applications. Throughout the chapters, you'll get equipped with XAI and anomaly detection knowledge that'll enable you to embark on a series of real-world projects. Whether you are building computer vision, natural language processing, or time series models, you'll learn how to quantify and assess their explainability.

By the end of this deep learning book, you'll be able to build a variety of deep learning XAI models and perform validation to assess their explainability.

Who this book is for

This book is for anyone who aspires to explore explainable deep learning anomaly detection, tenured data scientists or ML practitioners looking for XAI best practices, or business leaders looking to make decisions on the trade-off between the performance and interpretability of anomaly detection applications. A basic understanding of deep learning and anomaly detection-related topics using Python is recommended to get the most out of this book.

What this book covers

Chapter 1, *Understanding Deep Learning Anomaly Detection*, describes types of anomalies and real-world use cases for anomaly detection. It provides two PyOD example walk-throughs to illustrate fundamental concepts, including challenges, opportunities, and considerations when using deep learning for anomaly detection.

Chapter 2, *Understanding Explainable AI*, covers an overview of XAI, including its evolution since the US **Defense Advanced Research Project Agency** (**DARPA**) initiative, its significance in the *Right to Explanation* and regulatory compliance context, and a holistic approach to the XAI life cycle.

Chapter 3, *Natural Language Processing Anomaly Explainability*, dives deep into finding anomalies within textual data. You will complete two NLP example walk-throughs to detect anomalies using AutoGluon and Cleanlab and explain the model's output using **SHapley Additive exPlanations** (**SHAP**).

Chapter 4, *Time Series Anomaly Explainability*, introduces concepts and approaches to detecting anomalies within time series data. You will build a times series anomaly detector using **Long Short-Term Memory (LSTM)** and explain anomalies using OmniXAI's SHAP explainer.

Chapter 5, *Computer Vision Anomaly Explainability*, integrates visual anomaly detection with XAI. This chapter covers various techniques for image-level and pixel-level anomaly detection. The example walk-through shows how to implement a visual anomaly detector and evaluate discriminative image regions identified by the model using a **Class Activation Map (CAM)** and **Gradient-Weighted Class Activation Mapping (Grad-CAM)**.

Chapter 6, *Differentiating Intrinsic versus Post Hoc Explainability*, discusses intrinsic versus post hoc XAI methods at the local and global levels. The example walk-through further demonstrates the considerations when choosing either approach.

Chapter 7, *Backpropagation versus Perturbation Explainability*, reviews gradient-based backpropagation and perturbation-based XAI methods to determine feature importance for a model's decision. This chapter has two example walk-throughs covering the saliency map and **Local Interpretable Model-Agnostic Explanations (LIME)**.

Chapter 8, *Model-Agnostic versus Model-Specific Explainability*, evaluates how these two approaches work with example walk-throughs using Kernel SHAP and **Guided Integrated Gradients (Guided IG)**. This chapter also outlines a working-backward methodology for choosing the model-agnostic versus the model-specific XAI method, starting with analyzing and understanding stakeholder and user needs.

Chapter 9, *Explainability Evaluation Schemes*, describes fundamental XAI principles recommended by the **National Institute of Standards and Technology (NIST)**. This chapter reviews the existing XAI benchmarking landscape on how to quantify model explainability and assess the extent of interpretability.

To get the most out of this book

You will need a Jupyter environment with Python 3.8+ to run the example walk-throughs in this book. Each sample notebook comes with a `requirement.txt` file that lists the package dependencies. You can experiment with the sample notebooks on Amazon SageMaker Studio Lab (https://aws.amazon.com/sagemaker/studio-lab/). This free ML development environment provides up to 12 hours of CPU or 4 hours of GPU per user session and 15 GiB storage at no cost.

Software/hardware covered in the book	Operating system requirements
Python 3.8+	Windows, macOS, or Linux
TensorFlow 2.11+	Windows, macOS, or Linux
AutoGluon 0.6.1+	Windows, macOS, or Linux
Cleanlab 2.2.0+	Windows, macOS, or Linux

A valid email address is all you need to get started with Amazon SageMaker Studio Lab. You do not need to configure infrastructure, manage identity and access, or even sign up for an AWS account. For more information, please refer to `https://docs.aws.amazon.com/sagemaker/latest/dg/studio-lab-overview.html`. Alternatively, you can try the practical examples on your preferred **Integrated Development Environment** (IDE).

If you are using the digital version of this book, we advise you to type the code yourself or access the code from the book's GitHub repository (a link is available in the next section). Doing so will help you avoid any potential errors related to the copying and pasting of code.

A basic understanding of deep learning and anomaly detection-related topics using Python is recommended. Each chapter comes with example walk-throughs that help you gain hands-on experience, except for *Chapters 2* and *9*, which focus more on conceptual discussions. We suggest running the provided sample notebooks while reading a specific chapter. Additional exercises are available in *Chapters 3*, *4*, and *5* to reinforce your learning.

Download the example code files

You can download the example code files for this book from GitHub at `https://github.com/PacktPublishing/Deep-Learning-and-XAI-Techniques-for-Anomaly-Detection`. If there's an update to the code, it will be updated in the GitHub repository.

We also have other code bundles from our rich catalog of books and videos available at `https://github.com/PacktPublishing/`. Check them out!

Download the color images

We also provide a PDF file that has color images of the screenshots and diagrams used in this book. You can download it here: `https://packt.link/nWeUY`.

Conventions used

There are a number of text conventions used throughout this book.

`Code in text`: Indicates code words in text, database table names, folder names, filenames, file extensions, pathnames, dummy URLs, user input, and Twitter handles. Here is an example: "You can download the `export_food.csv` file from this data repository for the example walk-through."

A block of code is set as follows:

```
df = pd.read_csv('export_food.csv')
data = df[['reviews','ratings']]
data['reviews'] = data['reviews'].str.strip()
data.head(3)
```

> **Tips or important notes**
> Appear like this.

Get in touch

Feedback from our readers is always welcome.

General feedback: If you have questions about any aspect of this book, email us at customercare@packtpub.com and mention the book title in the subject of your message.

Errata: Although we have taken every care to ensure the accuracy of our content, mistakes do happen. If you have found a mistake in this book, we would be grateful if you would report this to us. Please visit www.packtpub.com/support/errata and fill in the form.

Piracy: If you come across any illegal copies of our works in any form on the internet, we would be grateful if you would provide us with the location address or website name. Please contact us at copyright@packt.com with a link to the material.

If you are interested in becoming an author: If there is a topic that you have expertise in and you are interested in either writing or contributing to a book, please visit authors.packtpub.com.

Share Your thoughts

Once you've read *Deep Learning and XAI Techniques for Anomaly Detection*, we'd love to hear your thoughts! Scan the QR code below to go straight to the Amazon review page for this book and share your feedback.

`https://packt.link/r/1-804-61775-X`

Your review is important to us and the tech community and will help us make sure we're delivering excellent quality content.

Download a free PDF copy of this book

Thanks for purchasing this book!

Do you like to read on the go but are unable to carry your print books everywhere?

Is your eBook purchase not compatible with the device of your choice?

Don't worry, now with every Packt book, you get a DRM-free PDF version of that book at no cost.

Read anywhere, any place, on any device. Search, copy, and paste code from your favorite technical books directly into your application.

The perks don't stop there; you can get exclusive access to discounts, newsletters, and great free content in your inbox daily,

Follow these simple steps to get the benefits:

1. Scan the QR code or visit the link below:

    https://packt.link/free-ebook/9781804617755

2. Submit your proof of purchase.
3. That's it! We'll send your free PDF and other benefits to your email directly.

Part 1 – Introduction to Explainable Deep Learning Anomaly Detection

Before embarking upon an AI journey to drive transformational business opportunities, it is essential to understand the compelling rationale for embracing and incorporating explainability throughout the process.

Part 1 introduces the usage of deep learning and the significant role of XAI in anomaly detection. By the end of *Part 1*, you will have gained a conceptual understanding with hands-on experience of where XAI fits in the bigger picture of the **machine learning** (**ML**) life cycle. Besides the awareness of executive accountability and increased regulatory pressure in AI adoption, you will learn how XAI can bring significant business benefits and turn your AI strategy into a competitive differentiator.

This part comprises the following chapters:

- *Chapter 1, Understanding Deep Learning Anomaly Detection*
- *Chapter 2, Understanding Explainable AI*

1
Understanding Deep Learning Anomaly Detection

Anomaly detection is an active research field widely applied to many commercial and mission-critical applications, including healthcare, fraud detection, industrial predictive maintenance, and cybersecurity. It is a process of discovering outliers, abnormal patterns, and unusual observations that deviate from established normal behaviors and expected characteristics in a system, dataset, or environment.

Many anomaly detection applications require domain-specific knowledge to extract actionable insights in a timely manner for informed decision-making and risk mitigation. For example, early detection of equipment performance degradation prevents unplanned downtime, whereas early discovery of disease threats prevents a pandemic outbreak.

The advent of cloud technologies, unlimited digital storage capacity, and a plethora of data have motivated deep learning research for anomaly detection. Detecting outliers requires an enormous dataset because anomalies are rare by nature in the presence of abundance. For example, detecting abnormal machinery vibrations and unusual power consumption or temperature increases allows companies to plan for predictive maintenance and avoid expensive downtime.

Deep learning anomaly detection has shown promising results in addressing challenges with the rare nature of anomalies, complex modeling of high-dimensional data, and identifying novel anomalous classes. The primary interest in anomaly detection is often focused on isolating undesirable data instances, such as product defects and safety risks, from the targeted domain. Other interests include improving model performance by removing noisy data or irrelevant outliers and identifying emerging trends from the dataset for a competitive advantage.

This chapter covers an overview of anomaly detection with the following topics:

- Exploring types of anomalies
- Discovering real-world use cases
- Considering when to use deep learning and what for
- Understanding challenges and opportunities

By the end of this chapter, you will have an understanding of the basics of anomaly detection, including real-world use cases, and the role of deep learning in accelerating outlier discovery. You will also have gained a sense of existing challenges and growth potential in leveraging deep learning techniques for anomaly detection.

Technical requirements

For this chapter, you will need the following components for the example walkthrough:

- PyOD – An open-source Python library for outlier detection on multivariate data
- Matplotlib – A plotting library for creating data visualizations
- NumPy – An open-source library that provides mathematical functions when working with arrays
- Pandas – A library that offers data analysis and manipulation tools
- Seaborn – A Matplotlib-based data visualization library
- TensorFlow – An open-source framework for building deep learning applications

Sample Jupyter notebooks and requirements files for package dependencies discussed in this chapter are available at https://github.com/PacktPublishing/Deep-Learning-and-XAI-Techniques-for-Anomaly-Detection/tree/main/Chapter1.

You can experiment with this example on Amazon SageMaker Studio Lab, https://aws.amazon.com/sagemaker/studio-lab/, a free ML development environment that provides up to 12 hours of CPU or 4 hours of GPU per user session and 15 GiB storage at no cost. Alternatively, you can try this on your preferred Integrated Development Environment (IDE).

Before exploring the sample notebooks, let's cover the types of anomalies in the following section.

Exploring types of anomalies

Before choosing appropriate algorithms, a fundamental understanding of what constitutes an anomaly is essential to enhance explainability. Anomalies manifest in many shapes and sizes, including objects, vectors, events, patterns, and observations. They can exist in static entities or temporal contexts. Here is a comparison of different types of anomalies:

- A **point anomaly** exists in any dataset where an individual data point is out of the boundary of normal distribution. For example, an out-of-norm expensive credit card purchase is a point anomaly.
- A **collective anomaly** only occurs when a group of related data records or sequences of observations appear collectively and significantly differ from the remaining dataset. A spike of errors from multiple systems is a collective anomaly that might indicate problems with downstream e-commerce systems.

- A **contextual anomaly** occurs when viewed against contextual attributes such as day and time. An example of a temporal contextual anomaly is a sudden increase in online orders outside of expected peak shopping hours.

An anomaly has at least one (univariate) or multiple attributes (multivariate) in numerical, binary, continuous, or categorical data types. These attributes describe the characteristics, features, and dimensions of an anomaly. *Figure 1.1* shows examples of common anomaly types:

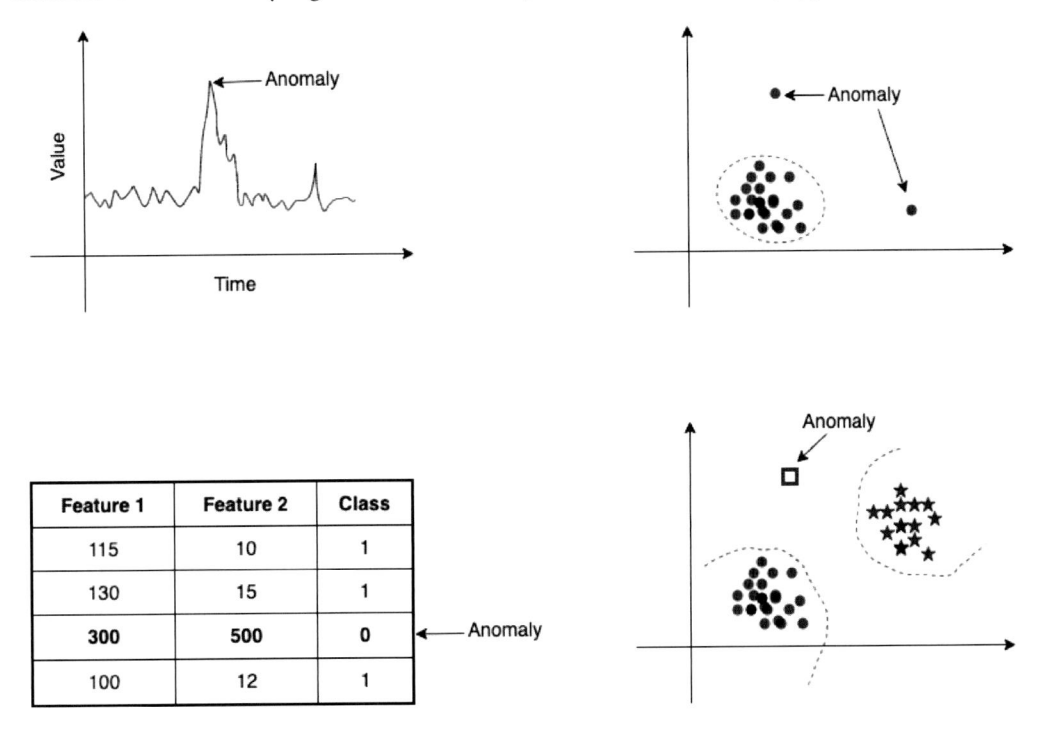

Feature 1	Feature 2	Class
115	10	1
130	15	1
300	500	0
100	12	1

Figure 1.1 – Types of anomalies

Defining an anomaly is not a straightforward task because boundaries between normal and abnormal behaviors can be domain-specific and subject to risk tolerance levels defined by the business, organization, and industry. For example, an irregular heart rhythm from **electrocardiogram** (**ECG**) time series data may signal cardiovascular disease risk, whereas stock price fluctuations might be considered normal based on market demand. Thus, there is no universal definition of an anomaly and no one-size-fits-all solution for anomaly detection.

Let's look at a point anomaly example using **PyOD** and a diabetes dataset from Kaggle, https://www.kaggle.com/datasets/mathchi/diabetes-data-set. PyOD, https://github.com/yzhao062/pyod. PyOD is an open source Python library that provides over 40 outlier detection algorithms, covering everything from outlier ensembles to neural network-based methods on multivariate data.

Sample Jupyter notebooks and requirements files for package dependencies discussed in this chapter are available at https://github.com/PacktPublishing/Deep-Learning-and-XAI-Techniques-for-Anomaly-Detection/tree/main/Chapter1.

You can experiment with this example on **Amazon SageMaker Studio Lab**, https://aws.amazon.com/sagemaker/studio-lab/, a free ML development environment that provides up to 12 hours of CPU or 4 hours of GPU per user session and 15 GiB storage at no cost. Alternatively, you can try this on your preferred **Integrated Development Environment (IDE)**. A sample notebook, *chapter1_pyod_point_anomaly.ipynb*, can be found in the book's GitHub repo. Let's get started:

1. First, install the required packages using provided requirements file.

   ```
   import sys
   !{sys.executable} -m pip install -r requirements.txt
   ```

2. Import essential libraries.

   ```
   %matplotlib inline

   import pandas as pd
   import numpy as np
   import warnings
   from pyod.models.knn import KNN
   from platform import python_version

   warnings.filterwarnings('ignore')

   print(f'Python version: {python_version()}')
   ```

3. Load and preview the dataset, as shown in *Figure 1.2*:

   ```
   df = pd.read_csv('diabetes.csv')
   df.head()
   ```

	Pregnancies	Glucose	BloodPressure	SkinThickness	Insulin	BMI	DiabetesPedigreeFunction	Age	Outcome
0	6	148	72	35	0	33.6	0.627	50	1
1	1	85	66	29	0	26.6	0.351	31	0
2	8	183	64	0	0	23.3	0.672	32	1
3	1	89	66	23	94	28.1	0.167	21	0
4	0	137	40	35	168	43.1	2.288	33	1

Figure 1.2 – Preview dataset

4. The dataset contains the following columns:

    - `Pregnancies`: Number of times pregnant
    - `Glucose`: Plasma glucose concentration in an oral glucose tolerance test
    - `BloodPressure`: Diastolic blood pressure (mm Hg)
    - `SkinThickness`: Triceps skin fold thickness (mm)
    - `Insulin`: 2-hour serum insulin (mu U/ml)
    - `BMI`: Body mass index (weight in kg/(height in m)^2)
    - `DiabetesPedigreeFunction`: Diabetes pedigree function
    - `Age`: Age (years)
    - `Outcome`: Class variable (0 is not diabetic and 1 is diabetic)

5. *Figure 1.3* shows the descriptive statistics about the dataset:

    ```
    df.describe()
    ```

	Pregnancies	Glucose	BloodPressure	SkinThickness	Insulin	BMI	DiabetesPedigreeFunction	Age	Outcome
count	768.000000	768.000000	768.000000	768.000000	768.000000	768.000000	768.000000	768.000000	768.000000
mean	3.845052	120.894531	69.105469	20.536458	79.799479	31.992578	0.471876	33.240885	0.348958
std	3.369578	31.972618	19.355807	15.952218	115.244002	7.884160	0.331329	11.760232	0.476951
min	0.000000	0.000000	0.000000	0.000000	0.000000	0.000000	0.078000	21.000000	0.000000
25%	1.000000	99.000000	62.000000	0.000000	0.000000	27.300000	0.243750	24.000000	0.000000
50%	3.000000	117.000000	72.000000	23.000000	30.500000	32.000000	0.372500	29.000000	0.000000
75%	6.000000	140.250000	80.000000	32.000000	127.250000	36.600000	0.626250	41.000000	1.000000
max	17.000000	199.000000	122.000000	99.000000	846.000000	67.100000	2.420000	81.000000	1.000000

Figure 1.3 – Descriptive statistics

6. We will focus on identifying point anomalies using the Glucose and Insulin features. Assign model feature and target column to the variables:

    ```
    X = df['Glucose']
    Y = df['Insulin']
    ```

7. *Figure 1.4* is a scatter plot that shows the original data distribution using the following code:

    ```
    import matplotlib.pyplot as plt
    plt.scatter(X, Y)
    plt.xlabel('Glucose')
    plt.ylabel('Blood Pressure')
    plt.show()
    ```

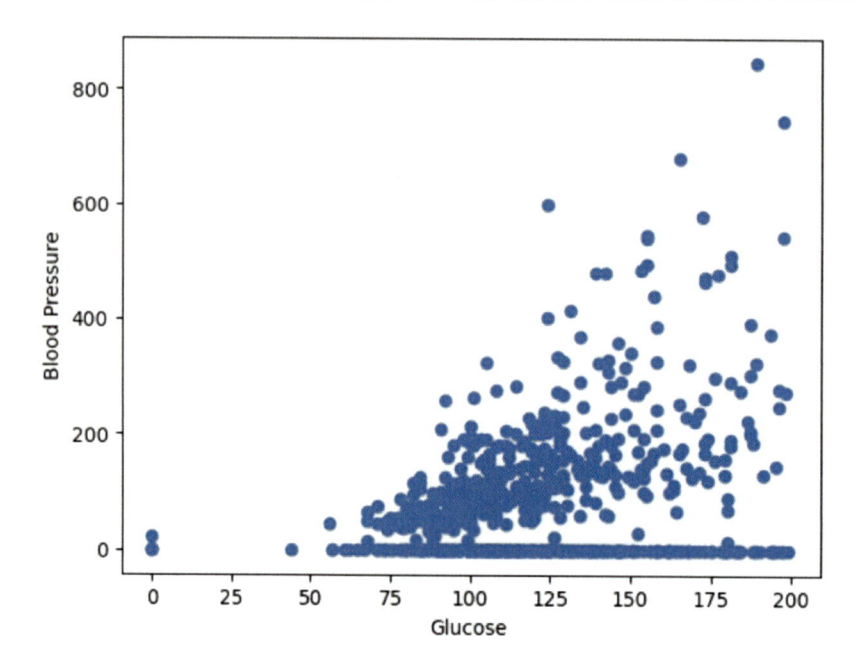

Figure 1.4 – Original data distribution

8. Next, load a **K-nearest neighbors** (**KNN**) model from PyOD. Before predicting outliers, we must reshape the target column into the desired input format for KNN:

```
from pyod.models.knn import KNN
Y = Y.values.reshape(-1, 1)
X = X.values.reshape(-1, 1)
clf = KNN()
clf.fit(Y)
outliers = clf.predict(Y)
```

9. List the identified outliers. You should see the output as shown in *Figure 1.5*:

```
anomaly = np.where(outliers==1)
anomaly
```

```
(array([  8,  13,  20,  31,  43,  52,  53,  54,  56,  73,  99, 111, 132,
        144, 153, 162, 182, 186, 199, 206, 220, 228, 231, 247, 248, 254,
        258, 286, 287, 296, 297, 323, 335, 359, 364, 370, 388, 392, 409,
        412, 415, 458, 485, 486, 487, 540, 545, 555, 574, 584, 606, 645,
        655, 673, 679, 695, 707, 710, 713, 715, 753]),)
```

Figure 1.5 – Outliers detected by KNN

Figure 1.6 shows a preview of the identified outliers:

	Pregnancies	Glucose	BloodPressure	SkinThickness	Insulin	BMI	DiabetesPedigreeFunction	Age	Outcome
8	2	197	70	45	543	30.5	0.158	53	1
13	1	189	60	23	846	30.1	0.398	59	1
20	3	126	88	41	235	39.3	0.704	27	0
31	3	158	76	36	245	31.6	0.851	28	1
43	9	171	110	24	240	45.4	0.721	54	1
52	5	88	66	21	23	24.4	0.342	30	0
53	8	176	90	34	300	33.7	0.467	58	1
54	7	150	66	42	342	34.7	0.718	42	0
56	7	187	68	39	304	37.7	0.254	41	1
73	4	129	86	20	270	35.1	0.231	23	0

Figure 1.6 – Preview outliers

10. Visualize the outliers and inliers distribution, as shown in *Figure 1.7*:

```
Y_outliers = Y[np.where(outliers==1)]
X_outliers = X[np.where(outliers==1)]
Y_inliers = Y[np.where(outliers==0)]
X_inliers = X[np.where(outliers==0)]

plt.scatter(X_outliers, Y_outliers,
edgecolor='black',color='red', label= 'Outliers')
plt.scatter(X_inliers, Y_inliers,
edgecolor='black',color='cyan', label= 'Inliers')
plt.legend()
plt.ylabel('Blood Pressure')
plt.xlabel('Glucose')
plt.savefig('outliers_distribution.png', bbox_inches='tight')
plt.show()
```

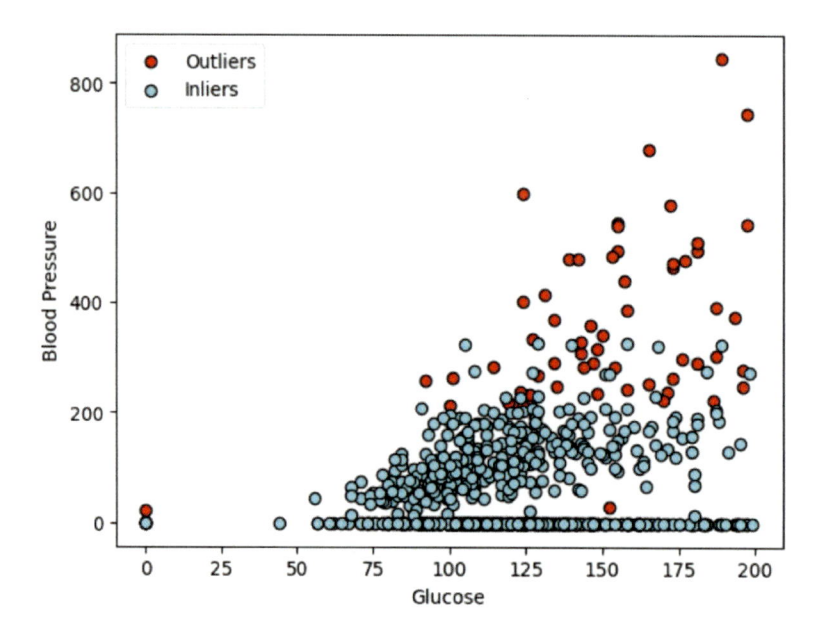

Figure 1.7 – Outliers versus inliers

11. PyOD computes anomaly scores using `decision_function` for the trained model. The larger the anomaly score, the higher the probability that the instance is an outlier:

    ```
    anomaly_score = clf.decision_function(Y)
    ```

12. Visualize the calculated anomaly score distribution with a histogram:

    ```
    n_bins = 5
    min_outlier_anomaly_score = np.floor(np.min(anomaly_score[np.where(outliers==1)])*10)/10

    plt.figure(figsize=(6, 4))
    values, bins, bars = plt.hist(anomaly_score, bins=n_bins, edgecolor='white')
    plt.axvline(min_outlier_anomaly_score, c='r')
    plt.bar_label(bars, fontsize=12)
    plt.margins(x=0.01, y=0.1)
    plt.xlabel('Anomaly Score')
    plt.ylabel('Number of Instances')
    plt.savefig('outliers_min.png', bbox_inches='tight')
    plt.show()
    ```

In *Figure 1.8*, the red vertical line indicates the minimum anomaly score to flag an instance as an outlier:

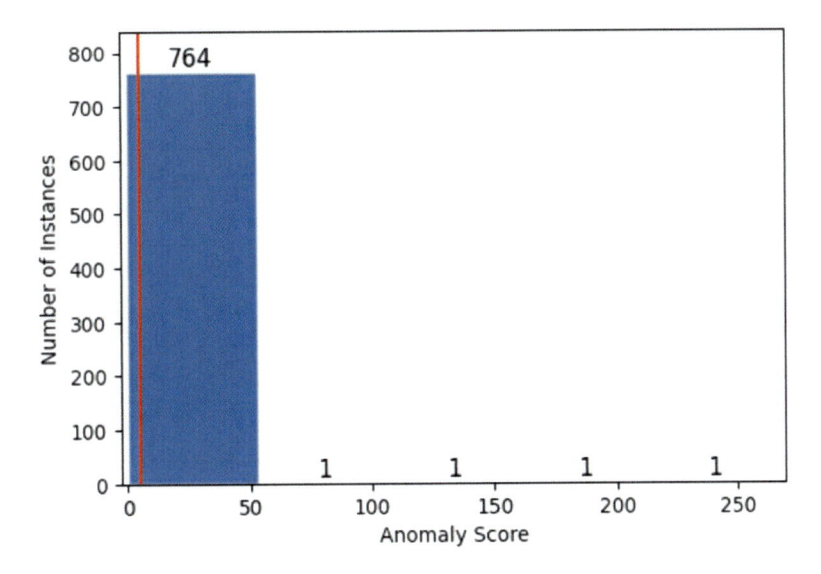

Figure 1.8 – Anomaly score distribution

13. We can change the anomaly score threshold. Increasing the threshold should reduce the number of outputs. In this case, we only have one outlier after increasing the anomaly score threshold to over 250, as shown in *Figure 1.9*:

    ```
    raw_outliers = np.where(anomaly_score >= 250)
    raw_outliers
    ```

	Pregnancies	Glucose	BloodPressure	SkinThickness	Insulin	BMI	DiabetesPedigreeFunction	Age	Outcome
13	1	189	60	23	846	30.1	0.398	59	1

Figure 1.9 – Outlier with a higher anomaly score

14. *Figure 1.10* shows another outlier distribution with a different threshold:

    ```
    n_bins = 5
    min_anomaly_score = 50
    values, bins, bars = plt.hist(anomaly_score, bins=n_bins, edgecolor='white', color='green')
    plt.axvline(min_anomaly_score, c='r')
    plt.bar_label(bars, fontsize=12)
    ```

```
plt.margins(x=0.01, y=0.1)
plt.xlabel('Anomaly Score')
plt.ylabel('Number of Instances')
plt.savefig('outliers_modified.png', bbox_inches='tight')
plt.show()
```

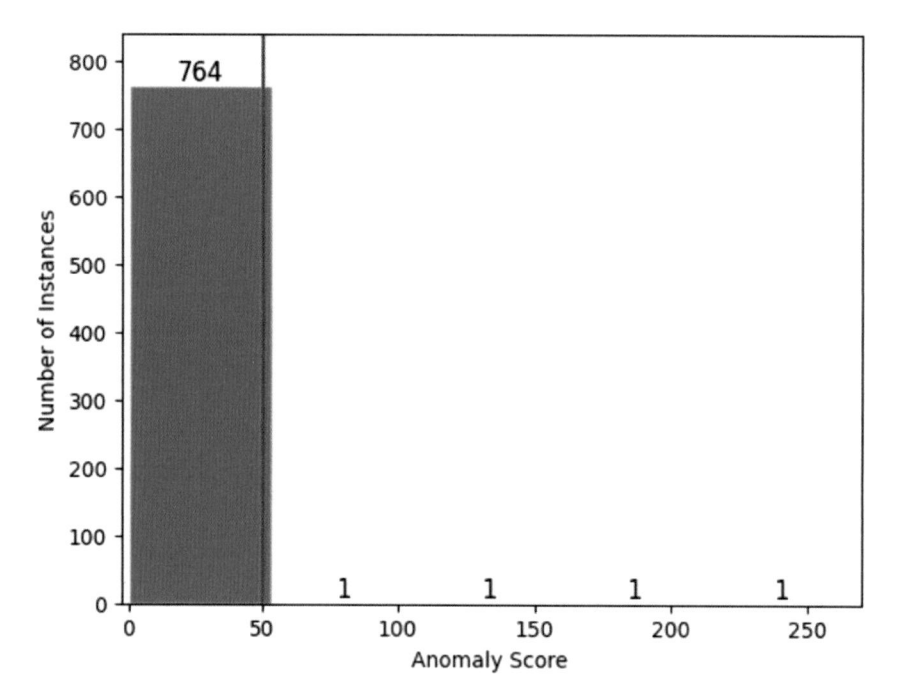

Figure 1.10 – Modified anomaly threshold

You completed a walk-through of point anomaly detection using a KNN model. Feel free to explore other outlier detection algorithms provided by PyOD. With a foundational knowledge of anomaly types, you are ready to explore various real-world use cases for anomaly detection in the following section.

Discovering real-world use cases

Anomaly detection plays a crucial role in extracting valuable insights for risk management. Over the years, anomaly detection applications have diversified across various domains, including medical diagnosis, fraud discovery, quality control analysis, predictive maintenance, security scanning, and threat intelligence. In this section, let's look at some practical industry use cases of anomaly detection, including the following:

- Detecting fraud
- Predicting industrial maintenance

- Diagnosing medical conditions
- Monitoring cybersecurity threats
- Reducing environmental impact
- Recommending financial strategies

Detecting fraud

The continued growth of the global economy and increased business demand for real-time and ubiquitous digital payment methods open the door to fraud exposure, causing electronic commerce systems to be vulnerable to organized crimes. Fraud prevention mechanisms that protect technological systems from potential fraud risks are insufficient to cover all possible fraudulent scenarios. Thus, fraud detection systems provide an additional layer of protection in detecting suspicious and malicious activities.

Discovery sampling is an auditing technique that determines whether to approve or reject a sampled audit population if the percentage error rate is below the defined minimum unacceptable threshold. Manual fraud audit techniques based on discovery sampling require domain knowledge across multiple disciplines and are time-consuming. Leveraging **machine learning** (ML) in fraud detection systems has proven to produce higher model accuracy and detect novel anomaly classes.

Fraud detection systems leverage behavioral profiling methods to prevent fraud by modeling individual behavioral patterns and monitoring deviations from the norms, such as daily banking activities, spending velocity, transacted foreign countries, and beneficiaries based on historical transactions. Nevertheless, an individual's spending habits are influenced by changes in income, lifestyle, and other external factors. Such unpredicted changes can introduce concept drift with the underlying model. Hence, a fraud detection model and an individual's transaction profiling must be recursively and dynamically updated by correlating input data changes and various parameters to enable adaptive behavioral profiling.

Let's review a fraud detection example using an anonymized multivariate credit card transactions dataset from `https://www.kaggle.com/datasets/whenamancodes/fraud-detection` and AutoEncoder provided by PyOD, `https://pyod.readthedocs.io/en/latest/pyod.models.html#module-pyod.models.auto_encoder`.

AutoEncoder is an unsupervised deep learning algorithm that can reconstruct high dimensional input data using a compressed latent representation of the input data. AutoEncoder helps detect abnormalities in the data by calculating the reconstruction errors.

Figure 1.11 shows a high-level AutoEncoder architecture that consists of three components:

- **Encoder** – Translates high dimensional input data into a low dimensional latent representation
- **Code** – Learns the latent-space representation of the input data
- **Decoder** – Reconstructs the input data based on the encoder's output

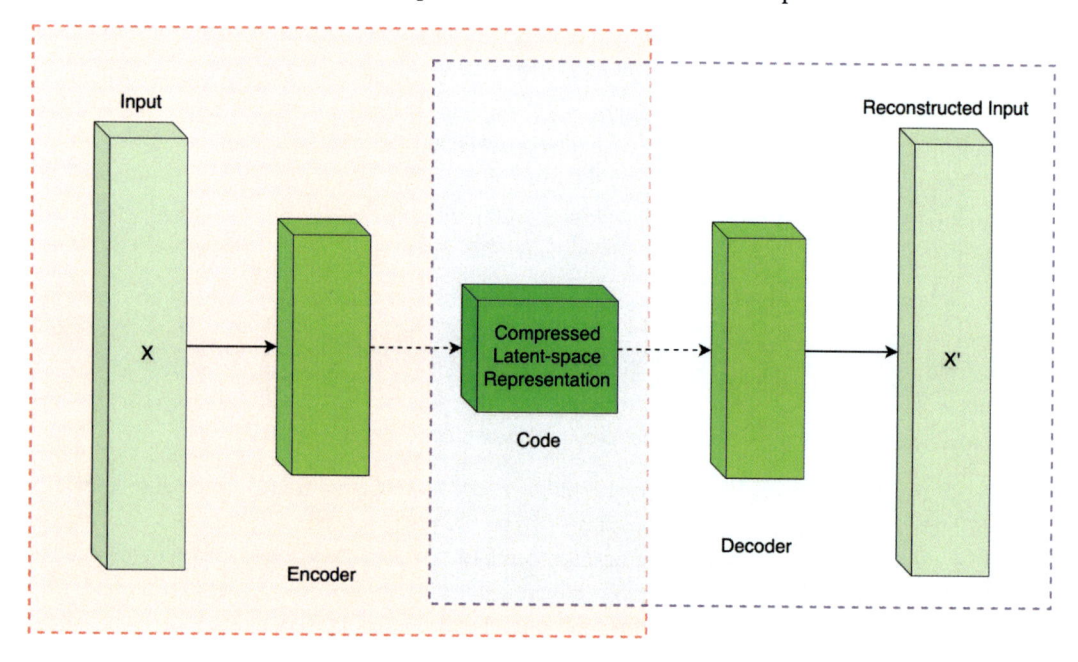

Figure 1.11 – The AutoEncoder architecture

A sample notebook, *chapter1_pyod_autoencoder.ipynb*, can be found in the book's GitHub repo.

You can also experiment with this example on Amazon SageMaker Studio Lab, https://aws.amazon.com/sagemaker/studio-lab/, a free notebook development environment that provides up to 12 hours of CPU or 4 hours of GPU per user session and 15 GiB storage at no cost. Alternatively, you can try this on your preferred IDE. Let's get started:

1. First, install the required packages using provided requirements.txt file.

   ```
   import sys
   !{sys.executable} -m pip install -r requirements.txt
   ```

2. Load the essential libraries:

   ```
   %matplotlib inline
   import pandas as pd
   ```

```python
import numpy as np
import matplotlib.pyplot as plt
import seaborn as sns
import os
from platform import import python_version
import tensorflow as tf
from pyod.models.auto_encoder import AutoEncoder
os.environ["TF_CPP_MIN_LOG_LEVEL"] = "3"
print(f'TensorFlow version: {tf.__version__}')
print(f'Python version: {python_version()}')
```

3. Load and preview the anonymized credit card transactions dataset:

```
df = pd.read_csv('creditcard.csv')
df.head()
```

The result will be as follows:

	Time	V1	V2	V3	V4	V5	...	V25	V26	V27	V28	Amount	Class
0	0.0	-1.359807	-0.072781	2.536347	1.378155	-0.338321	...	0.128539	-0.189115	0.133558	-0.021053	149.62	0
1	0.0	1.191857	0.266151	0.166480	0.448154	0.060018	...	0.167170	0.125895	-0.008983	0.014724	2.69	0
2	1.0	-1.358354	-1.340163	1.773209	0.379780	-0.503198	...	-0.327642	-0.139097	-0.055353	-0.059752	378.66	0
3	1.0	-0.966272	-0.185226	1.792993	-0.863291	-0.010309	...	0.647376	-0.221929	0.062723	0.061458	123.50	0
4	2.0	-1.158233	0.877737	1.548718	0.403034	-0.407193	...	-0.206010	0.502292	0.219422	0.215153	69.99	0

Figure 1.12 – Preview anonymized credit card transactions dataset

4. Assign model features and the target label to variables:

```
model_features = df.columns.drop('Class')
X = df[model_features]
y = df['Class']
```

5. View the frequency distribution for target labels. You should have 284,315 non-fraudulent transactions for class 0 and 492 fraudulent transactions for class 1:

```
y.value_counts()
```

6. Set the contamination rate for the amount of contamination or the proportion of outliers in the training dataset. The default contamination value is `0.1`. Here, we are setting `contamination` to the maximum value, `0.5`. PyOD uses this setting to calculate the threshold. Fix the number of epochs for training:

```
contamination = 0.5
epochs = 30
```

7. Set the number of neurons per hidden layer and initialize `AutoEncoder` for training:

```
hn = [64, 30, 30, 64]
clf = AutoEncoder(epochs=epochs,
contamination=contamination, hidden_neurons=hn)
clf.fit(X)
```

Figure 1.13 shows a model summary for AutoEncoder in this example:

Model: "sequential"

Layer (type)	Output Shape	Param #
dense (Dense)	(None, 30)	930
dropout (Dropout)	(None, 30)	0
dense_1 (Dense)	(None, 30)	930
dropout_1 (Dropout)	(None, 30)	0
dense_2 (Dense)	(None, 64)	1984
dropout_2 (Dropout)	(None, 64)	0
dense_3 (Dense)	(None, 30)	1950
dropout_3 (Dropout)	(None, 30)	0
dense_4 (Dense)	(None, 30)	930
dropout_4 (Dropout)	(None, 30)	0
dense_5 (Dense)	(None, 64)	1984
dropout_5 (Dropout)	(None, 64)	0
dense_6 (Dense)	(None, 30)	1950

Total params: 10,658
Trainable params: 10,658
Non-trainable params: 0

Figure 1.13 – The AutoEncoder model summary

8. Obtain predictions on outliers:

   ```
   outliers = clf.predict(X)
   ```

9. Filter outliers from the model's predictions. The `anomaly` variable contains the identified outliers:

   ```
   anomaly = np.where(outliers==1)
   anomaly
   ```

10. View the output of a particular instance. You should see the output is 1, indicating this is predicted as a fraudulent transaction. Validate the result with the ground truth:

    ```
    sample = X.iloc[[4920]]
    clf.predict(sample, return_confidence=False)
    ```

    The result displayed is shown in *Figure 1.14*:

    ```
    1/1 [==============================] - 0s 23ms/step
    array([1])
    ```

    `X.iloc[[4920]]`

	Time	V1	V2	V3	V4	V5	...	V25	V26	V27	V28	Amount
4920	4462.0	-2.30335	1.759247	-0.359745	2.330243	-0.821628	...	-0.156114	-0.542628	0.039566	-0.153029	239.93

    1 rows × 30 columns

    `y.iloc[[4920]]`

    ```
    4920    1
    Name: Class, dtype: int64
    ```

    Figure 1.14 – Prediction versus ground truth

11. Evaluate the model's prediction if using a perturbed dataset:

    ```
    clf.predict_confidence(sample)
    ```

12. Generate binary labels of the training data, where 0 means inliers and 1 means outliers:

    ```
    y_pred = clf.labels_
    ```

13. Call the `decision_scores_` function to calculate anomaly scores. Higher values represent a higher severity of abnormalities:

    ```
    y_scores = clf.decision_scores_
    ```

14. *Figure 1.15* shows anomaly scores calculated by `decision_scores_` using the threshold value based on the contamination rate using the following code. The red horizontal line represents the threshold in use:

    ```
    plt.rcParams["figure.figsize"] = (15,8)
    plt.plot(y_scores);
    plt.axhline(y=clf.threshold_, c='r', ls='dotted',
    label='threshold');
    plt.xlabel('Instances')
    plt.ylabel('Decision Scores')
    plt.title('Anomaly Scores with Auto-Calculated
    Threshold');
    plt.savefig('auto_decision_scores.png', bbox_
    inches='tight')
    plt.show()
    ```

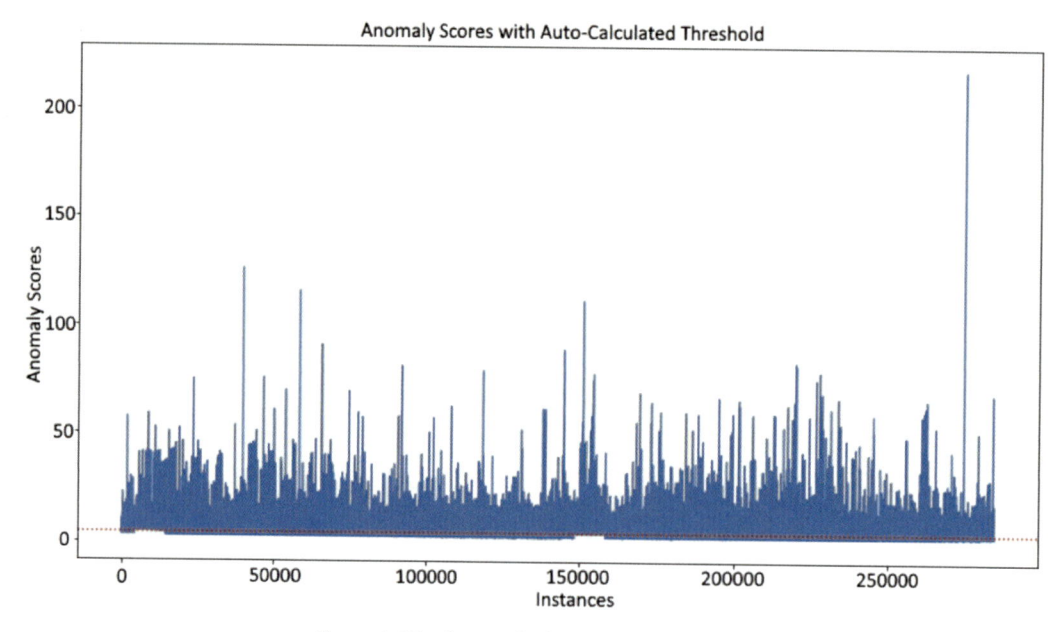

Figure 1.15 – Auto-calculated anomaly scores

15. *Figure 1.16* shows the modified threshold using the following code. The red horizontal line represents the new threshold:

    ```
    threshold = 50
    plt.rcParams["figure.figsize"] = (15,8)
    ```

```
plt.plot(y_scores, color="green");
plt.axhline(y=threshold, c='r', ls='dotted',
label='threshold');
plt.xlabel('Instances')
plt.ylabel('Anomaly Scores')
plt.title('Anomaly Scores with Modified Threshold');
plt.savefig('modified_threshold.png', bbox_
inches='tight')
plt.show()
```

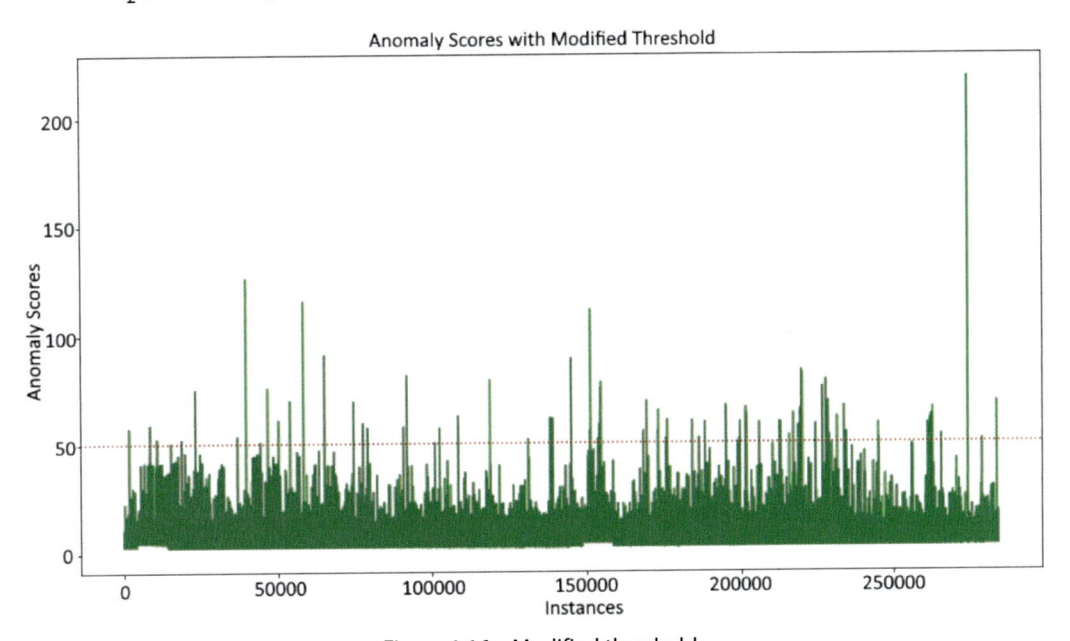

Figure 1.16 – Modified threshold

16. We will use the following code to determine the error loss history:

```
plt.rcParams["figure.figsize"] = (15,8)
pd.DataFrame.from_dict(clf.history_).plot(title='Error
Loss');
plt.savefig('error_loss.png', bbox_inches='tight')
plt.show()
```

Figure 1.17 shows the error loss history:

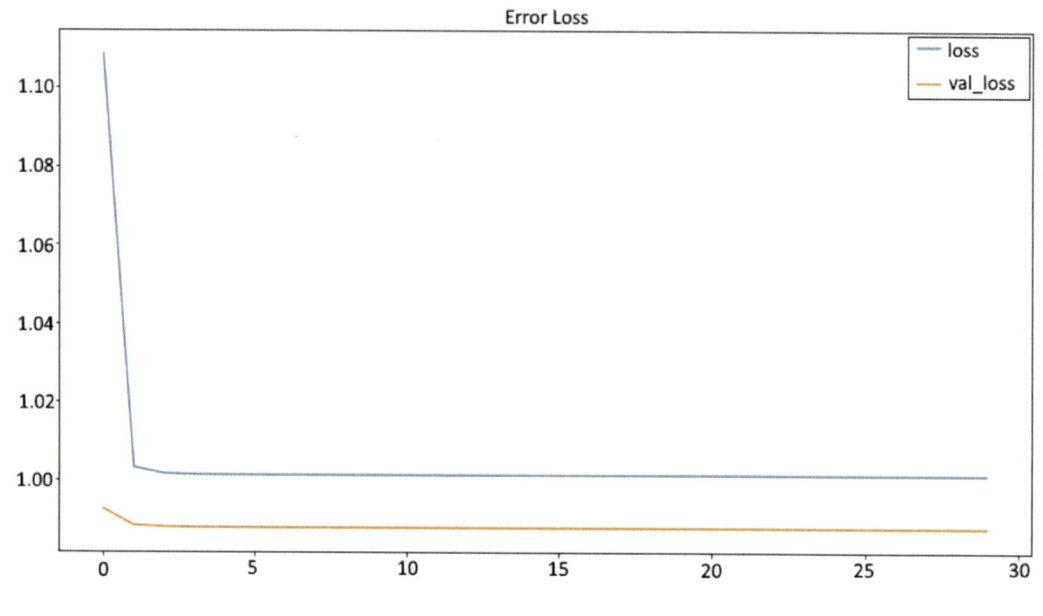

Figure 1.17 – Error loss history

17. Visualize anomaly scores and outliers by comparing Time and Amount with a scatter plot:

```
sns.scatterplot(x="Time", y="Amount", hue=y_scores,
data=df, palette="RdBu_r", size=y_scores);
plt.xlabel('Time (seconds elapsed from first
transaction)')
plt.ylabel('Amount')
plt.legend(title='Anomaly Scores')
plt.savefig('pca_anomaly_score.png', bbox_inches='tight')
plt.show()
```

The result is shown in *Figure 1.18*:

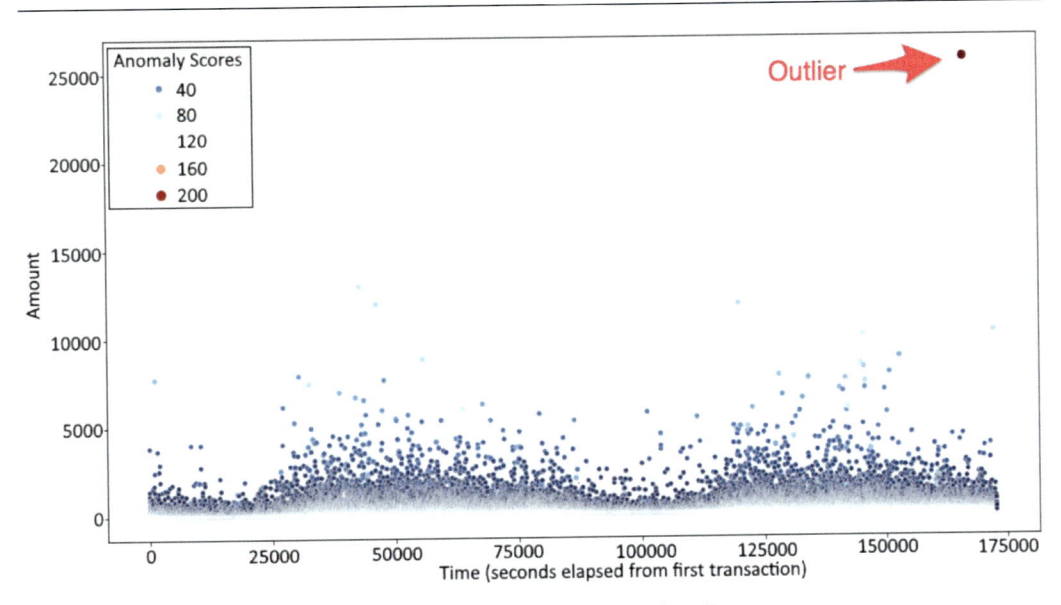

Figure 1.18 – Anomaly scores and outlier

You completed a walk-through of a fraud detection example using AutoEncoder. The following section discusses a few more real-world anomaly detection examples.

Predicting industrial maintenance

The rise of Industry 4.0 transformed manufacturing technologies focusing on interconnectivity between machines and industrial equipment using the **Internet of Things** (**IoT**). Real-time data produced by interconnected devices presents enormous opportunities for predictive analytics in structural health checks and anomaly detection.

Inadequate machine maintenance is the primary cause of unplanned downtime in manufacturing. Improving equipment availability and performance is critical in preventing unplanned downtime, avoiding unnecessary maintenance costs, and increasing productivity in industrial workloads.

Although equipment health can deteriorate over time due to regular use, early discovery of abnormal symptoms helps optimize performance and uptime over a machine's life expectancy and ensure business continuity.

Predictive maintenance techniques have evolved from reactive mode to ML approaches. Anomaly detection for predictive maintenance is challenging due to a lack of domain knowledge in defining anomaly classes and the absence of past anomalous behaviors in the available data. Many existing manufacturing processes can only detect a subset of anomalies, leaving the remaining anomalies undetected before the equipment goes into a nonfunctional state. Anomaly detection in predictive maintenance aims to predict the onset of equipment failure and perform prompt maintenance to avoid unnecessary downtime.

You can try implementing a predictive maintenance problem using PyOD with this dataset: `https://www.kaggle.com/datasets/shivamb/machine-predictive-maintenance-classification`.

Diagnosing medical conditions

The physiological data collection through medical diagnosis applications, such as **magnetic resonance imaging** (**MRI**), and wearable devices, such as glucose monitors, enables healthcare professionals to highlight abnormal readings that may be precursors of potential health risks to patients using anomaly detection approaches. Besides medical diagnosis, anomaly detection helps healthcare providers predict recovery rates and escalates medical risks by forecasting physiological signals, such as heart rate and blood pressure.

Detection and prediction accuracy is critical in medical anomaly detection as they involve time-sensitive decisions and life-and-death situations. Besides common challenges with class imbalance and scarcity of anomaly samples, medical anomaly detection faces challenges in distinguishing patient and demographic-specific characteristics.

Deep learning techniques have gained popularity in medical anomaly detection due to their feature learning and non-linearity modeling capabilities. However, current deep medical anomaly detection methods mainly correlate patients' symptoms with a known disease category based on annotated data. Medical experts will be skeptical of trusting decisions made by black-box models without quantifiable causal estimation or explanation. Hence, the role of **explainable artificial intelligence** (**XAI**) is crucial in providing end users visibility into how a deep learning model derives a prediction that leads to informed decision-making.

Monitoring cybersecurity threats

Detecting zero-day attacks or unforeseen threats is highly desirable in security applications. Therefore, unsupervised deep learning techniques using unlabeled datasets are widely applied in security-related anomaly detection applications such as **intrusion detection systems** (**IDSs**), web attack detection, video surveillance, and **advanced persistent threat** (**APT**).

Two categories of IDSs are host-based and network-based. Host-based IDSs detect collective anomalies such as malicious applications, policy violations, and unauthorized access by analyzing sequential call traces at the operating system level. Network-based IDSs analyze high-dimensional network data to identify potential external attacks for unauthorized network access.

Web applications are now an appealing target to cybercriminals as data becomes ubiquitous. Existing signature-based techniques using static rules no longer provide sufficient web attack protection because the quality of rulesets depends on known attacks in the signature dataset. Anomaly-based web attack detection methods distinguish anomalous web requests by measuring the probability threshold of attributes in the request to the established normal request profiles.

Reducing environmental impact

The widespread climate change driven by human activities has contributed to the rise of the earth's temperature by 0.14 degrees Fahrenheit or -17.7 degrees Celsius since 1880, and 2020 was marked as the second-warmest year according to the **National Oceanic Atmospheric Administration (NOAA)**. Irreversible consequences of climate change can lead to other impacts, such as intense droughts, water shortages, catastrophic wildfires, and severe flooding. Detecting abnormal weather patterns and climatic events, such as the frequency of heat and cold waves, cyclones, and floods, provides a scientific understanding of the behaviors and relationships of climatological variables.

With almost 80% of the world's energy produced by fossil fuels, it is crucial to develop green energy sources and reduce total energy consumption by identifying wasted energy using anomaly detection approaches through smart sensors. For example, buildings contribute 40% of global energy consumption and 33% of greenhouse gas emissions. Thus, reducing building energy consumption is a significant effort toward achieving net-zero carbon emissions by 2050.

Recommending financial strategies

Identifying anomalies in financial data, such as stock market indices, is instrumental for informed decision-making and competitive advantage. Characteristics of financial data include volume, velocity, and variety. For example, The **New York Stock Exchange (NYSE)** generates over one terabyte of stock market data daily that reflects continuous market changes at low latency. Market participants need a mechanism to identify anomalies in financial data that can cause misinterpretation of market behavior leading to poor trading decisions.

Now that we have covered some commercial and environmental use cases for anomaly detection, you are ready to explore various deep learning approaches and their appropriate use for detecting anomalies in the following section.

Considering when to use deep learning and what for

Deep learning forms the basis of neural networks in ML. A neural network contains many layers of densely interconnected neurons organized into input, hidden, and output layers. Information flows through a neural network in one direction and begins with the input layer receiving raw data for model training. The hidden layer uses backpropagation to calculate the gradient of errors and optimizes the learning process.

A neuron contains an activation function to produce prediction through the output layer. *Figure 1.19* shows a basic deep learning architecture:

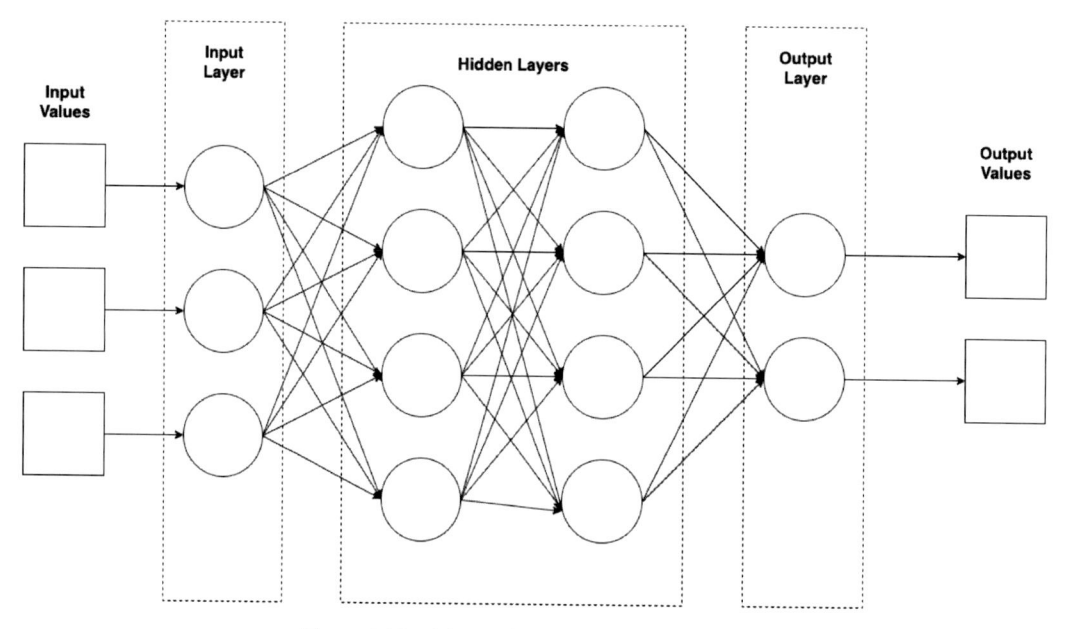

Figure 1.19 – A basic deep learning architecture

Anomaly detection techniques are generally available in three categories:

- **Supervised anomaly detection**: Train an ML model with an imbalanced labeled dataset where each data instance is categorized into a normal or abnormal class. This approach is viable if ground truth or actual observation is available. An anomaly detection model determines the class of unseen data assuming outliers follow the same distribution as the training dataset. Limitations of supervised anomaly detection include scarcity of anomaly samples and challenges in identifying precise representation of the normal class.

- **Semi-supervised anomaly detection**: Train an ML model with a large amount of unlabeled datasets supplemented by a small set of labeled data for expected behavior. This approach assumes outliers differ from training dataset distribution. Hence, semi-supervised is more applicable than supervised for detecting outliers since anomalies are rare.

- **Unsupervised anomaly detection**: Train an ML model with an unlabeled dataset that contains normal and abnormal observations. This approach assumes normal and abnormal observations typically isolated in high-density and low-density regions. An anomaly detector looks for instances or potential outliers in the low-density region.

Besides identifying the class of unseen data, anomaly detection algorithms can produce anomaly scores to quantify the severity, help businesses determine an acceptable impact threshold, and manage risk tolerance levels.

The significance of anomaly detection is evident across many mission-critical domains. When choosing deep learning versus traditional anomaly detection methods, consider business objectives, data size, and training time versus trade-offs such as algorithmic scalability, model flexibility, explainability, and interpretability.

Identifying an ML problem to address a specific business problem is essential before embarking on an ML journey. Knowing the inputs, outputs, and success criteria, such as accuracy over interpretability, is critical for choosing the appropriate algorithms and lineage tracking. Consider traditional methods such as KNN and decision trees if interpretability is a higher priority to your business for regulatory compliance or auditability needs. Explore deep learning methods if high accuracy triumphs over interpretability for your use case, as XAI continues to mature for deep learning models.

Deep learning methods are capable and ideal for handling large datasets and complex problems. Deep learning can extract and correlate relationships across many interdependent features if your business aims to discover hidden patterns in large datasets. Otherwise, traditional methods might be a good start if your data size is small.

Training a deep learning anomaly detection model can be compute-intensive and time-consuming, depending on the number of parameters involved and available infrastructure, such as **graphics processing units** (**GPUs**). More computing power is needed as the size and complexity grow with deep learning models. Conversely, traditional anomaly detection methods can run and train faster on cheaper hardware, within hours.

Traditional rule-based anomaly detection methods created manually by domain experts are not scalable enough to handle high-dimensional data and are difficult to maintain. For instance, it can be challenging to develop security rules for every possible malicious behavior and keep those rules up to date. In contrast, deep learning-based anomaly detection methods are more adaptive by learning and extracting features incrementally from data in a nested hierarchy through hidden layers.

This section covered the basics and general best practices of deep learning. In the following section, we will discuss known challenges of deep learning anomaly detection and future opportunities of XAI in this field.

Understanding challenges and opportunities

The abundance of computing resources and available data accelerated the evolution of anomaly detection techniques over the years. According to the **International Data Corporation** (**IDC**), `https://www.statista.com/statistics/871513/worldwide-data-created/`, less than 2% of 64.2 zettabytes of data created during the COVID-19 pandemic was retained into 2021, presenting enormous opportunities for big data analytics and anomaly detection. However, challenges such as high false positives, scarcity of anomaly samples, and imbalanced distribution remain prevalent.

Establishing the boundary of normal versus abnormal behaviors is vital in anomaly detection. Nevertheless, this is not always a straightforward task due to the dynamic nature of anomalies. For example, defining normal behaviors is a moving target task when malicious adversaries adapt and appear as justifiable acts to anomaly detection algorithms. Noise and mislabeled data can cause a benign record to appear as an abnormal observation. An anomaly record might be undetected due to aggregated data or masking of hidden trends. Furthermore, concept drift can occur with input data and feature changes, causing the current notion of normal behavior invalid.

Generally, businesses believe ML improves decision-making and operational efficiency. With increased predictive accuracy and complexity, companies struggle to identify optimal trade-offs between model performance and interpretability for auditability and regulatory compliance. For example, individuals are entitled to the *Right to Explanation* under the **European Union (EU) General Data Protection Regulation (GDPR)**. Therefore, there is a growing awareness of explainability across different maturity levels of ML adoption among enterprises.

Knowing the key challenges, let's explore some future research focuses and opportunities for the next generation of deep learning anomaly detection practices. Instead of exclusively fitting limited labeled anomaly samples with a supervised technique or training with unlabeled data using unsupervised methods, there is an increasing interest in deep weakly-supervised anomaly detection using partially labeled anomaly data in the hope of getting the best of both worlds. Deep weakly-supervised anomaly detection aims to enhance model learning by training with a small set of accurately labeled anomaly samples and continuing to explore possible anomalies in unseen data.

Most existing deep learning methods focus on point anomalies. Complex interconnected devices such as climate control and electromechanical systems that generate continuous multidimensional data streams pose a new opportunity for multimodal anomaly detection. Multidimensional anomalies can occur when one or more dimensions exceed or fall below the expected range of values, or multiple dimensions no longer correlate.

XAI is an emerging research field that studies the tools and frameworks to provide human-legible explanations and increase confidence in model prediction with quantifiable factors. The earlier days of XAI in anomaly detection can be seen in rule-based expert systems where human experts formulated the rules and system knowledge, resulting in its inherent explainability. Further research on interpretable and actionable deep learning anomaly detection is significant in explaining model decisions and mitigating potential bias.

Summary

Despite the previously mentioned challenges, anomaly detection is highly applicable to various domains and will remain a diverse research field. In this chapter, you learned about the basics of anomaly detection, practical industry use cases, and considerations of deep learning versus traditional anomaly detection approaches. You also completed two example walkthroughs and explored challenges and exciting opportunities in this space. You also explored challenges and exciting opportunities in this space. In the next chapter, we will discuss XAI and its significance for anomaly detection in more depth.

2
Understanding Explainable AI

The breakthrough of ImageNet in 2012 accelerated the deep learning revolution, which evolved into the call for **Explainable Artificial Intelligence** (**XAI**) in 2015, initiated by the **United States** (**U.S.**) **Defense Advanced Research Project Agency** (**DARPA**), due to increased research interests in these opaque systems. Realizing the gap between rationalizing AI systems for human users and concerns about hidden risks for high-stakes situations, DARPA launched the XAI program in May 2017, intending to develop AI systems that end users can understand and trust.

In the past several decades, AI has evolved at an unprecedented rate to the extent that it almost requires no human intervention. While deep learning is increasingly sophisticated in solving complex problems, these advancements raise concerns about AI's social impacts and ethical implications.

XAI is an emerging research field focused on studying approaches, methods, tools, and frameworks to explain the inner workings of AI systems. The goal of XAI is to satisfy various stakeholders' interests and expectations. For example, this paper, `https://ieeexplore.ieee.org/document/9785199`, discussed an XAI case study that provided sonologists and dermatologists with information and explanations on how an ML model detects anomalies for melanoma skin cancer or nevus-mole like skin lesions. The model encapsulates knowledge from a dataset that contains 10,000 images from the **International Skin Imaging Collaboration** (**ISIC**). Besides detecting skin lesion abnormalities using the **Disentangled Inferred Prior Variational Autoencoder** (**DIP-VAE**), the model provides explanations based on medical guidelines in evaluating the asymmetry, border, color, and diameter of skin conditions.

In this chapter, we will explore the following XAI topics:

- Understanding the basics of XAI
- Reviewing XAI significance
- Choosing XAI techniques

By the end of this chapter, you will learn more about XAI and its significance for anomaly detection, including business implications, social impacts, and regulatory compliance.

Understanding the basics of XAI

AI systems extract patterns from input data and derive perceptions based on trained knowledge. The increased use of AI systems and applications in our everyday lives has prompted a growing demand for interpretability and accountability to justify model outputs for broader AI adoption. Unlike traditional human-made, rule-based systems that are self-explanatory, many deep learning algorithms are inherently opaque and overly complex for human interpretability.

XAI is a multidisciplinary field that spans psychology, computer science, and engineering, as pictured in *Figure 2.1*. Applying algorithmic, psychology, and cognitive science concepts, XAI aims to provide explainable AI decisions, allowing users without ML backgrounds to comprehend model behavior.

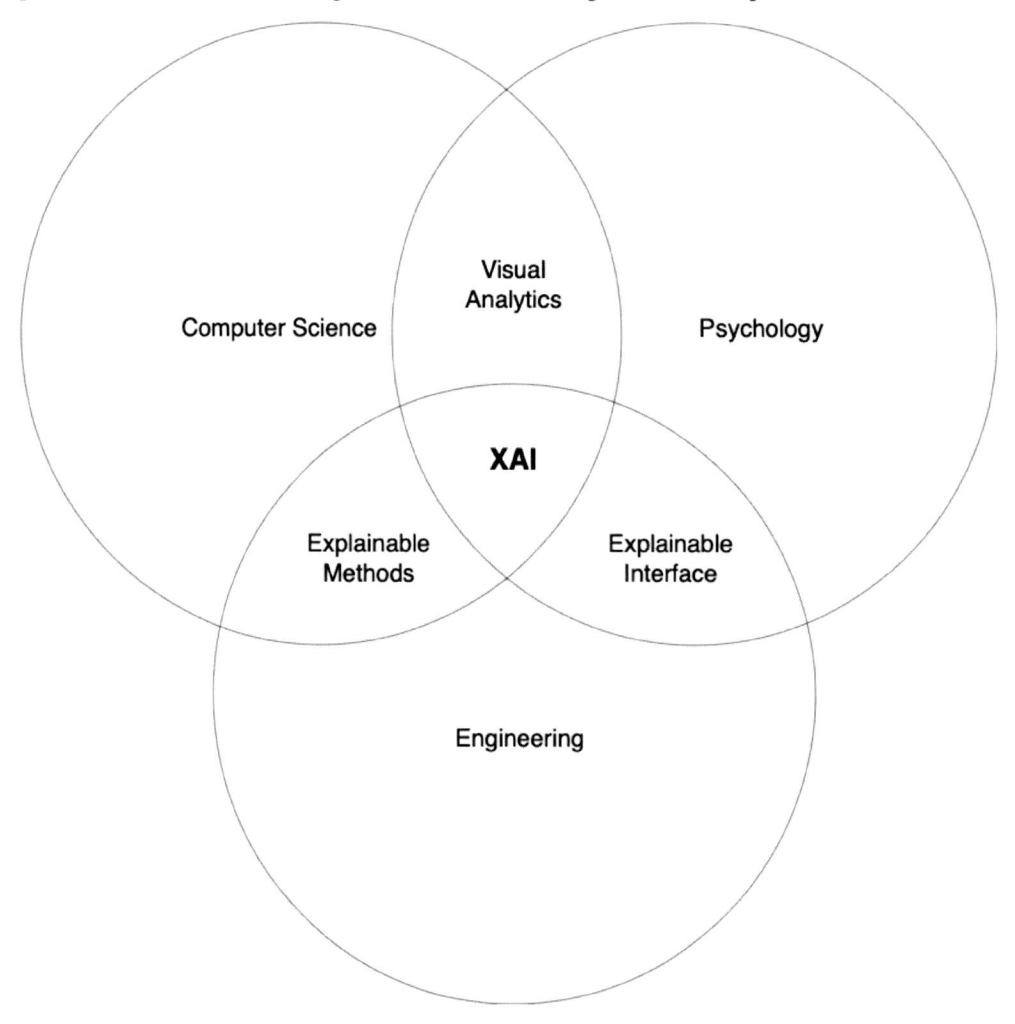

Figure 2.1 – XAI as a multidisciplinary field

DARPA's initial focus was to evaluate XAI in two problem areas – that is, data analytics and autonomy. They believe summarizing AI systems' inner logic is inadequate to address operational challenges, such as helping intelligence analysts filter false positives from model outputs and deciding when and where to apply AI-enabled warfighter capabilities. DARPA's XAI program follows a user-centered approach to produce more explainable models, design explainable user interfaces, and create adequate explanations based on psychological requirements. They employed human-in-the-loop psychologic experiments to evaluate user satisfaction, a mental model, perception, task performance, and the level of trust. To identify more explainable models, DARPA focuses on the following three main areas:

- **Deep explanation**: Examining deep explanation by reviewing deep learning design choices, including sources of training data, architecture complexity, training sequences, regularization, loss functions, and optimization techniques
- **Interpretable models**: Exploring interpretable models such as Bayesian rule lists to learn causal relationships and interpretable structure
- **Model induction**: Inferencing an explainable model by approximating a black-box model

Besides rationalizing AI systems, DARPA's XAI program aims to characterize the strengths and weaknesses of learned models to assess future AI evolution. The 4-year DARPA XAI program ended in 2021 with an open source **Explainable AI Toolkit** (**XAITK**), `https://xaitk.org/`, as the final deliverable, containing program artifacts that included code, papers, and reports. The goals of XAITK included consolidating DARPA XAI research into a single publicly accessible repository and providing operational capabilities for future research by interested contributors. You can read more about DARPA's XAI in this paper: `https://onlinelibrary.wiley.com/doi/10.1002/ail2.61`.

Since then, the following motivations have constituted XAI's growth:

- **User interests**: Explains a model output to a user – for example, why is a student denied a college admission application?
- **Social trust**: Explanations for the general public to foster trust and acceptance in AI systems – for example, does the public trust an AI system following ethical guidelines when recommending a candidate for a job?
- **Regulatory compliance**: Explains algorithmic logic to auditors or regulators to meet legal and ethical requirements – for example, can an AI system explain why certain transactions are flagged as abnormal in accounting?
- **Model debugging**: Explanations on model artifacts, enabling technical professionals to debug model decay
- **Business interests**: Explanations to justify business decisions based on model prediction – for example, an online retailer wanting to understand how AI systems make product recommendations to improve customer experience

An ML model can be partially or fully explainable. Fully interpretable models are generally more structured and follow domain knowledge by using correlated variables to provide transparent explanations of how a decision is derived. In contrast, partially interpretable models often are not bound by domain constraints and only reveal essential elements of a reasoning process. *Figure 2.2* compares ML algorithms based on model accuracy and interpretability.

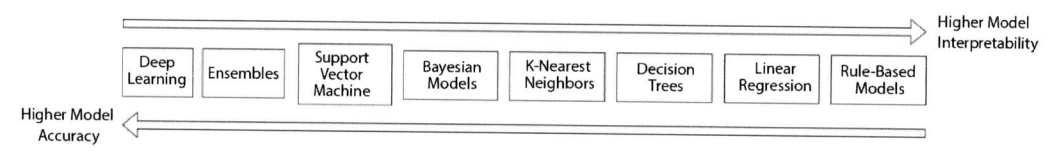

Figure 2.2 – Model accuracy versus interpretability

Simpler models with more structured functional details, such as decision trees, rule-based algorithms, and linear regression models, are intrinsically interpretable, simulatable, and decomposable. In contrast, complex ML algorithms such as deep learning neural networks with millions of parameters or weights are considered black-box models, since they are not understood by humans.

The current XAI maturity level has yet to identify the exact root cause leading to a model decision or prediction. Nevertheless, existing XAI methods focus primarily on local and global explainability, which we will discuss in more depth in *Chapter 6*. Here is an introduction to the two concepts:

- **Local explainability** explains how an ML model reaches an individual decision or predicts a specific outcome. This approach focuses on explaining to a user the reasoning behind a model's decision – for example, a bank might be audited to demonstrate explainability when declining a loan application based on an AI-generated decision.

- **Global explainability** provides a holistic view of the overall model behavior by investigating model learning, including the choice of data and algorithms. This approach explains to a user what elements influence a model's decision-making – for example, a company's marketing team might want to know how an ML model predicts the likelihood of a customer enrolling in a paid subscription.

XAI techniques apply to various data modalities, including images, text, and tabular data. Choosing the appropriate XAI technique for the relevant data type is crucial in capturing the learned knowledge as a source of explanations. We will walk through in detail how to build explainable anomaly detectors for **natural language processing** (NLP), time series, and computer vision in *Part 2* of the book.

This section highlights the inflection point and motivations of XAI. The following section compares two key aspects of XAI, explainability and interpretability.

Differentiating explainability versus interpretability

There are two main XAI concepts, explainability and interpretability. Knowing the differences between these terms, often used interchangeably in the literature, is essential.

In machine learning, explainability refers to human-understandable explanations of a model's working mechanisms to derive a prediction – for example, a fraud detection model predicts a transaction to be fraudulent, and we want to know how and why the model arrived at this conclusion.

In contrast, interpretability refers to the contextual understanding of a prediction – for example, we want to understand the severity and risks of a credit card transaction flagged as fraudulent to users, such as quantifying fraud and event correlation. Simply put, explainability focuses on the *how* and *why*, while interpretability emphasizes the *so what?*.

Table 2.1 summarizes the comparisons between explainability and interpretability, where explainability produces reasoning of the model's decisions while interpretability measures the extent of understanding the model's behavior:

Explainability	Interpretability
Human-understandable explanations for working mechanisms of models deriving a prediction	Contextual understanding of a prediction
After model training, perform post hoc explainability to assess a model's local and global explainability	Intrinsically interpretable algorithms such as decision trees and linear models, with more structured functional details
How does a model predict fraud? What parameters lead to predicted fraud?	What kind of fraud? How bad is the fraud?

Table 2.1 – Comparing explainability and interpretability

The explainability and interpretability of an ML model can result in profound implications for end users. For example, understanding how an AI system detects anomalous tissue samples for cancer screenings and how the system presents output to end users can impact survival prediction and guide physicians on diagnosis and treatment. With the aforementioned case study, an AI system explains how the model detects abnormal skin lesions based on asymmetry, border, color, and diameter measurements. Sonologists and dermatologists who receive AI-generated explanations can interpret the model following medical guidelines in diagnosing skin disorders.

In short, explainability tells us how the model behaves in human terms. In contrast, interpretability assesses whether the given explanations of how the model behaves make sense in real-world practice.

Now that you understand the differences between explainability and interpretability, the following section discusses target personas on the receiving end of XAI output.

Contextualizing stakeholder needs

Understanding and contextualizing individual stakeholder needs are essential to cultivating trust in AI systems and helping users, as shown in *Figure 2.3*, assess risks before accepting a model decision. Like informed consent, a healthcare provider informs patients about treatment plans and guides them to evaluate the risks and benefits, based on their medical conditions, before proceeding with a procedure. Informed users have higher situational awareness and are empowered to make better decisions.

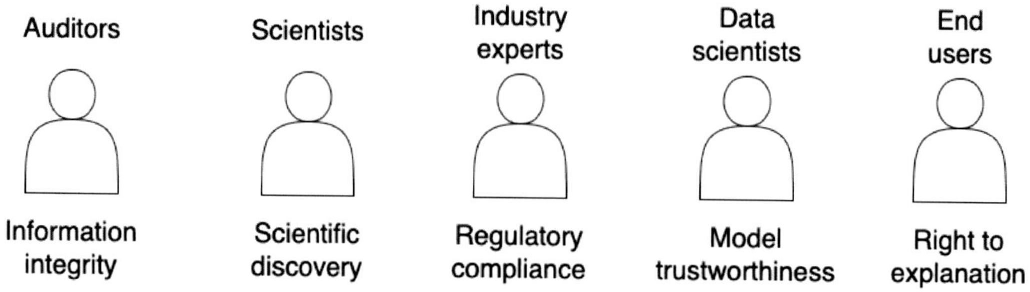

Auditors	Scientists	Industry experts	Data scientists	End users
Information integrity	Scientific discovery	Regulatory compliance	Model trustworthiness	Right to explanation

Figure 2.3 – XAI personas

XAI stakeholder personas with diverse viewpoints include the following:

- **Auditors**: While navigating increasingly complex laws and regulations, auditors must ensure information integrity throughout the audit process to validate the accuracy and reliability of the model output. As AI matures, XAI helps auditors understand the model's input, processing, and output to meet auditing standards.

- **Research scientists**: AI systems have made tremendous progress in approximating and generalizing unseen data based on the trained model. XAI helps research scientists enhance their knowledge based on information extracted by the model, leading to novel scientific discoveries.

- **Industry experts**: Simpler models are generally preferred over black-box models due to their interpretability to meet regulatory requirements. XAI helps lower the barrier to AI adoption for industry experts when considering model performance and interpretability trade-offs.

- **Data scientists**: Model development is an iterative process. XAI helps data scientists identify potential algorithmic and data bias throughout ML life cycles to improve trustworthiness in AI systems.

- **End users**: Since its inception in 2016, the **European Union (EU) General Data Protection Regulation (GDPR)** has enforced a "right to explanation" that entitles a data subject to obtain an explanation from automated decision-making systems. Individuals can request human intervention to challenge an unfair decision that affects their legal and financial rights – for example, an individual being denied a loan is entitled to demand an explanation to justify the decision.

Explanations provided by AI systems mainly serve as artifacts to guide users in deciding what to do next based on model output. Generally, users informed on both model results and reasoning take a shorter decision time than those who are only given the model results. *Figure 2.4* illustrates the current and ideal future XAI state where the user can identify the best course of action given an AI-generated explanation.

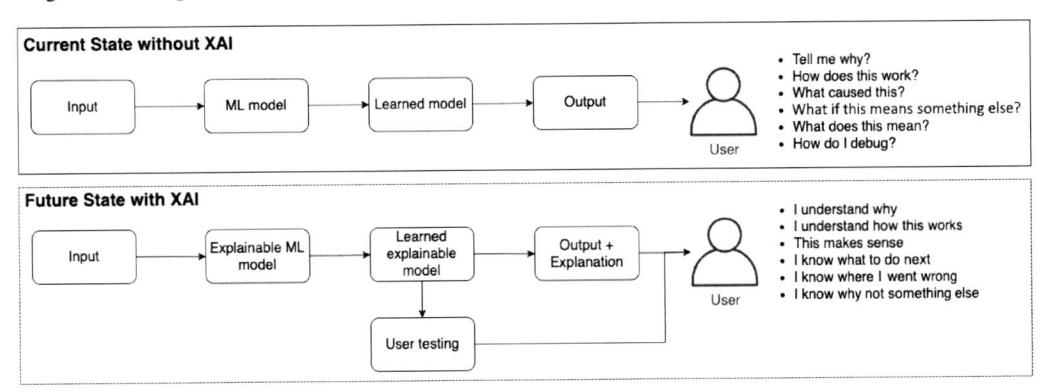

Figure 2.4 – The future state of XAI

AI systems must produce meaningful explanations for users. However, the definition of meaningful might vary for different user groups. For example, explanations that are meaningful to data scientists might not apply to auditors. In this case, data scientists might care more about algorithmic nuances, while auditors typically look for reasonable assurance. Hence, it is essential to gather direct user feedback and perform user testing to validate acceptance criteria. Note that users' perspectives on meaningful explanations can evolve as users become more comfortable and familiar with AI systems.

Now that you understand the user explainability needs, let's explore how to apply XAI for anomaly detection in the following section.

Implementing XAI

Explainability is key to building a deep learning solution for anomaly detection. Qualitative measures of XAI effectiveness often involve subjective ratings and polling user feedback on the clarity of explanations. Quantitative methods such as infidelity and sensitivity are used as objective evaluation measures for saliency map explainability, based on how well an explanation captures the predictor behavior in response to perturbations.

34   Understanding Explainable AI

The ML life cycle involves a cyclic iterative process of identifying business goals, framing specific ML problems, data preparation, model development, and deployment. Incorporating XAI in the ML life cycle enables contextual understanding and adds interpretability. *Figure 2.5* illustrates an end-to-end explainable deep learning anomaly detection life cycle.

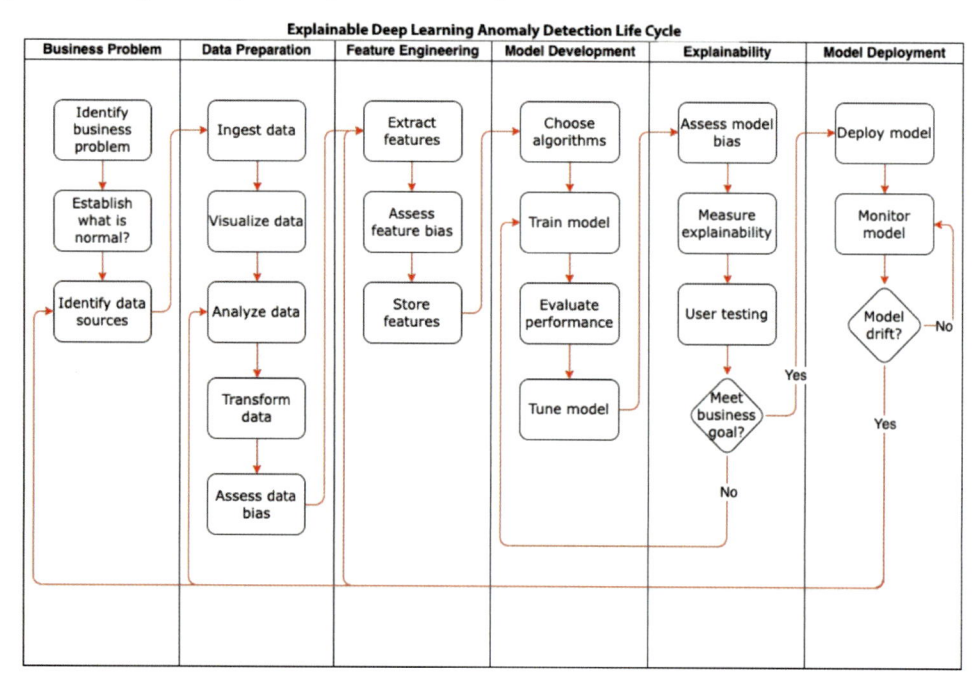

Figure 2.5 – The explainable deep learning anomaly detection life cycle

Let's review each phase of the life cycle:

- **Business Problem**: An organization considering building an AI system for anomaly detection should be able to identify clear problems, and measure business value against quantifiable success criteria. An organization must frame an ML problem around the business problem, including data modalities, target prediction, normal versus abnormal observations, and performance metrics.

- **Data Preparation**: After identifying reliable data sources, an organization must perform data processing tasks to ingest, clean, visualize, analyze, and transform input data to mitigate potential bias.

- **Feature Engineering**: Clean data is now ready for feature engineering to extract relevant attributes for model training. Be mindful of detecting feature bias where attributes such as gender, ethnic characteristics, or social status might have a detrimental effect on model predictions.

- **Model Development**: This stage involves model building, training, tuning, and performance evaluation to achieve prediction accuracy.

- **Explainability**: If the model is not inherently interpretable, this stage assesses model bias by detecting systematic error within the algorithm resulting from erroneous assumptions. Besides choosing the appropriate XAI techniques, an organization must benchmark AI-generated explanations to meet business goals and user intuition. No matter how robust your algorithm is, identifying false positive and negative results through XAI is crucial to determine an optimal trade-off.

- **Model Deployment**: A trained, tuned, and validated model is ready for deployment and inferences. Monitor the model for concept and data drifts to maintain the desired level of model performance.

As you may have noticed, XAI can be applied before, during, and after the model development process. *Figure 2.6* highlights some examples of XAI approaches when building an ML model.

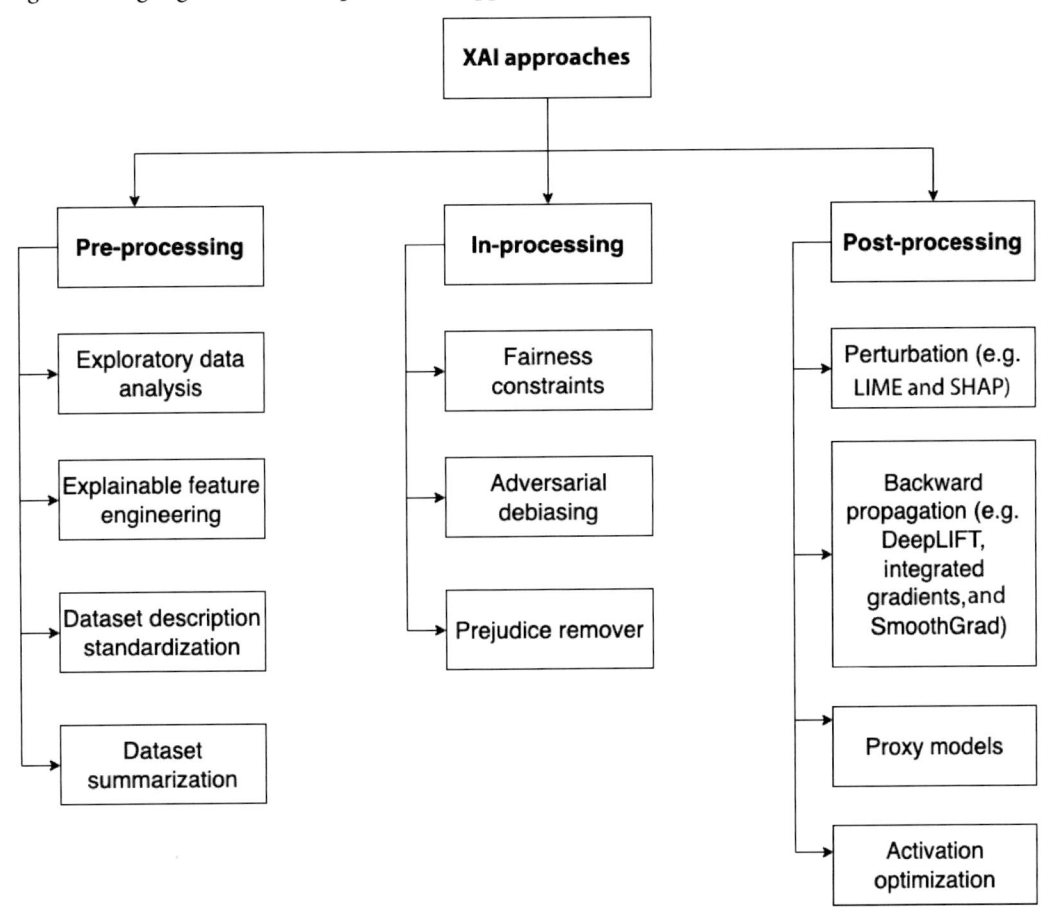

Figure 2.6 – Incorporating XAI when building ML models

Let's review these approaches:

- **Pre-processing XAI techniques**: These focus on removing bias before the model learning process, including modifying feature weighting to avoid discrimination against sensitive variables or ensuring a balanced and inclusive representation of diversity in the input data. Examples include exploratory data analysis, explainable feature engineering, dataset description standardization, and dataset summarization methods.

- **In-processing XAI techniques**: One dilemma of XAI in constructing an explanation is to protect confidential information from being exposed to adversarial attacks, which could alter model output by manipulating input based on a given explanation. In-processing XAI techniques are implemented during model training to optimize target variable prediction while minimizing feature prediction. For example, the fairness constraints framework restricts model behavior by enforcing fairness conditions within a model, adversarial debiasing reduces exposure of protected attributes from model predictions, and the prejudice remover adds discrimination-aware regularization to eliminate bias.

- **Post-processing XAI techniques**: These are applied after a model is trained without changing the input data. Common methodologies include perturbation, backward propagation, and activation optimization. We will cover backpropagation and perturbation in more depth in *Chapter 7*.

Reviewing XAI significance

Sophisticated and trained deep learning algorithms are capable of performing many tasks. Nevertheless, humans often cannot comprehend how AI systems make decisions due to their opaque nature. Fundamental questions to consider on why we need XAI are who built AI and who AI is built for. Hence, XAI has been viewed as a significant effort to keep the momentum going in the AI research field. As Albert Einstein said, "If you can't explain it simply, you don't understand it well enough." Without adequate understanding, humans cannot translate valuable insights produced by AI systems into actionable real-world knowledge. This section covers the following topics to help us understand the significance of XAI for continuous advancements toward trustworthy AI:

- Considering the right to explanation
- Driving inclusion with XAI
- Mitigating business risks

Considering the right to explanation

Since its inception in 2016, the GDPR's mission has been to unify data protection laws across EU member countries. Data protection is part of the EU Charter of Fundamental Rights to protect any personally identifiable data created through digital platforms. The legislation reaches beyond EU boundaries. Businesses collecting and processing EU residents' data are subject to GDPR regulatory requirements, regardless of where the data processing occurs or where a company resides.

Examples of GDPR articles relevant to XAI include the following:

- **Article 12**: *"Transparent information, communication and modalities for the exercise of the rights of the data subject"* (`https://gdpr-info.eu/art-12-gdpr/`). This requires businesses to communicate concisely intelligible information to data subjects in their natural language.

- **Article 15**: *"Right of access by the data subject"* (`https://gdpr-info.eu/art-15-gdpr/`). This states that the data subject is entitled to obtain explanations about the logic involved with automated decision-making systems.

- **Article 22**: *"Automated individual decision-making, including profiling"* (`https://gdpr-info.eu/art-22-gdpr/`). This grants individuals the right to request human intervention to validate AI decisions. Considering the implications of the right to explanation in *Article 15* and the right to human intervention in *Article 22*, businesses must have a clear picture of how their automated systems work to comply with GDPR.

This paper, `https://doi.org/10.1093/idpl/ipab020`, discussed how GDPR Article 22 could pose challenges to accountability in an AI-based anomaly detection system, due to automated decision-making. For example, a user might be surprised to find their bank account frozen due to an abnormal spending pattern, detected by their bank using an anomaly detection algorithm. Under the GDPR provision, this user is entitled to request human intervention in validating an automated decision and obtain explanations on what triggered such an action.

Violating the GDPR can result in financial liability of up to 4% of total annual revenue or 20 million euros, whichever is higher. Furthermore, a company will be subject to negative reputational consequences. Besides the GDPR, other regulations follow suit to enforce explainability. For example, the Equal Credit Opportunity Act demands businesses to provide a statement of reasons for denied credit applications. With increased enforcement of the right to explanation across regulations, firms must perform due diligence on XAI to improve user experience, establish user trust, and minimize business risks.

ML algorithms primarily focus on statistical correlations to estimate probability without providing the causal relationship between variables. Besides reviewing potential data and algorithmic bias, firms must be aware of explainability capabilities to support the continued use of existing AI systems. Rather than a one-size-fits-all approach, businesses should focus on producing user-centered explanations, as described by the GDPR articles.

Now that you understand the legal implications of the right to explanation for anomaly detection, let's review the social impacts of XAI in the following section.

Driving inclusion with XAI

The skills gap and AI diversity remain prominent in the AI field. Building a successful AI team requires a versatile skill set and diverse representation across various protected characteristics, including age, gender, race, national origin, religion, marital status, disability, and sexual orientation. In-demand AI skills include machine learning, statistics, probability, data analytics and visualization, programming, cloud computing, and cognitive science.

Historically, AI systems have been made by highly skilled researchers and technologists in a male-dominated industry. According to the World Economic Forum at, https://www3.weforum.org/docs/WEF_GGGR_2018.pdf, 78% of worldwide AI talents are male, and only 22% are female. This skills gap affects underrepresented groups, such as girls and women, who might not have AI educational opportunities. Furthermore, developing countries are underrepresented in the AI revolution due to the growing global digital divide. According to United Nations, about 3.7 billion people, or 50% of the world's population, do not have access to modern technological tools or communication devices. While AI continues to make strides, an inclusion effort is needed to ensure that AI is for everyone and benefits people who cannot afford the technology.

For example, the authors of this paper, http://jonathan-hersh.com/wp-content/uploads/2022/12/XAI_skills_gap.pdf, conducted an XAI experiment with 685 bank employees with mixed ML experiences to assess how the digital divide could affect AI adoption and the significance of XAI in establishing user trust. The experiment generated AI predictions to classify whether a loan will incur late disbursement and presented the outcomes to respondents with and without explanations, using Shapley values. The surveyed employees were asked to provide feedback on whether they trust AI predictions and what factors constitute their trust. The results indicated that respondents without ML backgrounds were reluctant to trust AI predictions but found the given explanations helpful. This experiment suggests that ML models designed with explainability could benefit everyday users.

A complex organizational structure may hinder AI-driven decision-making, with individual business units taking different stances and holding diverging perspectives. Businesses want to ensure the reliability of AI systems and prevent any negative impact over time. XAI can accelerate a company's AI maturity by bridging the gap in understanding AI algorithms among stakeholders and improving time to decision.

Technology leaders constantly explore and invest in new possibilities to enhance business outcomes. According to a McKinsey report at, https://www.mckinsey.com/business-functions/quantumblack/our-insights/global-survey-the-state-of-ai-in-2021, regulatory compliance, explainability, and equity and fairness are the top AI risks identified by surveyed respondents. Top performers with the highest returns from AI adoption are those who mitigate AI risks, including detecting underrepresentation of protected characteristics and identifying potential bias throughout data life cycles and model development stages. Some top performers established a central governance committee that facilitates collaboration between legal and risk professionals and data scientists to determine the impact of bias and protected classes.

This section covered XAI as an essential element in improving user experience. The following section discusses increased public awareness of XAI's significance in mitigating business risks.

Mitigating business risks

With AI adoption rising, regulators are enforcing stricter policies that mandate explainability and interpretability with AI systems to protect citizens from harmful effects. Hence, firms are required to adhere to strict regulatory compliance.

Besides regulatory compliance, firms that embrace XAI gain increased AI adoption. According to McKinsey at, `https://www.mckinsey.com/business-functions/quantumblack/our-insights/global-survey-the-state-of-ai-in-2020`, a global material manufacturer found its frontline workers did not trust AI decisions to operate a piece of heavy and potentially dangerous equipment after a significant investment in AI systems. To increase workers' confidence in AI and enable explainability, the manufacturer opted for more transparent models to improve **Return on Investment** (**ROI**).

Many companies accelerated their analytics strategy during COVID-19 by embracing AI technologies. According to Gartner at, `https://www.gartner.com/en/newsroom/press-releases/2021-09-07-gartner-identifies-four-trends-driving-near-term-artificial-intelligence-innovation`, all AI roles should demonstrate responsible AI expertise by 2023. Greater insights come with greater risks and responsibility. Business and technology leaders are increasingly aware of probable consequences and liability caused by bad decisions made by AI systems. Furthermore, failure to address public perception of bias and concerns over unfairness in AI systems can hinder AI adoption.

We learned about the implications of XAI due to public awareness in this section. Next, let's explore a methodology for choosing the appropriate XAI technique for deep learning anomaly detection solutions.

Choosing XAI techniques

Fundamental XAI principles warrant AI systems to provide some forms of explanations, evidence, and information apprehensible by humans to justify model output. The main objective of XAI is to make AI decisions comprehensible to everyday users. Choosing an XAI technique for deep learning anomaly detection requires careful deliberation and thorough analysis of the following aspects:

- **Analyze stakeholders and scope of explainability**: Know your audience, understand their roles, and discover what matters to them. Gather functional and non-functional requirements using questionnaires or existing documentation – for example, what qualifies as an anomaly in their business domain? What is an acceptable threshold when detecting outliers? What will they do with the explanations? Do they need reasoning for every prediction or aggregated explanation to understand the overall model behavior?

- **Identify data modalities**: XAI techniques differ by the data input they explain – for example, explaining images focuses more on the visual saliency of superpixels, while explaining text relies on highlighting key phrases contributing to the model prediction.

- **Choosing XAI algorithms**: There are two main categories of XAI algorithms for explaining deep learning models – perturbation and gradient-based algorithms. While the perturbation-based XAI technique produces intuitive explanations such as attribution maps, the output can be sensitive to even tiny perturbations. In contrast, while the gradient-based XAI method generates more robust explanations, they might not be faithful to the original model. *Chapter 7* covers perturbation and gradient-based XAI techniques in more depth.

- **Determine success criteria**: Perceptions of interpretability can be subjective with respect to a user's personality traits, experiences, subject matter knowledge, beliefs, and cultural influence. An organization must decide what explanations generated by an AI system it should present to stakeholders and users and how to do so. How often do they need access to this information? What should be a well-designed human-centered XAI user interface? Are the explanations simulatable and reproducible? *Chapter 9* covers explainability evaluation schemes in more detail.

The general public consensus is that better performance with AI algorithms leads to complexity and lower interpretability. Most high-performing techniques, such as deep learning, are often less explainable. Conversely, most explainable methods, such as decision trees, suffer accuracy. Nevertheless, interpretability can be subjective to users, and the satisfactory level of explainability can vary depending on people and their perceptions.

Despite ongoing research on benchmarking XAI methods, there is no unified approach to measure the quality of explanations, since XAI approaches can vary depending on use cases, data modalities, and algorithm choices. Thus, a better understanding of inner logic helps to correct potential deficiencies, implement quality control of input variables, ensure impartial decision-making, and detect vulnerabilities for adversarial perturbations that could manipulate model prediction.

Implementing XAI at scale extends beyond technology. Companies must define a sound business strategy to balance the trade-offs between prediction accuracy and explainability to meet compliance requirements. Therefore, it is essential to understand the fundamentals of XAI and related concepts when choosing appropriate explainability frameworks and tools.

Summary

While the advent of AI has pushed the boundary of what's possible, interpretability makes it more accessible by providing relevant model metrics to satisfy the needs of company stakeholders. Future XAI advancements require further testing on the validity of existing explainability frameworks and careful engineering to communicate human-comprehensible explanations and drive effective interpretability.

This chapter concludes *Part 1* of the book. You gained an overview of deep learning and XAI for anomaly detection, including their significance and best practices. In *Part 2*, we will cover practical examples of building deep learning anomaly detectors, starting with NLP.

Part 2 – Building an Explainable Deep Learning Anomaly Detector

Part 2 dives into building deep learning anomaly detectors in three major application domains using various data modalities, with step-by-step example walk-throughs. By the end of *Part 2*, you will have learned how to quickly develop sophisticated anomaly detectors using state-of-the-art frameworks such as AutoGluon and Cleanlab, and be able to apply XAI techniques to extend the model's explainability in these domains.

This part comprises the following chapters:

- *Chapter 3, Natural Language Processing Anomaly Explainability*
- *Chapter 4, Time Series Anomaly Explainability*
- *Chapter 5, Computer Vision Anomaly Explainability*

3
Natural Language Processing Anomaly Explainability

The evolution of **Natural Language Processing** (**NLP**) began in the 1950s with machine translation converting Russian into English. The advent of computing power and big data motivated NLP innovation, leading to a new subfield of linguistics, computer science, and artificial intelligence. *Figure 3.1* shows the intersections of NLP with other disciplines:

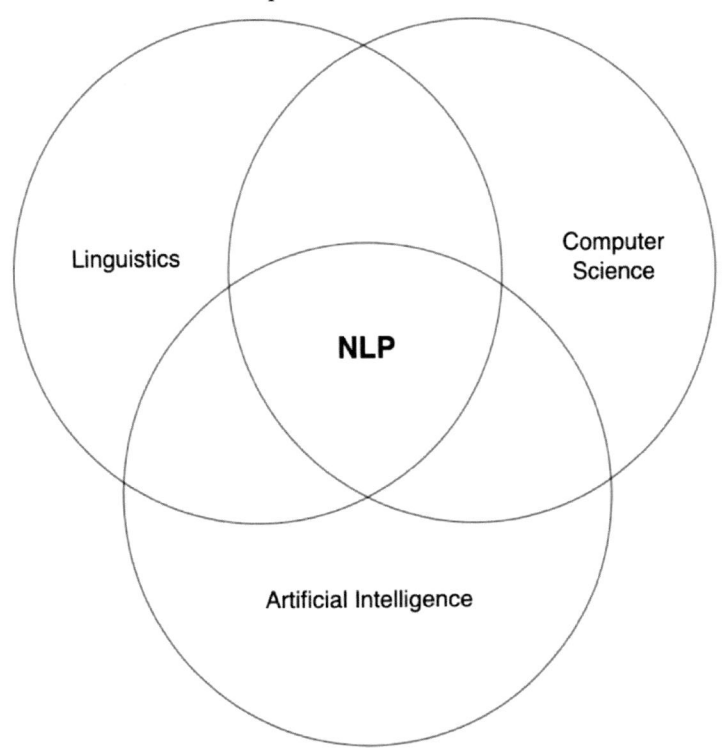

Figure 3.1 – NLP Venn diagram

There is abundant unstructured textual data around us for NLP tasks, such as text classification, topic modeling, and intent detection. NLP enables computers to understand and analyze massive amounts of written and verbal human language at scale. The goal is to contextualize language nuances and extract useful information to derive valuable insights.

Deep learning has revolutionized many NLP applications, including text summarization, machine translation, and question-answering. However, despite high accuracy, industry experts challenge the interpretability and credibility of deep learning model predictions due to their opaque nature. Furthermore, common linguistic challenges such as sarcasm, slang, and polysemy in textual data add complexity to handling lexical and syntactic ambiguity. NLP explainability aims to uncover the interpretability of word embedding models and understand the internal representations of neural networks for NLP, such as transformer models.

There are two example walk throughs in this chapter to cover NLP anomaly explainability:

- Using the public Amazon Customer Reviews dataset, `https://doi.org/10.7910/DVN/W96OFO`, you will learn the basics of NLP by building a text classifier for multiclass text classification with **AutoGluon**, `https://github.com/autogluon/autogluon`, an open source **automated machine learning** (**AutoML**) library developed by Amazon.

- For the NLP explainability example, you will use the same dataset to detect anomalies in text data using **Cleanlab**, `https://github.com/cleanlab/cleanlab`, an open source library that can find potential label errors for multiclass text classification and assess the quality of predictions using **SHapley Additive exPlanations** (**SHAP**), `https://github.com/slundberg/shap`.

By the end of this chapter, you will have gained a deeper understanding of evaluating explainability for NLP anomaly detection. Next, let's discuss the technical requirements for this chapter.

Technical requirements

You will need the following Python packages for the example walkthrough:

- **Matplotlib**: A plotting library for creating data visualizations
- **NumPy**: An open source library that provides mathematical functions when working with arrays
- **pandas**: A library that offers data analysis and manipulation tools
- **Imbalanced-learn**: An open source library imported as `imblearn` that provides tools to handle imbalanced datasets
- **MXNet**: An open source deep learning framework
- **TensorFlow**: An open source framework for building deep learning applications
- **AutoGluon**: An open source AutoML library that automates **machine learning** (**ML**) tasks

- **Cleanlab**: An open source library that automatically detects anomalies and finds data errors in a text dataset
- **SciPy**: An open source Python library for scientific computing
- **SciKeras**: Provides scikit-learn compatible wrappers for Keras models
- **Transformers**: Provides pre-trained models for ML tasks
- **Scikit-learn**: An ML library for predictive data analysis
- **SHAP**: A Python library that explains an ML output using Shapley values

The sample Jupyter notebook and requirements files for package dependencies discussed in this chapter are available at `https://github.com/PacktPublishing/Deep-Learning-and-XAI-Techniques-for-Anomaly-Detection/tree/main/Chapter3`.

You can experiment with these examples on Amazon SageMaker Studio Lab, `https://aws.amazon.com/sagemaker/studio-lab/`, a free notebook development environment that provides up to 12 hours of CPU or 4 hours of GPU per user session and 15 GiB storage at no cost. Alternatively, you can try this on your preferred **integrated development environment** (IDE).

Understanding natural language processing

Text classification is an NLP task that analyzes and categorizes text into groups using predefined labels. Common business use cases for text classification include sentiment analysis, topic detection, and language detection. Classifying content provides valuable business insights into customer preferences, personalized experience, content moderation, emerging market segments, and social sentiment.

For an overview of NLP, we will train a multiclass text classification model using AutoGluon, `https://auto.gluon.ai/`, and a public data repository for Amazon customer reviews, `https://doi.org/10.7910/DVN/W96OFO`, maintained by Harvard Dataverse. The data repository contains 7 text datasets collected between 2008 and 2020, with 5,000 reviews each. You can download the `export_food.csv` file from this data repository for the example walk through.

The following section gives an overview of AutoGluon.

Reviewing AutoGluon

AutoGluon is an open source AutoML library developed by Amazon that automates deep learning and ML applications for text, tabular, and image data. Without prior ML experience, users can train state-of-the-art and highly accurate models for text classification, tabular data prediction, and image classification with a few lines of code and minimal setup.

AutoGluon works by ensembling and stacking multiple models in layers. Without much data preprocessing, AutoGluon can infer a given dataset's ML task based on the label column's value type. For example, non-numeric string values in the label column indicate a classification problem, whereas repeated numeric values in the label column indicate a regression problem.

AutoGluon's **TextPredictor** formats NLP datasets in tables consisting of text columns and label columns to predict text. Each row represents a training example with discrete categorical value for classification or continuous values for regression. Furthermore, TextPredictor supports multilingual problems and multimodal data tables combining text, numeric, and categorical columns. You can read more about AutoGluon at https://arxiv.org/abs/2003.06505.

Now we are ready to build a text classifier with AutoGluon. A sample notebook, chapter3_autogluon_nlp.ipynb, is available at the book's GitHub repo:

1. First, install the required packages:

   ```
   import sys
   !{sys.executable} -m pip install -r requirements.txt
   ```

2. Next, load essential libraries and validate package dependencies:

   ```
   %matplotlib inline
   import numpy as np
   import warnings
   import matplotlib.pyplot as plt
   import pandas as pd
   import tensorflow as tf
   from platform import python_version
   from autogluon.tabular.version import __version__

   warnings.filterwarnings('ignore')
   np.random.seed(42)

   print(f'TensorFlow version: {tf.__version__}')
   print(f'Python version: {python_version()}')
   print(f'AutoGluon version: {__version__}')
   ```

3. Display full text for column values:

   ```
   pd.set_option("display.max_colwidth", None)
   ```

4. Load the raw dataset. Remove any leading and trailing characters. Then, preview the data:

```
df = pd.read_csv('export_food.csv')
data = df[['reviews','ratings']]
data['reviews'] = data['reviews'].str.strip()
data.head(3)
```

Figure 3.2 shows a preview of the dataset:

	reviews	ratings
0	I've been ordering this product monthly for over a year. These past few shipments have been off, and the packaging is different. It is obvious they are from two different manufacturers. The full bottle is the imposter and has no pink ribbon on the label, the label photo is different, and if you look at the bottle, you can see on the back that the legitimate product has a 3% Juice Content label on the back up top, and the imposter has a 1% Juice Content. There are also other differences on the label. See Photos for comparison. Two different products, and the IMPOSTER is absolutely undrinkable and tastes nothing like the original product.I contacted Amazon and they are pulling this flavor, Red Grapefruit, off the shelf while they investigate this issue. They also issued me a full credit. I hope they can get this figured out because this is my favorite flavor and I drink it everyday.	4
1	I used to drink these Sparkling Ice waters in all flavors every day. They all taste GREAT, my favorite was Black Raspberry. However, I just discovered that they contain sucralose which is just another harmful artificial sweetener. The only safe sweeteners are Stevia, Agave, and Raw Honey. I have stopped drinking/eating anything with harmful artificial sweeteners since they have been linked to many diseases, including dementia and the increase in Atzheimers disease patients.	5

Figure 3.2 – Preview dataset

5. Review information about the DataFrame, including index dtypes, columns, non-null values, and memory usage:

   ```
   data.info()
   ```

   Figure 3.3 shows the DataFrame information:

   ```
   <class 'pandas.core.frame.DataFrame'>
   RangeIndex: 5000 entries, 0 to 4999
   Data columns (total 2 columns):
    #   Column   Non-Null Count  Dtype
   ---  ------   --------------  -----
    0   reviews  5000 non-null   object
    1   ratings  5000 non-null   int64
   dtypes: int64(1), object(1)
   memory usage: 78.2+ KB
   ```

   Figure 3.3 – DataFrame information

6. View the unique classes for the target column:

   ```
   data['ratings'].unique()
   ```

   Figure 3.4 shows the unique classes in the dataset:

   ```
   array([4, 5, 1, 2, 3])
   ```

   Figure 3.4 – Unique classes

7. View the counts of records in each class:

   ```
   data['ratings'].value_counts()
   ```

   Figure 3.5 shows the class frequency distribution:

   ```
   5    3402
   4     683
   1     677
   3     134
   2     104
   Name: ratings, dtype: int64
   ```

   Figure 3.5 – Class frequency distribution

8. Plot a visualization of class frequency distribution:

   ```
   data['ratings'].value_counts().plot(kind = 'bar')
   ```

   Figure 3.6 shows the visualization of class frequency distribution:

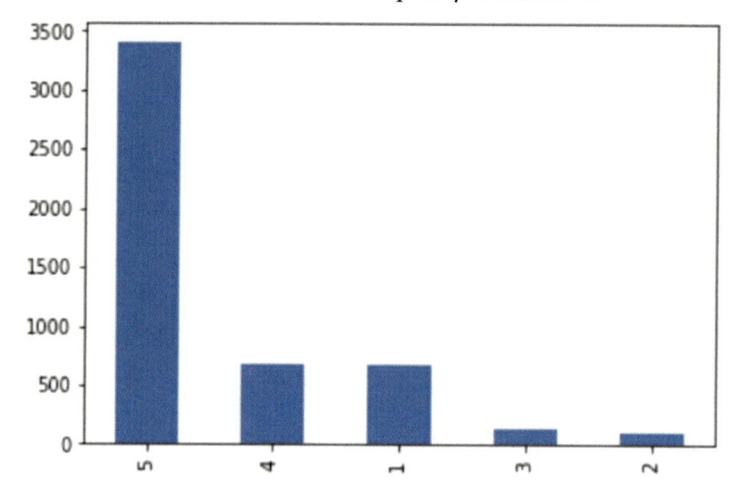

   Figure 3.6 – Original class frequency distribution

9. As you can see, the original dataset is highly imbalanced. For demo purposes, we will use `RandomOverSampler` to duplicate examples randomly in the minority class:

   ```
   from imblearn.over_sampling import RandomOverSampler

   X = data[['reviews']]
   y = data[['ratings']]
   ```

```
ros = RandomOverSampler(sampling_strategy='minority')
X_res, y_res = ros.fit_resample(X, y)

RandomOverSampler(sampling_strategy='minority')
```

10. Visualize the class frequency distribution again after oversampling. We have now increased the samples for the two-star rating class:

    ```
    y_res.value_counts().plot(kind = 'bar')
    ```

    After oversampling, you should see a new class frequency distribution as shown in *Figure 3.7*:

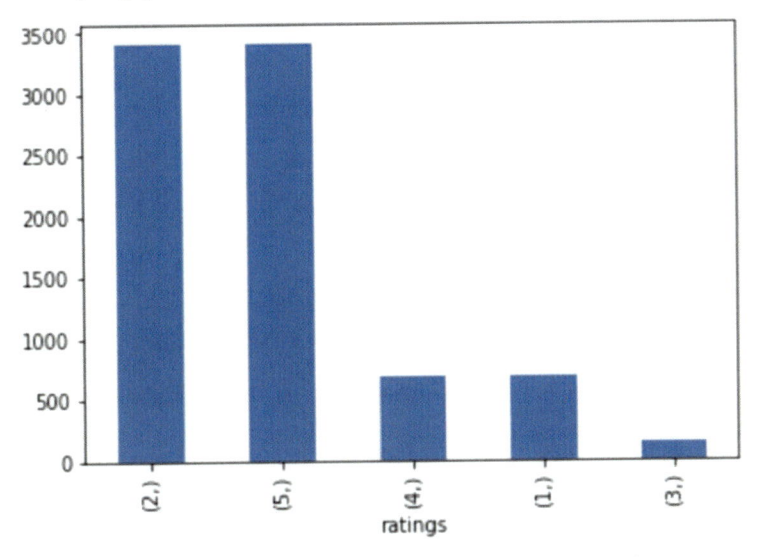

Figure 3.7 – After oversampling

11. Merge the rebalanced data:

    ```
    rebalanced_data = X_res.join(y_res)
    rebalanced_data.head(3)
    ```

12. Split the rebalanced dataset into an 80:20 ratio for training and testing:

    ```
    from sklearn.model_selection import train_test_split

    X_train, X_test = train_test_split(rebalanced_data, test_size=0.2, random_state=42)
    ```

13. View the train and test data shape:

    ```
    print(f'Train shape: {X_train.shape}')
    print(f'Test shape: {X_test.shape}')
    ```

    Figure 3.8 shows the train and test shape:

    ```
    Train shape: (6638, 2)
    Test shape: (1660, 2)
    ```

    Figure 3.8 – Train and test shape result

14. We are now ready to train a model using AutoGluon's TextPredictor. Let's define a directory named `ag_food_reviews` for saving the trained model output and logs. Remove any existing folder with the same output folder name:

    ```
    OUTPUT_DIR = 'ag_food_reviews'

    DO_DELETE = True

    if DO_DELETE:
      try:
        tf.compat.v1.gfile.DeleteRecursively(OUTPUT_DIR)
      except:
        pass

    tf.io.gfile.makedirs(OUTPUT_DIR)
    print(f'Model output directory: {OUTPUT_DIR}')
    ```

15. Let's call `TextPredictor` to fit the train data. Here, we are defining the `ratings` column as the target label, `multiclass` as `problem_type`, accuracy as an evaluation metric, and an output directory that we previously configured. Then, we call `predictor.fit` to train with the full train data to get a model with the best possible quality. Note that training time increases depending on the size of the data you are using. Alternatively, you can reduce the training time by setting `time_limit` in seconds. For example, `predictor_fit(X_train, time_limit=300)`:

    ```
    from autogluon.text import TextPredictor

    predictor = TextPredictor(label='ratings', problem_type='multiclass', eval_metric='acc', path=OUTPUT_DIR)

    predictor.fit(X_train)
    ```

16. Here, we can see some information about the model, including the number of trainable parameters and estimated model size. When the training completes, you can see the list of accepted hyperparameters, shown in *Figure 3.9*, saved by the predictor in `config.yaml` under the output folder:

```
Global seed set to 123
GPU available: False, used: False
TPU available: False, using: 0 TPU cores
IPU available: False, using: 0 IPUs
HPU available: False, using: 0 HPUs

  | Name              | Type                      | Params
-----------------------------------------------------------
0 | model             | HFAutoModelForTextPrediction | 108 M
1 | validation_metric | Accuracy                  | 0
2 | loss_func         | CrossEntropyLoss          | 0
-----------------------------------------------------------
108 M     Trainable params
0         Non-trainable params
108 M     Total params
435.582   Total estimated model params size (MB)
```

Figure 3.9 – AutoGluon model summary

17. *Figure 3.10* shows the training results. TextPredictor fits individual transformer neural network models directly to the raw text and handles numeric and categorical columns. It optimizes prediction based on accuracy evaluation metrics and saves a trained model as `model.ckpt` to the output folder:

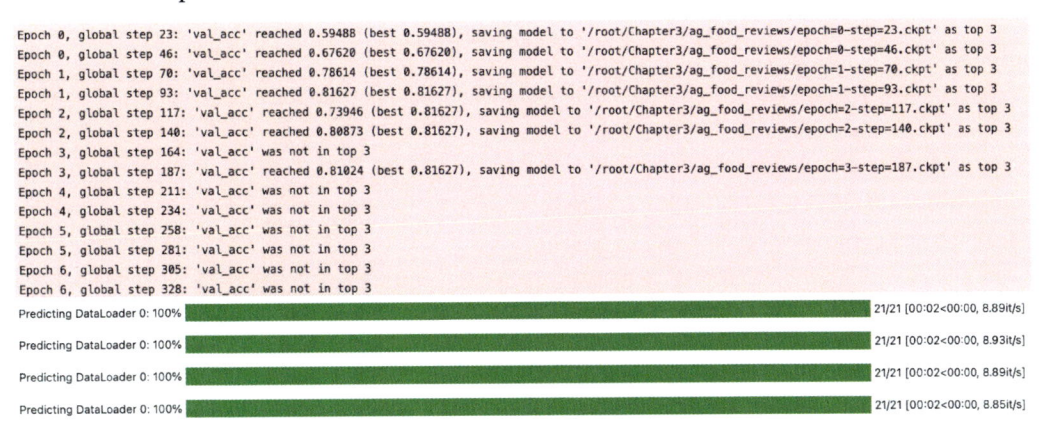

```
Epoch 0, global step 23:  'val_acc' reached 0.59488 (best 0.59488), saving model to '/root/Chapter3/ag_food_reviews/epoch=0-step=23.ckpt' as top 3
Epoch 0, global step 46:  'val_acc' reached 0.67620 (best 0.67620), saving model to '/root/Chapter3/ag_food_reviews/epoch=0-step=46.ckpt' as top 3
Epoch 1, global step 70:  'val_acc' reached 0.78614 (best 0.78614), saving model to '/root/Chapter3/ag_food_reviews/epoch=1-step=70.ckpt' as top 3
Epoch 1, global step 93:  'val_acc' reached 0.81627 (best 0.81627), saving model to '/root/Chapter3/ag_food_reviews/epoch=1-step=93.ckpt' as top 3
Epoch 2, global step 117: 'val_acc' reached 0.73946 (best 0.81627), saving model to '/root/Chapter3/ag_food_reviews/epoch=2-step=117.ckpt' as top 3
Epoch 2, global step 140: 'val_acc' reached 0.80873 (best 0.81627), saving model to '/root/Chapter3/ag_food_reviews/epoch=2-step=140.ckpt' as top 3
Epoch 3, global step 164: 'val_acc' was not in top 3
Epoch 3, global step 187: 'val_acc' reached 0.81024 (best 0.81627), saving model to '/root/Chapter3/ag_food_reviews/epoch=3-step=187.ckpt' as top 3
Epoch 4, global step 211: 'val_acc' was not in top 3
Epoch 4, global step 234: 'val_acc' was not in top 3
Epoch 5, global step 258: 'val_acc' was not in top 3
Epoch 5, global step 281: 'val_acc' was not in top 3
Epoch 6, global step 305: 'val_acc' was not in top 3
Epoch 6, global step 328: 'val_acc' was not in top 3
Predicting DataLoader 0: 100%|████████████| 21/21 [00:02<00:00, 8.89it/s]
Predicting DataLoader 0: 100%|████████████| 21/21 [00:02<00:00, 8.93it/s]
Predicting DataLoader 0: 100%|████████████| 21/21 [00:02<00:00, 8.89it/s]
Predicting DataLoader 0: 100%|████████████| 21/21 [00:02<00:00, 8.85it/s]
```

Figure 3.10 – AutoGluon training process

18. After training, we can evaluate the model performance using the test dataset. By default, the `evaluate()` function reports the previously defined metric, `accuracy`. You can include additional metrics, such as the `f1_micro` score, for evaluation:

    ```
    test_score = predictor.evaluate(X_test,
    metrics=['accuracy', 'f1_micro'])
    print(test_score)
    ```

    Figure 3.11 shows the `accuracy` and `f1_micro` score:

    ```
    {'accuracy': 0.8012048192771084, 'f1_micro': 0.8012048192771084}
    ```

    Figure 3.11 – Evaluation metrics

19. We are now ready to make predictions from the trained model by calling the `predictor.predict()` function. First, we will identify some samples from the test data with positive and negative reviews. Here, we categorize reviews with at least a three-star rating as positive and less than a three-star rating as negative:

    ```
    positive_reviews = X_test.query('ratings > 3')
    negative_reviews = X_test.query('ratings <= 3')
    ```

20. Preview the list of positive reviews with the following code:

    ```
    with pd.option_context('display.max_colwidth', None):
        display(positive_reviews)
    ```

    Figure 3.12 shows a preview of positive reviews:

	reviews	ratings
4985	They taste really good and I would recommend it to anyone	4
3994	Tastes really good.	5
2820	Did not like the ginger taste.	5
2280	My favorite flavor. Like sparkling lemonade....So refreshing!	5
3149	Refreshing	5
...	...	...
620	We love this and had been paying more per bottle at the grocery. I love being able to get this for cheaper and like the combination of flavors.	5
4745	Product came pre-opened with two inches of product missing.	4
4313	good taste n price	5

809 rows × 2 columns

Figure 3.12 – Positive reviews

Understanding natural language processing   53

21. Preview the negative reviews with the following code:

```
with pd.option_context('display.max_colwidth', None):
    display(negative_reviews)
```

Figure 3.13 shows a preview of the negative reviews:

Product Review: Sparkling ICE is the best! They are tasty, calorie free, bubbly, and inexpensive. Buying on amazon is less expensive than at the grocery store, so I order these all the time.
Predicted Rating: 5
Product Review: I have been ordering this for months but this last batch was old or bad and faded I had to return
Predicted Rating: 2

Besides predicted classes, we can obtain predicted class-probabilities.

Figure 3.13 – Negative reviews

22. Let's predict the target label for the following selected reviews:

```
review1 = "Sparkling ICE is the best! They are tasty, calorie free, bubbly, and inexpensive. Buying on amazon is less expensive than at the grocery store, so I order these all the time."
review2 = "I have been ordering this for months but this last batch was old or bad and faded I had to return"

predictions = predictor.predict({'reviews': [review1, review2]})
print(f'Product Review: {review1} \nPredicted Rating: {predictions.iloc[0]}')
print(f'Product Review: {review2} \nPredicted Rating: {predictions.iloc[1]}')
```

Figure 3.14 shows two predicted reviews:

Product Review: Sparkling ICE is the best! They are tasty, calorie free, bubbly, and inexpensive. Buying on amazon is less expensive than at the grocery store, so I order these all the time.
Predicted Class-Probabilities:
1   0.158037
2   0.250578
3   0.042650
4   0.133276
5   0.415459

Figure 3.14 – Predicted ratings

23. We can also obtain predicted class probabilities:

```
probs = predictor.predict_proba({'reviews': [review1, review2]})
print(f'Product Review: {review1} \nPredicted Class-Probabilities:\n{probs.iloc[0]}')
print(f'Product Review: {review2} \nPredicted Class-Probabilities:\n{probs.iloc[1]}')
```

Figure 3.15 shows the class probabilities:

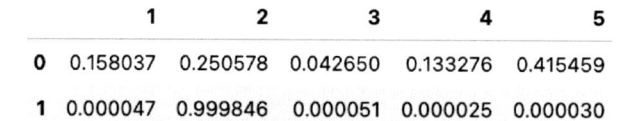

	1	2	3	4	5
0	0.158037	0.250578	0.042650	0.133276	0.415459
1	0.000047	0.999846	0.000051	0.000025	0.000030

Figure 3.15 – Predicted class probabilities

24. Let's produce predictions over the entire test data:

```
test_predictions = predictor.predict(X_test)
```

25. The `fit` function automatically saves the trained predictor at the end of the training process. We can reload it for prediction:

```
loaded_predictor = TextPredictor.load('ag_food_reviews')
loaded_predictor.predict_proba({'reviews': [review1, review2]})
```

Figure 3.16 shows the output probabilities for each class:

	1	2	3	4	5
0	0.158037	0.250578	0.042650	0.133276	0.415459
1	0.000047	0.999846	0.000051	0.000025	0.000030

Figure 3.16 – Output probabilities

26. Alternatively, by calling the `save` function, you can save the trained model to a desired location:

```
loaded_predictor.save('my_saved_dir')
loaded_predictor2 = TextPredictor.load('my_saved_dir')
loaded_predictor2.predict_proba({'reviews': [review1, review2]})
```

27. We can use a trained predictor to extract embeddings that map each data table row to an intermediate neural network representation of the row:

    ```
    embeddings = predictor.extract_embedding(X_test)
    print(embeddings)
    ```

28. *Figure 3.17* shows the embeddings used by the predictor:

```
Predicting DataLoader 0: 100%|████████████████████████████████| 52/52 [00:05<00:00, 9.27it/s]
[[-0.6521491  -0.26700833  0.09421055 ...  0.29980472  0.44825974
   0.7461777 ]
 [ 0.00520702  0.68804175  0.02289832 ...  0.5043433   0.2496965
  -0.26859117]
 [ 0.14096348  0.6670949   0.0537451  ...  0.46771514  0.09381741
  -0.37640372]
 ...
 [ 0.2750097  -0.34764984  0.1748297  ... -0.64605737  0.5334411
   0.12582716]
 [ 0.19423327  0.51381886  0.03548399 ...  0.3546247   0.25145265
  -0.6742987 ]
 [-0.65595    -0.77710974 -0.42872536 ... -0.7155813   0.6250126
   0.1075721 ]]
```

Figure 3.17 – Embeddings

29. Using **t-distributed stochastic neighbor embedding** (**t-SNE**), we can see the extracted embeddings of test data corresponding to five target labels, as shown in *Figure 3.18*:

    ```
    from sklearn.manifold import TSNE

    plt.rcParams["figure.figsize"] = (20,10)

    X_embedded = TSNE(n_components=2, random_state=123).fit_
    transform(embeddings)
    for val, color in [(1, 'red'), (2, 'purple'), (3,
    'blue'), (4, 'orange'), (5, 'green')]:
        idx = (X_test['ratings'].to_numpy() == val).nonzero()
        plt.scatter(X_embedded[idx, 0], X_embedded[idx, 1],
    c=color, label=f'label={val}')
    plt.legend(loc='best')
    ```

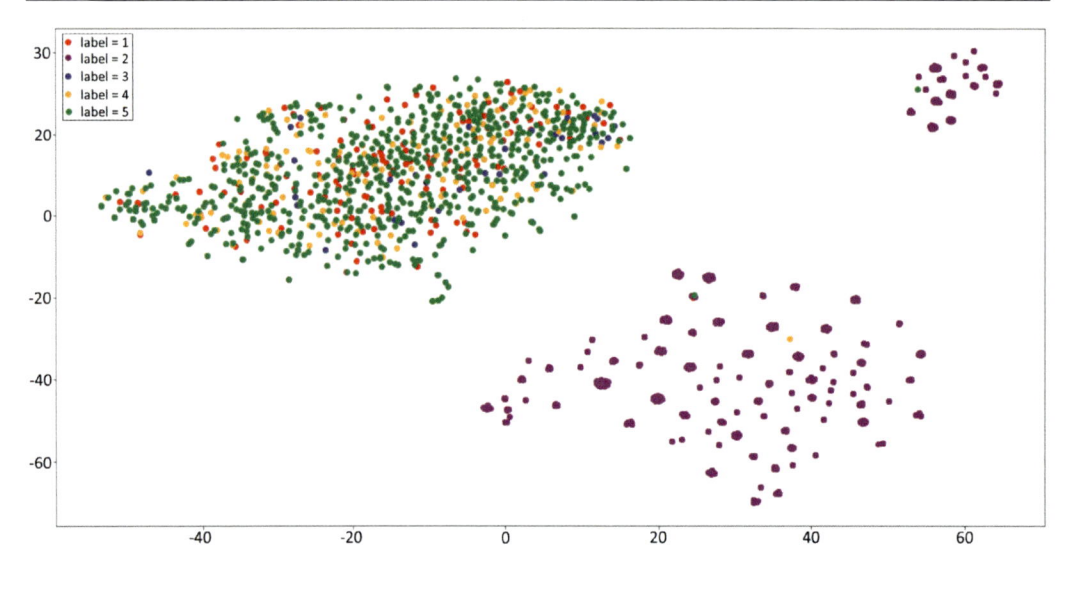

Figure 3.18 – t-SNE

You have completed an NLP text classification task by analyzing the Amazon Customer Reviews dataset and building a classifier with AutoGluon. Next, let's extend our knowledge by reviewing an example of NLP anomaly detection and assessing the interpretability quality.

Problem

NLP explainability typically involves removing or masking random words from a dataset. Extending the same Amazon Customer Reviews dataset, we will review an NLP anomaly detection example using Cleanlab, https://github.com/cleanlab/cleanlab, an open source library, to find potential label errors for text data. Then, we will use SHAP, https://github.com/slundberg/shap, to evaluate post hoc local explainability for model predictions by visualizing feature attributions of individual classes based on computed SHAP values.

Post hoc local explainability means assessing how a particular decision or prediction is made after model training. Using a fine-tuned **bidirectional encoder representations from transformers** (**BERT**) model, we will classify positive versus negative sentiments for the Amazon Customer Reviews dataset and compare predicted label errors.

The following section provides an end-to-end solution walk-through.

Solution walk-through

Let's review the steps from the `chapter3_nlp_shap.ipynb` notebook, available at the book's GitHub repo:

1. First, let's install the required packages:

   ```
   import sys
   !{sys.executable} -m pip install -r requirements.txt
   ```

2. Next, load the essential libraries:

   ```
   import os
   import random
   import numpy as np
   import pandas as pd
   import tensorflow as tf
   import re
   import string
   from platform import python_version

   os.environ["TF_CPP_MIN_LOG_LEVEL"] = "3"

   SEED = 42
   np.random.seed(SEED)
   random.seed(SEED)

   print(f'TensorFlow version: {tf.__version__}')
   print(f'Python version: {python_version()}')
   ```

   Figure 3.19 shows the TensorFlow and Python package dependencies:

   ```
   TensorFlow version: 2.11.0
   Python version: 3.9.10
   ```

   Figure 3.19 – Package dependencies

3. Set to display full-text reviews:

   ```
   pd.set_option("display.max_colwidth", None)
   ```

4. Read the raw text dataset from `export_food.csv` to extract the `reviews` and `ratings` columns. View the unique target labels:

```
df = pd.read_csv("export_food.csv")
df = df[['reviews','ratings']]
df['reviews'] = df['reviews'].str.strip()
df['ratings'].unique()
```

You should see the following result, as shown in *Figure 3.20*:

```
array([4, 5, 1, 2, 3])
```

Figure 3.20 – Unique classes

5. Cleanlab requires zero-indexed target labels. Therefore, we will normalize the `ratings` column and assign it to a new `categorical_ratings` column:

```
from sklearn import preprocessing

le = preprocessing.LabelEncoder()
le.fit(df['ratings'])
df['categorical_ratings'] = le.transform(df['ratings'])

df.head(5)
```

Figure 3.21 shows the encoded categorical target labels:

	reviews	categorical_ratings
0	I've been ordering this product monthly for over a year. These past few shipments have been off, and the packaging is different. It is obvious they are from two different manufacturers. The full bottle is the imposter and has no pink ribbon on the label, the label photo is different, and if you look at the bottle, you can see on the back that the legitimate product has a 3% Juice Content label on the back up top, and the imposter has a 1% Juice Content. There are also other differences on the label. See Photos for comparison. Two different products, and the IMPOSTER is absolutely undrinkable and tastes nothing like the original product.I contacted Amazon and they are pulling this flavor, Red Grapefruit, off the shelf while they investigate this issue. They also issued me a full credit. I hope they can get this figured out because this is my favorite flavor and I drink it everyday.	3
1	I used to drink these Sparkling Ice waters in all flavors every day. They all taste GREAT, my favorite was Black Raspberry. However, I just discovered that they contain sucralose which is just another harmful artificial sweetener. The only safe sweeteners are Stevia, Agave, and Raw Honey. I have stopped drinking/eating anything with harmful artificial sweeteners since they have been linked to many diseases, including dementia and the increase in Atzheimers disease patients.	4

Figure 3.21 – Encoded target labels

6. Create a new dataset using the `categorical_ratings` column as the target label:

```
raw_full_ds = df[['reviews','categorical_ratings']]
raw_full_ds.head(5)
```

Figure 3.22 shows the new dataset using the encoded `categorical_ratings` column:

	reviews	categorical_ratings
0	False	False
1	False	False
2	False	False
...	...	...
4997	False	False
4998	False	False
4999	False	False

5000 rows × 2 columns

Figure 3.22 – New dataset with the categorical_ratings column

7. Remove any rows with missing values:

```
raw_full_ds = raw_full_ds.dropna()
raw_full_ds.isna()
```

Figure 3.23 validates that there are no rows with missing values:

	reviews	categorical_ratings
0	False	False
1	False	False
2	False	False
...	...	...
4997	False	False
4998	False	False
4999	False	False

5000 rows × 2 columns

Figure 3.23 – Result showing no rows with missing values

8. Assign `categorical_ratings` as the new target column:

    ```
    raw_full_texts = raw_full_ds['reviews']
    full_labels = raw_full_ds['categorical_ratings']
    ```

9. Set the number of classes:

    ```
    num_classes = len(set(full_labels))
    print(f'Number of classes: {num_classes}')
    print(f'Categorical classes: {set(full_labels)}')
    ```

10. Review the shape and features data:

    ```
    print(f'Dataset shape: {raw_full_ds.shape}')
    print(f'Dataset features: {raw_full_ds.columns}')
    ```

Figure 3.24 validates the data shape and features that we will be using:

```
Dataset shape: (5000, 2)
Dataset features: Index(['reviews', 'categorical_ratings'], dtype='object')
```

Figure 3.24 – Data shape and features

11. Convert the DataFrame into NumPy arrays:

    ```
    raw_full_texts_arr = raw_full_texts.to_numpy(dtype=str)
    raw_full_texts_arr
    ```

Figure 3.25 shows the output after the conversion:

```
Example Label: 4
Example Text: Great but cheaper at the store
```

Figure 3.25 – Preview reviews after the NumPy conversion

12. Preview a sample review and rating, as shown in *Figure 3.26*:

    ```
    i = 4995
    print(f"Example Label: {full_labels[i]+1}")
    print(f"Example Text: {raw_full_texts[i]}")
    ```
    The result is:

    ```
    Example Label: 4
    Example Text: Great but cheaper at the store
    ```

Figure 3.26 – Result of the sample review

13. Create a function to clean the data by converting all characters to lowercase and removing HTML tags and punctuation:

    ```
    def preprocess_text(input_data):
        lowercase = tf.strings.lower(input_data)
        stripped_html = tf.strings.regex_replace(lowercase, "<br />", " ")
        return tf.strings.regex_replace(stripped_html, f"[{re.escape(string.punctuation)}]", "")
    ```

14. Map text features to integer sequences:

    ```
    from tensorflow.keras import layers

    tf.keras.utils.set_random_seed(SEED)

    max_features = 10000
    sequence_length = 250

    vectorize_layer = layers.TextVectorization(
        standardize=preprocess_text,
        max_tokens=max_features,
        output_mode="int",
        output_sequence_length=sequence_length,
    )
    ```

15. Apply preprocessing to the dataset by calling adapt:

    ```
    vectorize_layer.adapt(raw_full_texts_arr)
    full_texts = vectorize_layer(raw_full_texts_arr)
    full_texts = full_texts.numpy()
    ```

16. Create a simple neural network for multiclass text classification:

    ```
    from tensorflow.keras import losses, metrics
    from tensorflow.keras.optimizers import Adam

    def get_net():
        net = tf.keras.Sequential(
    ```

```
        [tf.keras.Input(shape=(None,), dtype="int64"),
        layers.Embedding(max_features + 1, 16),
        layers.Dropout(0.2),
        layers.GlobalAveragePooling1D(),
        layers.Dropout(0.2),
        layers.Dense(num_classes),
        layers.Softmax()]
    )

    net.compile(
        optimizer="adam",
        loss=losses.SparseCategoricalCrossentropy(),
        metrics=metrics.CategoricalAccuracy(),
    )
    return net
```

17. Wrap the neural network with SciKeras as some features from Cleanlab must be scikit-learn-compatible. We are also setting 10 epochs here:

    ```
    from scikeras.wrappers import KerasClassifier
    model = KerasClassifier(get_net(), epochs=10)
    ```

18. Cleanlab requires predicted probabilities for each data point from a deep learning model. These predicted probabilities can be overfitting. Hence, Cleanlab uses out-of-sample predicted probabilities via held-out datapoints from training. Here, we use k-fold cross-validation to produce out-of-sample predicted probabilities, where every training copy from defined *K* copies is trained with different unseen data subsets. You can try adjusting num_crossval_folds for better results:

    ```
    from sklearn.model_selection import cross_val_predict

    num_crossval_folds = 5

    pred_probs = cross_val_predict(
        model,
        full_texts,
        full_labels,
        cv=num_crossval_folds,
        method="predict_proba",
    )
    ```

Solution walk-through   63

19. Calculate `log_loss`, this is the score to evaluate probabilistic predictions, lower values are better:

    ```
    from sklearn.metrics import log_loss

    loss = log_loss(full_labels, pred_probs)
    print(f"Cross-validated estimate of log loss: {loss:.3f}")
    ```

20. Based on the predicted probability, sort the indices of identified label issues by self-confidence scores to measure the quality of a given label:

    ```
    from cleanlab.filter import find_label_issues

    ranked_label_issues = find_label_issues(
        labels=full_labels, pred_probs=pred_probs, return_indices_ranked_by="self_confidence"
    )
    ```

21. Cleanlab identified 1,556 potential label errors with this dataset. Let's list the top 10 indices of predicted label anomalies:

    ```
    print(
        f"Cleanlab identified {len(ranked_label_issues)} potential label errors.\n Indices of the top 10 most likely errors: \n {ranked_label_issues[:10]}"
    )
    ```

    Figure 3.27 shows the potential label errors detected by Cleanlab:

    ```
    Cleanlab identified 1556 potential label errors.
    Indices of the top 10 most likely errors:
    [4270 4366 4443 4872 4112 4327 4804 4496 4009 3792]
    ```

    Figure 3.27 – Top predicted label errors

22. Create a function to view the top-ranked label anomalies:

    ```
    def get_anomaly(index):
    return pd.DataFrame({"Reviews": raw_full_texts[index], "Categorical labels": full_labels[index]+1}, [index])
    ```

23. View a predicted label anomaly:

    ```
    get_label_anomaly(4270)
    ```

It seems unusual for this review to have a two-star rating, as shown in *Figure 3.28*:

	Reviews	Labels
4270	Great price	2

Figure 3.28 – Detected label anomaly

24. Let's pick a different predicted anomaly:

    ```
    get_anomaly(4443)
    ```

    Figure 3.29 shows another questionable rating:

	Reviews	Labels
4443	Great alternative for soda! I love it	2

Figure 3.29 – Label anomaly

25. Manually inspecting and fixing potential label errors can be time-consuming. We can train a better model using Cleanlab to filter noisy data. First, let's split the dataset into an 80:20 ratio:

    ```
    from sklearn.model_selection import train_test_split

    raw_train_texts, raw_test_texts, train_labels, test_labels = train_test_split(raw_full_texts, full_labels, test_size=0.2, random_state=42)

    raw_train_texts.to_numpy(dtype=str)
    raw_test_texts.to_numpy(dtype=str)
    ```

26. Next, examine the data shape:

    ```
    print(f'raw_train_texts shape: {raw_train_texts.shape}')
    print(f'train_labels shape: {train_labels.shape}')
    print(f'raw_test_texts shape: {raw_test_texts.shape}')
    print(f'test_labels shape: {test_labels.shape}')
    ```

    Review the data split, as shown in *Figure 3.30*:

    ```
    raw_train_texts shape: (4000,)
    train_labels shape: (4000,)
    raw_test_texts shape: (1000,)
    test_labels shape: (1000,)
    ```

    Figure 3.30 – Review the data split

Solution walk-through | 65

27. Vectorize the text:

```
vectorize_layer.reset_state()
vectorize_layer.adapt(raw_train_texts)

train_texts = vectorize_layer(raw_train_texts)
test_texts = vectorize_layer(raw_test_texts)

train_texts = train_texts.numpy()
test_texts = test_texts.numpy()
```

28. Train and evaluate the original neural network that we created earlier:

```
from sklearn.metrics import accuracy_score

model = KerasClassifier(get_net(), epochs=10)
model.fit(train_texts, train_labels)
preds = model.predict(test_texts)
acc_og = accuracy_score(test_labels, preds)

print(f'Test accuracy of original neural net: {acc_og}')
```

Figure 3.31 shows the training result:

```
Epoch 1/10
125/125 [==============================] - 1s 3ms/step - loss: 1.3862 - categorical_accuracy: 0.0075
Epoch 2/10
125/125 [==============================] - 0s 3ms/step - loss: 1.0653 - categorical_accuracy: 0.0000e+00
Epoch 3/10
125/125 [==============================] - 0s 3ms/step - loss: 1.0118 - categorical_accuracy: 0.0000e+00
Epoch 4/10
125/125 [==============================] - 0s 3ms/step - loss: 0.9991 - categorical_accuracy: 0.0000e+00
Epoch 5/10
125/125 [==============================] - 0s 4ms/step - loss: 0.9967 - categorical_accuracy: 0.0000e+00
Epoch 6/10
125/125 [==============================] - 0s 4ms/step - loss: 0.9994 - categorical_accuracy: 0.0000e+00
Epoch 7/10
125/125 [==============================] - 0s 4ms/step - loss: 0.9957 - categorical_accuracy: 0.0000e+00
Epoch 8/10
125/125 [==============================] - 0s 3ms/step - loss: 0.9910 - categorical_accuracy: 0.0000e+00
Epoch 9/10
125/125 [==============================] - 0s 4ms/step - loss: 0.9958 - categorical_accuracy: 0.0000e+00
Epoch 10/10
125/125 [==============================] - 0s 4ms/step - loss: 0.9940 - categorical_accuracy: 0.0000e+00
32/32 [==============================] - 0s 1ms/step
Test accuracy of original neural net: 0.698
```

Figure 3.31 – Training result

29. The `CleanLearning` wrapper class trains the original model with cross-validation to produce predicted probabilities for potential label errors. The noisy data with label errors is removed from the dataset before retraining the original model with the remaining clean data. The Cleanlab-trained model behaves the same as the original model to make predictions. We can see that the model is now trained with a lower log loss:

```
from cleanlab.classification import CleanLearning

model = KerasClassifier(get_net(), epochs=10)
cl = CleanLearning(clf=model, seed=SEED)

_ = cl.fit(train_texts, train_labels)
```

Figure 3.32 shows the evaluation metric:

```
Epoch 10/10
87/87 [==============================] - 0s 4ms/step - loss: 0.5372 - categorical_accuracy: 0.0043
```

Figure 3.32 – Evaluation metric

30. Obtain new prediction accuracy after removing the noisy data:

```
Pred_labels = cl.predict(test_texts)
acc_cl = accuracy_score(test_labels, pred_labels)
print(f'Test accuracy of Cleanlab\'s neural net: {acc_cl}')
```

Figure 3.33 shows the test result:

```
32/32 [==============================] - 0s 1ms/step
Test accuracy of Cleanlab's neural net: 0.696
```

Figure 3.33 – Test accuracy

31. Next, let's evaluate the post hoc local explainability for the model predictions. First, load the essential libraries and data. Then, set the relevant feature and target columns:

```
import pandas as pd
import numpy as np
import scipy as sp
import matplotlib.pyplot as plt
import transformers
import shap
```

```
dataset = pd.read_csv('export_food.csv')
data = pd.DataFrame({'text':dataset['reviews'],'senti-
ment':dataset['ratings']})
```

32. Load a fine-tuned `distilbert-base-uncased-finetuned-sst-2-english` NLP transformer model:

```
import transformers

model = transformers.pipeline(
    'sentiment-analysis',
    model='distilbert-base-uncased-finetuned-sst-2-
english',
    top_k=None
)
```

33. Pass the transformer pipeline object directly to SHAP:

```
explainer = shap.Explainer(model)
```

34. Pass a predicted anomalous review to the SHAP explainer. For example, the 4270 sample was flagged as a top-ranked label anomaly by Cleanlab:

```
shap_values = explainer(df['reviews'][4111:4113])
```

35. We will now visualize the feature attributions computed by SHAP:

```
shap.plots.text(shap_values)
```

Figure 3.34 shows feature attributions toward each class. You can hover over an output class in the Jupyter notebook to see the explanation for a predicted output class. The base value represents the model outputs when the full input text is removed or masked. The $f_{outputclass}(inputs)$ is the output for the entire original input. SHAP values show that the impact of unmasking each word deviates from the base value. A SHAP force plot indicates the influence of each word on the prediction.

For example, the word **price** pushes the prediction to be a negative review, whereas the word **love** pushes the prediction to be a positive review:

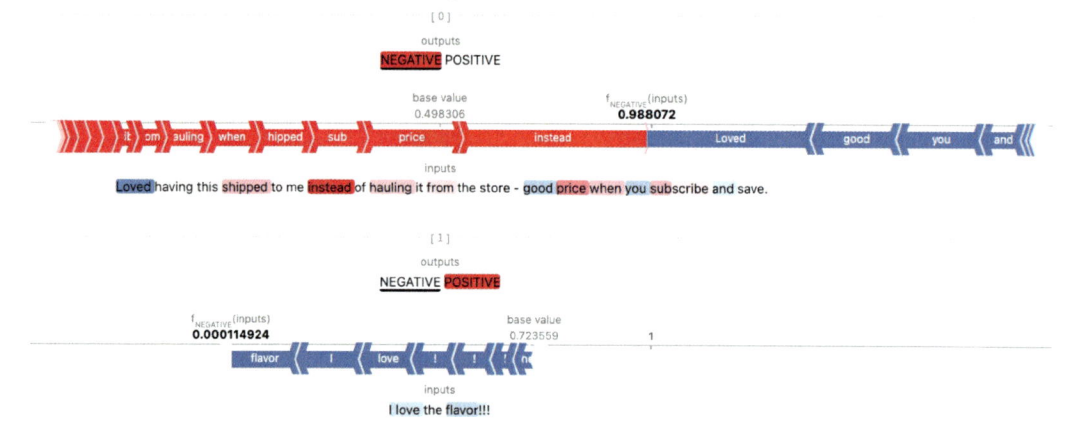

Figure 3.34 – A SHAP force plot

36. Similarly, we can highlight words that result in predicting a review to be positive. For example, removing the word `price` pushed the prediction to be positive:

    ```
    shap.plots.text(shap_values[:, :, "POSITIVE"])
    ```

    Figure 3.35 shows a SHAP force plot for predicted positive reviews:

Figure 3.35 – A SHAP force plot for positive reviews

37. Let's also pull the words that result in predicting negative reviews. In this case, removing the word `love` made the prediction negative:

    ```
    shap.plots.text(shap_values[:, :, "NEGATIVE"])
    ```

Figure 3.36 shows a SHAP force plot for predicted negative reviews:

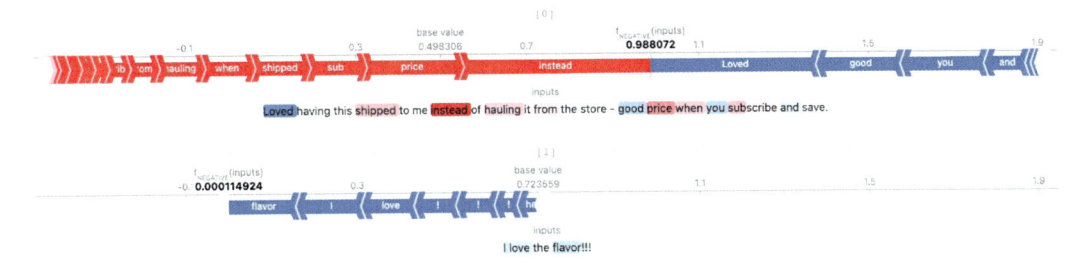

Figure 3.36 – A SHAP force plot for negative reviews

38. Let's visualize the top words that influence the positive class predictions:

    `shap.plots.bar(shap_values[:,:,"POSITIVE"].mean(0))`

    Figure 3.37 shows the SHAP bar plot for predicted positive reviews:

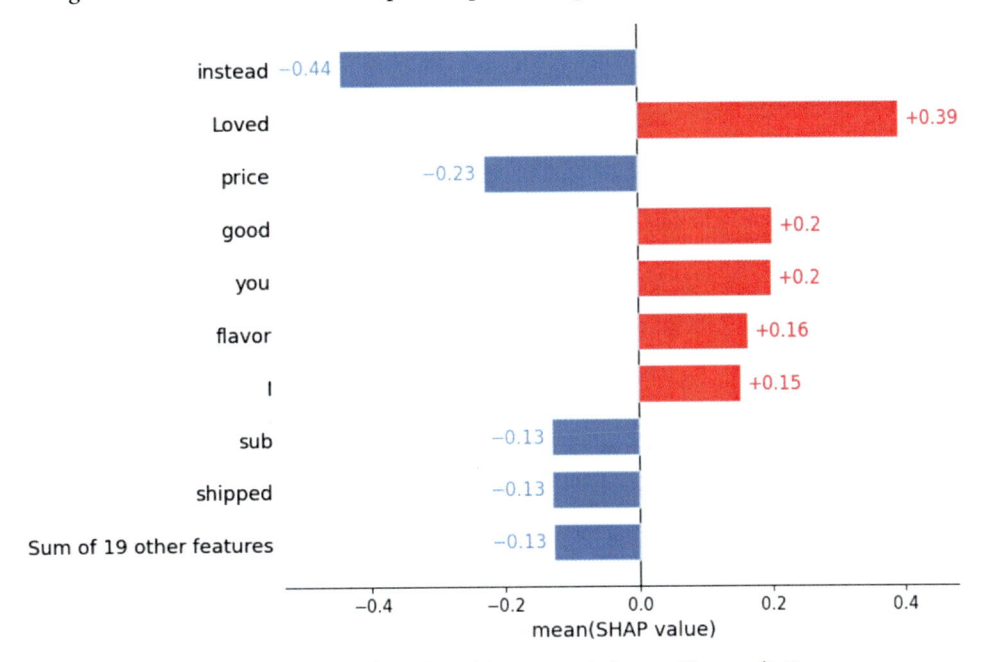

Figure 3.37 – A SHAP bar plot with top words for positive predictions

39. Here, we visualize the words that influence the negative class predictions:

    ```
    shap.plots.bar(shap_values[:,:,"NEGATIVE"].mean(0))
    ```

    Figure 3.38 shows the SHAP bar plot for predicted negative reviews:

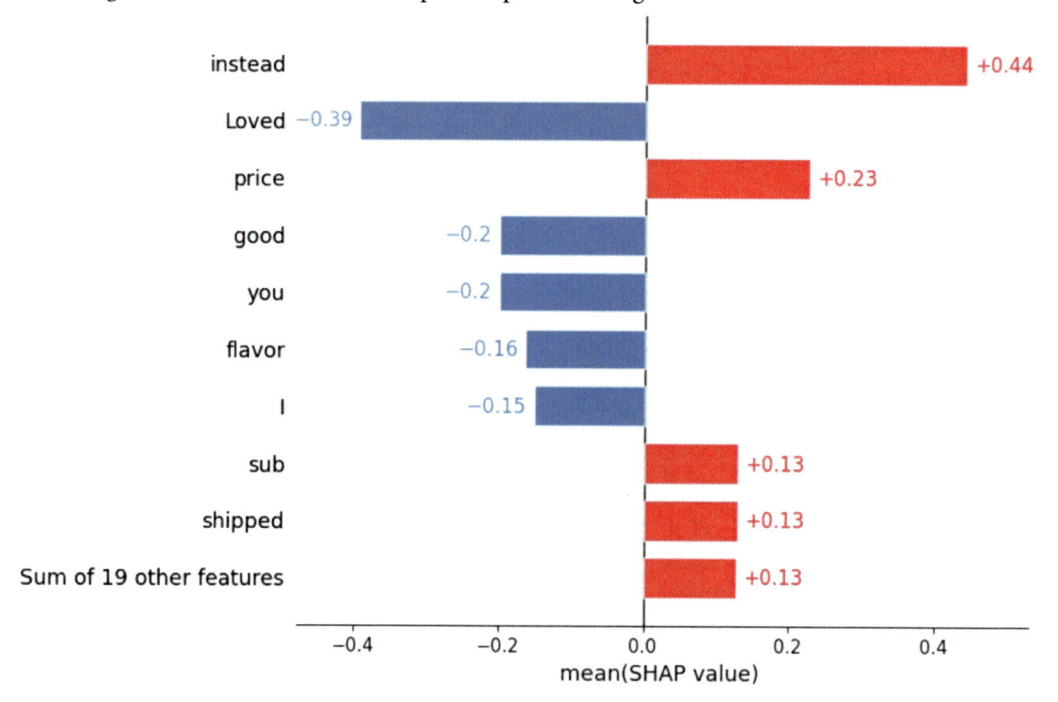

Word	mean(SHAP value)
instead	+0.44
Loved	−0.39
price	+0.23
good	−0.2
you	−0.2
flavor	−0.16
I	−0.15
sub	+0.13
shipped	+0.13
Sum of 19 other features	+0.13

Figure 3.38 – A SHAP bar plot with top words for negative predictions

40. We can sort the bar plot in descending order for better visualization:

    ```
    shap.plots.bar(shap_values[:,:,"POSITIVE"].mean(0),
    order=shap.Explanation.argsort)
    ```

    Figure 3.39 shows the bar plot sorted in descending order:

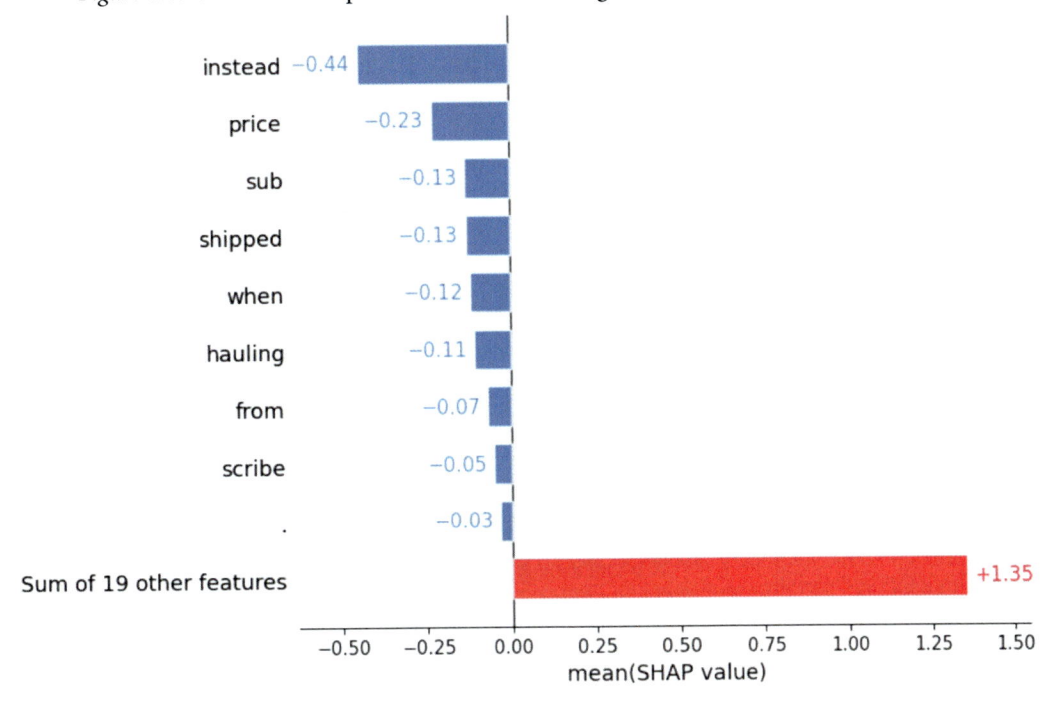

Feature	mean(SHAP value)
instead	−0.44
price	−0.23
sub	−0.13
shipped	−0.13
when	−0.12
hauling	−0.11
from	−0.07
scribe	−0.05
	−0.03
Sum of 19 other features	+1.35

    Figure 3.39 – A SHAP bar plot sorted in descending order

41. Here is the ascending order of the SHAP bar plot:

    ```
    shap.plots.bar(shap_values[:,:,"POSITIVE"].mean(0),
    order=shap.Explanation.argsort.flip)
    ```

    Figure 3.40 shows the bar plot sorted in ascending order:

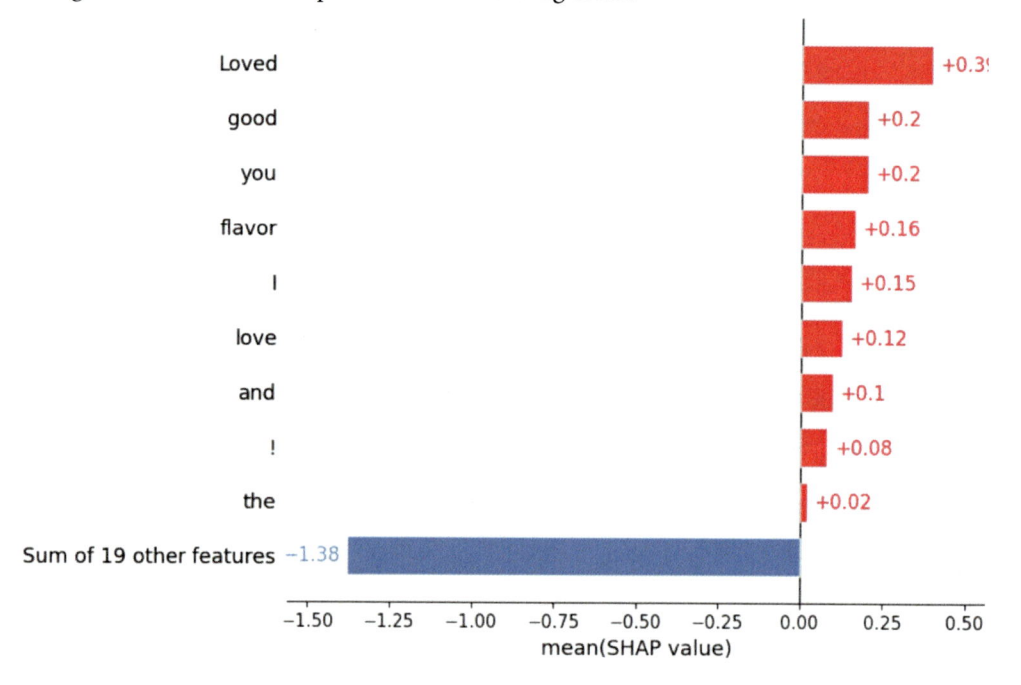

	mean(SHAP value)
Loved	+0.39
good	+0.2
you	+0.2
flavor	+0.16
I	+0.15
love	+0.12
and	+0.1
!	+0.08
the	+0.02
Sum of 19 other features	−1.38

    Figure 3.40 – A SHAP bar plot sorted in ascending order

Congratulations on completing a full walk-through of the NLP anomaly explainability example. In this section, you used Cleanlab to detect label anomalies in the Amazon Customer Reviews dataset and explained the anomalies using SHAP. In the *Exercise* section, your challenge is to explore Amazon's open source text dataset, named **MASSIVE**. This dataset contains 1 million labeled utterances in 51 languages. Can you apply what you learned in this chapter to find abnormal intent labels from this dataset?

Exercise

Amazon released a new MASSIVE dataset in 2022, `https://www.amazon.science/blog/amazon-releases-51-language-dataset-for-language-understanding`, containing 1 million labeled utterances in 51 languages, available at `https://github.com/alexa/massive`.

MASSIVE provides tools and open source code for multilingual **natural language understanding** (NLU) modeling, such as intent classification. You can read more about MASSIVE's paper at arXiv, `https://doi.org/10.48550/arXiv.2204.08582`.

Using this dataset, you can practice with the `chapter3_MASSIVE_get_started.ipynb` exercise notebook, available at the GitHub repo. After downloading and decompressing the MASSIVE dataset, load a JSON Lines (`.jsonl`) file containing a specific language's utterances. For example, `en-US.jsonl` contains utterances in English. Let's cover the getting started steps in the sample notebook:

1. Load the language-specific JSON Lines file:

    ```
    import json
    with open('en-US.jsonl') as f:
        data = [json.loads(line) for line in f]
    ```

    Figure 3.41 shows a preview of the first three utterances:

    ```
    [{'id': '0',
      'locale': 'en-US',
      'partition': 'test',
      'scenario': 'alarm',
      'intent': 'alarm_set',
      'utt': 'wake me up at five am this week',
      'annot_utt': 'wake me up at [time : five am] [date : this week]',
      'worker_id': '1'},
     {'id': '1',
      'locale': 'en-US',
      'partition': 'train',
      'scenario': 'alarm',
      'intent': 'alarm_set',
      'utt': 'wake me up at nine am on friday',
      'annot_utt': 'wake me up at [time : nine am] on [date : friday]',
      'worker_id': '1'},
     {'id': '2',
      'locale': 'en-US',
      'partition': 'train',
      'scenario': 'alarm',
      'intent': 'alarm_set',
      'utt': 'set an alarm for two hours from now',
      'annot_utt': 'set an alarm for [time : two hours from now]',
      'worker_id': '1'}]
    ```

    Figure 3.41 – Preview of the utterances in the MASSIVE dataset

2. Convert the JSON into a pandas DataFrame:

    ```
    import pandas as pd
    df = pd.DataFrame(data, columns = ['id', 'locale',
    ```

```
'partition', 'scenario', 'intent', 'utt', 'annot_utt',
'worker_id'])
```

Figure 3.42 shows a preview of the MASSIVE dataset:

	id	locale	partition	scenario	intent	utt	annot_utt	worker_id
0	0	en-US	test	alarm	alarm_set	wake me up at five am this week	wake me up at [time : five am] [date : this week]	1
1	1	en-US	train	alarm	alarm_set	wake me up at nine am on friday	wake me up at [time : nine am] on [date : friday]	1
2	2	en-US	train	alarm	alarm_set	set an alarm for two hours from now	set an alarm for [time : two hours from now]	1
3	3	en-US	test	audio	audio_volume_mute	quiet	quiet	1
4	4	en-US	train	audio	audio_volume_mute	olly quiet	olly quiet	1

Figure 3.42 – Preview of the MASSIVE dataset

3. The en-US.jsonl dataset contains 16,521 records and 60 unique labels for the intent target column:

```
df.describe()
```

Figure 3.43 shows the dataset statistics:

	id	locale	partition	scenario	intent	utt	annot_utt	worker_id
count	16521	16521	16521	16521	16521	16521	16521	16521
unique	16521	1	3	18	60	16432	16434	691
top	0	en-US	train	calendar	calendar_set	do i have any new email	do i have any new email	0
freq	1	16521	11514	2370	1150	3	3	228

Figure 3.43 – Dataset statistics for the MASSIVE dataset

4. Here is a list of the unique classes for the intent target column, as shown in *Figure 3.44*:

```
df['intent'].unique()
array(['alarm_set', 'audio_volume_mute', 'iot_hue_lightchange',
       'iot_hue_lightoff', 'iot_hue_lighton', 'iot_hue_lightdim',
       'iot_cleaning', 'calendar_query', 'play_music', 'general_quirky',
       'general_greet', 'datetime_query', 'datetime_convert',
       'takeaway_query', 'alarm_remove', 'alarm_query', 'news_query',
       'music_likeness', 'music_query', 'iot_hue_lightup',
       'takeaway_order', 'weather_query', 'music_settings',
       'audio_volume_down', 'general_joke', 'music_dislikeness',
       'audio_volume_other', 'iot_coffee', 'audio_volume_up',
       'iot_wemo_on', 'iot_wemo_off', 'qa_stock', 'play_radio',
       'social_post', 'recommendation_locations', 'cooking_recipe',
       'qa_factoid', 'recommendation_events', 'calendar_set',
       'play_audiobook', 'play_podcasts', 'social_query',
       'transport_query', 'email_sendemail', 'transport_ticket',
       'recommendation_movies', 'lists_query', 'play_game', 'email_query',
       'transport_traffic', 'cooking_query', 'qa_definition',
       'calendar_remove', 'lists_remove', 'email_querycontact',
       'lists_createoradd', 'email_addcontact', 'transport_taxi',
       'qa_maths', 'qa_currency'], dtype=object)
```

Figure 3.44 – Unique intent classes

5. *Figure 3.45* shows the class frequency distribution for the MASSIVE dataset. We can see `calendar_set` is the most queried intent while the `cooking_query` intent has the least frequency:

```
%matplotlib inline
import matplotlib.pyplot as plt
plt.rcParams["figure.figsize"] = (20,15)
df['intent'].value_counts().plot(kind = 'barh').invert_yaxis()
plt.savefig('massive_dist.png', bbox_inches="tight")
```

Figure 3.45 shows the intent class distribution:

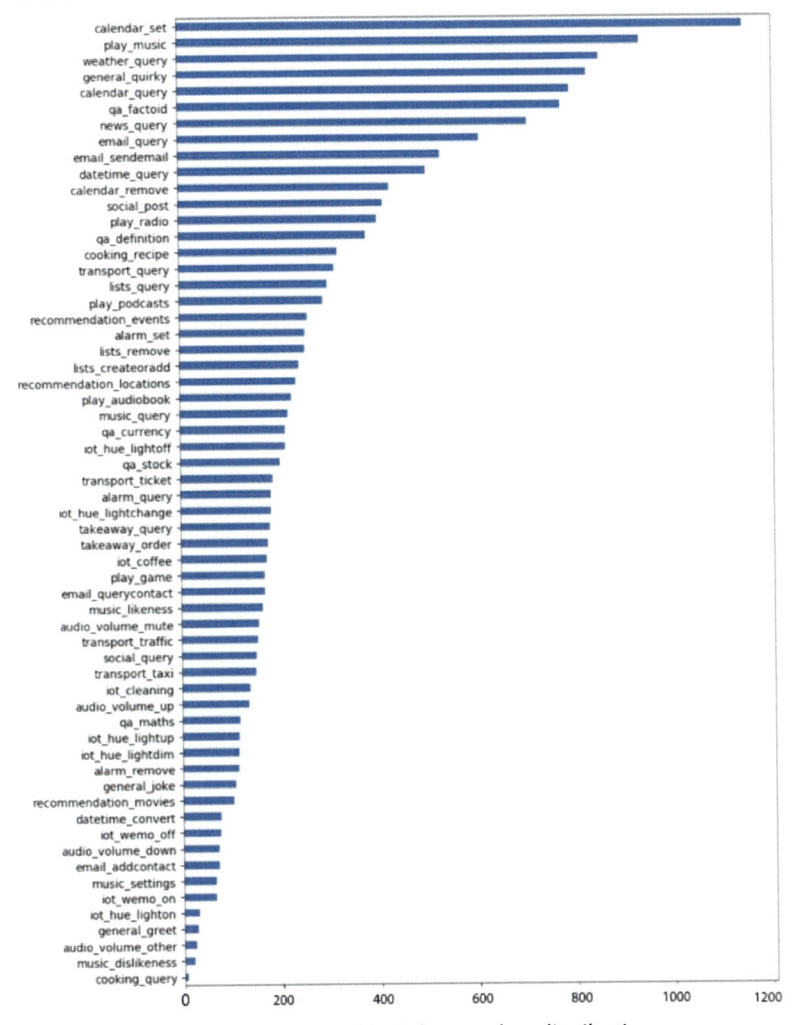

Figure 3.45 – The MASSIVE dataset class distribution

Give this exercise a try. I hope you discover something new from this analysis.

Summary

NLP explainability is an emerging field, and many tools are still being developed. One major challenge in **explainable artificial intelligence** (**XAI**) is ensuring that explanations are faithful and accurately represent the model reasoning process. In this chapter, you learned how to build a state-of-the-art deep learning NLP model using AutoGluon. You also successfully identified label anomalies using Cleanlab and explained the words contributing to the predicted labels using SHAP. In the next chapter, we will explore time series anomaly explainability.

4
Time Series Anomaly Explainability

Time series is a stream of continuous, sequential, indexed, and timestamped data points often plotted in temporal line charts to correlate trends, detect seasonality patterns, create forecasting, and identify anomalies. Time series data is ubiquitous. Examples of time series data are daily stock prices, weekly COVID-19 confirmed cases, monthly rainfall measurements, and annual sales revenue.

The advent of connected technology, storage affordability, and increasing business demand for insights enables many systems to generate more data than most organizations can consume. According to Statista, (`https://www.statista.com/statistics/871513/worldwide-data-created/`), only 2% of 64.2 zettabytes produced globally in 2020 was retained into 2021.

Finding anomalies in time series presents significant business values and applies to many real-world use cases. For example, companies proactively monitor manufacturing equipment metrics for industrial predictive maintenance to prevent economic loss. Government emergency management agencies forecast natural disasters to issue alerts and avoid casualties. Security experts evaluate unusual web traffic to detect malicious activities. The healthcare industry applies time series analysis for public health observations, such as predicting the spread of COVID-19.

Since anomalies are rare by nature, finding anomalies in time series data is akin to searching for a needle in a haystack. Furthermore, a multivariate time series requires considerations across multiple time-dependent variables simultaneously.

Deep learning has made promising advancements across diverse fields in recent years, including tackling complex challenges in anomaly detection using time series data. Despite high performance, the opaque nature of deep learning presents drawbacks in interpretability and slows down practical deployment.

This chapter covers deep learning anomaly detection explainability for time series data. First, we will cover the basics of time series and various deep learning approaches for anomaly detection. Then, we will explore a time series dataset to detect, visualize, and explain anomalies using **SHapley Additive exPlanations** (**SHAP**), provided by **Omni eXplainable AI** (**OmniXAI**). By the end of this chapter, you will understand various approaches to building and evaluating time series anomaly explainability with deep learning.

Understanding time series

Anomaly detection with time series data is crucial for detecting novel and unexpected outliers in many real-world use cases, including healthcare, manufacturing, and cybersecurity. Hence, it has been an active research domain since the 1960s. As computing power increases and deep learning advances, neural networks can learn expressive feature representation using complex and multidimensional time series data with higher performance than traditional approaches.

Let's discuss the taxonomy of time series data to help us understand deep learning approaches for time series anomaly detection. A time series dataset consists of observations collected and indexed sequentially over a pre-determined period. These time series data points can be univariate or multivariate:

- **Univariate time series** refers to a series of one-dimensional timestamped data, with a single column of values that changes around a single variable. For example, a univariate time series of monthly precipitation can be used to predict rainfall and unexpected downpours.

- **Multivariate time series** refers to a series of multidimensional timestamped data, with multiple columns of values that change over time. These variables might have temporal or spatial dependencies on each other. A variable with temporal dependence might be influenced by another variable's past or current behavior. In contrast, a variable with spatial dependence represents the dynamic relationships between a specific observation and nearby data points. For example, a multivariate time series containing precipitation, water temperature, humidity, and discharge can be used to extract climate patterns.

As time series measurements can occur at regular or irregular intervals, we can observe different trends or movements for relationship correlation. *Figure 4.1* shows the components that represent various trends in time series:

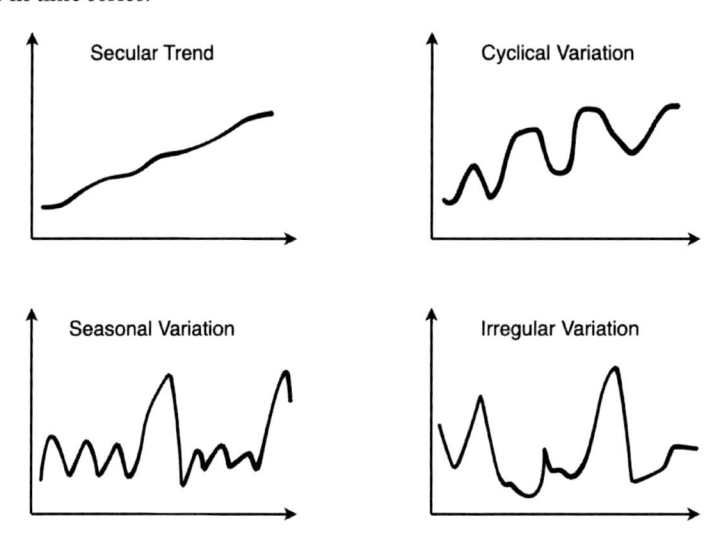

Figure 4.1 – Time series components

Let us learn what each trend represents:

- A **secular trend** represents a long-term trend that maintains a predictable trajectory or continues moving in a stable increasing or decreasing direction for the foreseeable future. Examples of secular trends include an aging population and computing power.
- A **cyclical fluctuation** represents the gradual ups or downs without a fixed frequency, resulting in successive expansion or contraction cycles. For example, consumer spending increases as the economy expands or unemployment decreases.
- A **seasonal variation** represents systematic or expected variation at a fixed frequency. For example, retail revenue typically increases during the holidays, and higher electric bills occur in the summer.
- An **irregular variation** refers to random, non-uniform, and non-seasonal patterns. Examples of irregular variations include abnormal **electrocardiogram** (**ECG**) readings or unusual account withdrawals from an **automated teller machine** (**ATM**).

With a foundational understanding of time series structure, let's discuss deep learning anomaly detection approaches in the following section.

Understanding explainable deep anomaly detection for time series

Because anomalies are rare by nature, many deep learning models learn the feature representation from normal observations and detect anomalies by measuring deviations from known behavior. Deep learning employs different approaches, such as supervised, semi-supervised, and unsupervised, depending on the availability of labeled observations. Please refer to *Chapter 1* for comparisons of these approaches.

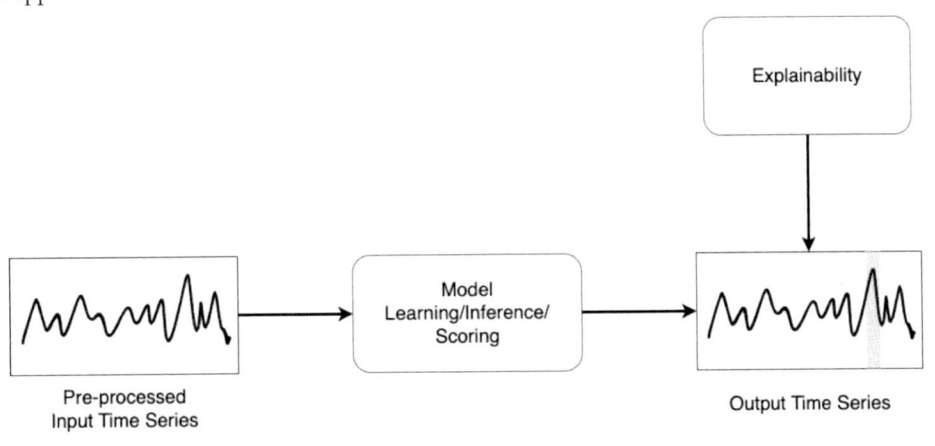

Figure 4.2 – Deep learning anomaly detection for time series

Figure 4.2 shows a high-level workflow of deep learning anomaly detection for time series with the following stages:

1. A deep learning model takes input data as either a timestep or a sliding window. A **timestep** represents an individual data point, whereas a **sliding window** refers to a sequence of timesteps with historical information. Generally, input data requires preprocessing tasks, such as imputing missing values and normalization, to extract the optimal sliding window.

2. Anomalies can surface in point or subsequence form, and not every observation is necessarily an outlier. Hence, a model calculates anomaly scores based on a defined loss function to determine whether the prediction deviates from the rest of the data and should be flagged as an anomaly. Essentially, an anomaly score indicates the degree of an anomaly, using a threshold value identified by risk assessment.

3. XAI aims to provide reasoning behind a model's prediction. Post hoc explainability methods such as SHAP are popular for assessing the quality of the model's predictions.

There are three types of deep learning models for time series anomaly detection in the preceding workflow:

- **Forecasting-based models** predict whether an incoming point or sliding window is an outlier by comparing the deviations of their predicted values against their actual values. The deviation values become the anomalous values to identify abnormal behavior.

- **Reconstruction-based models** capture time series embedding by encoding subsequences of normal sliding window input to provide temporal context during reconstruction. The model generates reconstruction errors, since they are only trained with normal observations. Reconstruction errors become the anomalous value to rank anomalies, based on a threshold value.

- **Hybrid models** combine forecasting and reconstruction-based models to achieve better learning in time series, using timestamp prediction from forecasting and latent representations from the reconstruction approach.

Following this overview of deep learning approaches for time series anomaly detection, let's explore an example of detecting time series anomalies using a reconstruction-based model and evaluating prediction quality with the SHAP XAI method in the next section.

Technical requirements

You need the following Python packages for the example walk-through in this chapter:

- **Keras**: An open source library for building neural networks
- **Matplotlib**: A plotting library for creating data visualizations
- **NumPy**: An open source library that provides mathematical functions when working with arrays

- **OmniXAI**: An open source XAI library that provides various XAI methods through a unified interface
- **pandas**: A library that offers data analysis and manipulation tools
- **Seaborn**: A Matplotlib-based data visualization library
- **Sklearn**: A machine learning tool library for predictive data analysis
- **TensorFlow**: An open source framework for building deep learning applications

A sample Jupyter notebook, a requirements file for package dependencies, and a sample dataset for the example discussed in this chapter are available at `https://github.com/PacktPublishing/Deep-Learning-and-XAI-Techniques-for-Anomaly-Detection/tree/main/Chapter4`.

Next, let's explore the dataset for this example.

The problem

This section reviews an anomaly detection problem using the NYC Taxi Traffic dataset from Kaggle (`https://www.kaggle.com/datasets/julienjta/nyc-taxi-traffic`), sourced from the NYC Taxi and Limousine Commission. This dataset contains univariate time series observations of the total number of taxi passengers between July 2014 and January 2015, aggregated at 30-minute intervals. The data include five anomalies during the NYC Marathon, Thanksgiving, Christmas, New Year's Day, and a snowstorm.

You will implement end-to-end anomaly detection by analyzing the NYC Taxi Traffic dataset, creating a **Long Short Term Memory (LSTM)** model to predict outliers, and explaining anomalies using an OmniXAI SHAP explainer.

The following section reviews a step-by-step walk-through for this example.

Solution walkthrough

This section aims to step through an example of creating an LSTM model to detect anomalies in a time series dataset and generate local explanations for predictions, using a SHAP explainer provided by OmniXAI. You can read more about OmniXAI at `https://arxiv.org/pdf/2206.01612.pdf`:

1. Install the essential libraries using the provided requirements file:

   ```
   import sys
   !{sys.executable} -m pip install -qr requirements.txt
   ```

2. Load the essential libraries:

```
%matplotlib inline
import numpy as np
import pandas as pd
import matplotlib.pyplot as plt
import matplotlib.dates as mdates
import seaborn as sns
from sklearn.preprocessing import StandardScaler
from sklearn.model_selection import train_test_split
import tensorflow as tf
from tensorflow import keras
from tensorflow.keras.layers import LSTM, Dense, RepeatVector, Dropout, TimeDistributed
import os
from platform import python_version
import warnings

warnings.simplefilter(action='ignore', category=FutureWarning)
os.environ['TF_CPP_MIN_LOG_LEVEL'] = '3'
print(f'TensorFlow version: {tf.__version__}')
print(f'Python version: {python_version()}')
```

Figure 4.3 shows the TensorFlow and Python dependencies:

```
TensorFlow version: 2.11.0
Python version: 3.9.10
```

Figure 4.3 – Package dependencies

3. Load and preview the NYC Taxi Traffic dataset:

```
data = pd.read_csv('nyc.csv')
data['date'] = pd.to_datetime(data['date'], infer_datetime_format=True)
data = pd.DataFrame.reindex(data, columns = ['date','value'])
data.head(5)
```

The result is shown in *Figure 4.4*:

	date	value
0	2014-07-01 00:00:00	10844
1	2014-07-01 00:30:00	8127
2	2014-07-01 01:00:00	6210
3	2014-07-01 01:30:00	4656
4	2014-07-01 02:00:00	3820

Figure 4.4 – The dataset preview

4. To view the dataset statistic, use the following code:

```
data.describe()
```

Figure 4.5 shows the dataset statistics:

	value
count	10320.000000
mean	15137.569380
std	6939.495808
min	8.000000
25%	10262.000000
50%	16778.000000
75%	19838.750000
max	39197.000000

Figure 4.5 – The dataset statistics

5. Standardize the data using `StandardScaler`:

```
scaler = StandardScaler()
scaler.fit(data[['value']])
data['scaled_value'] = scaler.transform(data[['value']])
data.head(5)
```

Figure 4.6 shows a dataset preview with a new `scaled_value` column:

	date	value	scaled_value
0	2014-07-01 00:00:00	10844	-0.618745
1	2014-07-01 00:30:00	8127	-1.010291
2	2014-07-01 01:00:00	6210	-1.286549
3	2014-07-01 01:30:00	4656	-1.510496
4	2014-07-01 02:00:00	3820	-1.630971

Figure 4.6 – Standardized data

6. Let us now compare the raw and scaled values:

```
x_year = data['date']
y_total = data['value']
y_scaled = data['scaled_value']

fig, axs = plt.subplots(2,sharex=False, sharey=False, figsize=(20,8))

plt.gca().xaxis.set_major_formatter(mdates.DateFormatter('%b-%Y'))
plt.minorticks_off()

axs[0].plot(x_year, y_total)
axs[0].set_title('Raw Total Taxi Passengers')

axs[1].plot(x_year, y_scaled)
axs[1].set_title('Scaled Total Taxi Passengers')

fig.autofmt_xdate()

plt.savefig('raw_scaled_ts.png', bbox_inches='tight')
plt.show()
```

Solution walkthrough   85

Let's visualize and compare the raw and scaled values. *Figure 4.7* shows the raw and scaled values. A quick visual assessment shows apparent spikes in the total number of taxi passengers at the beginning of November and January, which corresponded to the 2014 NYC Marathon on November 2 and the New Year's Day timeline. The drop in the total number of passengers toward the end of January coincided with the 2014 snowstorm around the New York area:

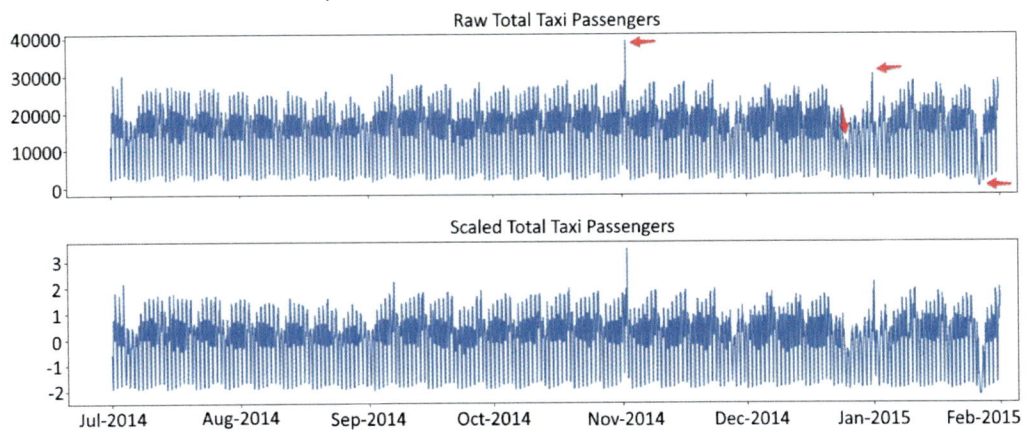

Figure 4.7 – Raw versus scaled values

7. Visualize the data distribution with a histogram:

    ```
    sns.histplot(data=data, x ='value', kde=True)
    ```

Figure 4.8 shows a histogram of data distribution with the **kernel density estimate (KDE)** parameter enabled:

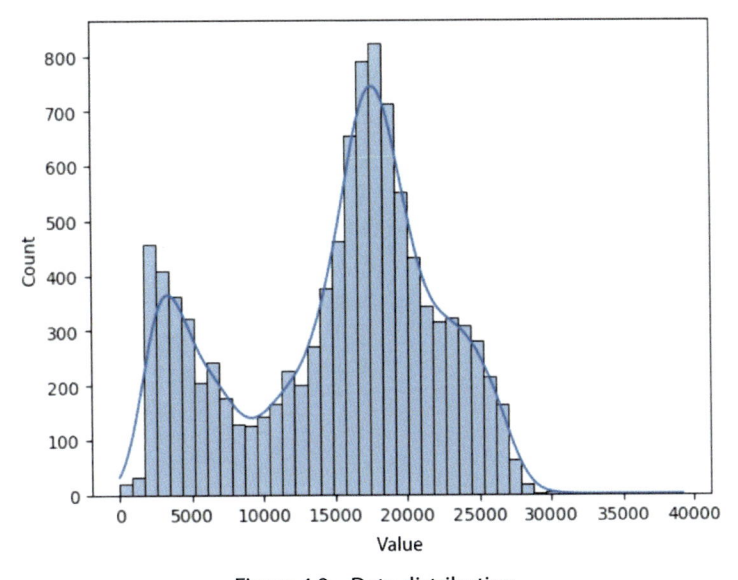

Figure 4.8 – Data distribution

8. Set timesteps to train on hourly trends, since the dataset is aggregated at a 30-minute interval:

   ```
   TIMESTEPS = 2
   train_data, test_data = train_test_split(data, train_
   size=0.8, shuffle=False, random_state=42)
   train_data.sort_index(inplace=True)
   test_data.sort_index(inplace=True)
   print(f'Train shape: {train_data.shape}')
   print(f'Test shape: {test_data.shape}')
   ```

   You should see the following output shape for train and test splits, as shown in *Figure 4.9*:

   ```
   Train shape: (8256, 3)
   Test shape: (2064, 3)
   ```

   Figure 4.9 – The output shape for train and test splits

9. Prepare new datasets using the predefined `timesteps` value:

   ```
   def newdataset(df, timesteps, feature):
       df_x, df_y = [], []

       for i in range(timesteps, len(df)):
           df_x.append(df.iloc[i-timesteps:i]
   [[feature]].values)
           df_y.append(df.iloc[i][feature])
       df_x = np.array(df_x)
       df_y = np.array(df_y)
       return df_x, df_y

   train_x, train_y = newdataset(train_data, TIMESTEPS,
   'scaled_value')
   test_x, test_y = newdataset(test_data, TIMESTEPS,
   'scaled_value')

   train_x.shape, train_y.shape, test_x.shape, test_y.shape
   ```

10. Create a simple LSTM model by initializing a sequential model, adding LSTM encoder and decoder layers, applying dropout, repeating the inputs with `RepeatVector`, and adding a `TimeDistributed` dense output layer. We will use the **Mean Absolute Error** (**MAE**) loss function as an evaluation metric and the Adam optimizer:

```
LSTM_units = 64
model = keras.Sequential()
model.add(LSTM(LSTM_units, input_shape=(train_x.shape[1],
train_x.shape[2]), return_sequences=False,name='encoder_
lstm'))
model.add(Dropout(0.2, name='encoder_dropout'))
model.add(RepeatVector(train_x.shape[1], name='decoder_
repeater'))
model.add(LSTM(LSTM_units, return_sequences=True,
name='decoder_lstm'))
model.add(Dropout(rate=0.2, name='decoder_dropout'))
model.add(TimeDistributed(Dense(train_x.
shape[2],name='decoder_dense_output')))
model.compile(loss='mae', optimizer='adam')
model.summary()
```

Figure 4.10 shows the model summary:

```
Model: "sequential_1"
_____
Layer (type)                 Output Shape              Param #
=================================================================
encoder_lstm (LSTM)          (None, 64)                16896

encoder_dropout (Dropout)    (None, 64)                0

decoder_repeater (RepeatVec  (None, 2, 64)             0
tor)

decoder_lstm (LSTM)          (None, 2, 64)             33024

decoder_dropout (Dropout)    (None, 2, 64)             0

time_distributed (TimeDistr  (None, 2, 1)              65
ibuted)

=================================================================
Total params: 49,985
Trainable params: 49,985
Non-trainable params: 0
_____
```

Figure 4.10 – The model summary

11. Train the model for 20 epochs:

```
%time
history = model.fit(
    train_x,
    train_x,
    epochs=20,
    batch_size=32,
    validation_split=0.1,
    shuffle=False
)
```

Figure 4.11 shows the information on the training process:

```
CPU times: user 3 µs, sys: 0 ns, total: 3 µs
Wall time: 8.34 µs
Epoch 1/20
233/233 [==============================] - 10s 8ms/step - loss: 0.2356 - val_loss: 0.1076
Epoch 2/20
233/233 [==============================] - 1s 5ms/step - loss: 0.1199 - val_loss: 0.1023
Epoch 3/20
233/233 [==============================] - 1s 5ms/step - loss: 0.1162 - val_loss: 0.0996
Epoch 4/20
233/233 [==============================] - 1s 5ms/step - loss: 0.1090 - val_loss: 0.0793
Epoch 5/20
233/233 [==============================] - 1s 5ms/step - loss: 0.0876 - val_loss: 0.0458
Epoch 6/20
233/233 [==============================] - 1s 5ms/step - loss: 0.0713 - val_loss: 0.0387
Epoch 7/20
233/233 [==============================] - 1s 5ms/step - loss: 0.0693 - val_loss: 0.0182
Epoch 8/20
233/233 [==============================] - 1s 5ms/step - loss: 0.0663 - val_loss: 0.0265
Epoch 9/20
233/233 [==============================] - 1s 5ms/step - loss: 0.0658 - val_loss: 0.0193
Epoch 10/20
233/233 [==============================] - 1s 5ms/step - loss: 0.0648 - val_loss: 0.0219
Epoch 11/20
233/233 [==============================] - 1s 5ms/step - loss: 0.0635 - val_loss: 0.0166
Epoch 12/20
233/233 [==============================] - 1s 5ms/step - loss: 0.0647 - val_loss: 0.0185
Epoch 13/20
233/233 [==============================] - 1s 5ms/step - loss: 0.0623 - val_loss: 0.0189
Epoch 14/20
233/233 [==============================] - 1s 5ms/step - loss: 0.0633 - val_loss: 0.0177
Epoch 15/20
233/233 [==============================] - 1s 5ms/step - loss: 0.0614 - val_loss: 0.0226
Epoch 16/20
233/233 [==============================] - 1s 5ms/step - loss: 0.0626 - val_loss: 0.0257
Epoch 17/20
233/233 [==============================] - 1s 5ms/step - loss: 0.0614 - val_loss: 0.0294
Epoch 18/20
233/233 [==============================] - 1s 5ms/step - loss: 0.0622 - val_loss: 0.0156
Epoch 19/20
233/233 [==============================] - 1s 5ms/step - loss: 0.0611 - val_loss: 0.0256
Epoch 20/20
233/233 [==============================] - 1s 5ms/step - loss: 0.0606 - val_loss: 0.0218
```

Figure 4.11 – Model training process

12. Let's evaluate training versus validation loss:

    ```
    plt.plot(history.history['loss'], label='training_loss')
    plt.plot(history.history['val_loss'], label='validation_
    loss')
    plt.legend()
    plt.show()
    ```

    Figure 4.12 shows the model performance:

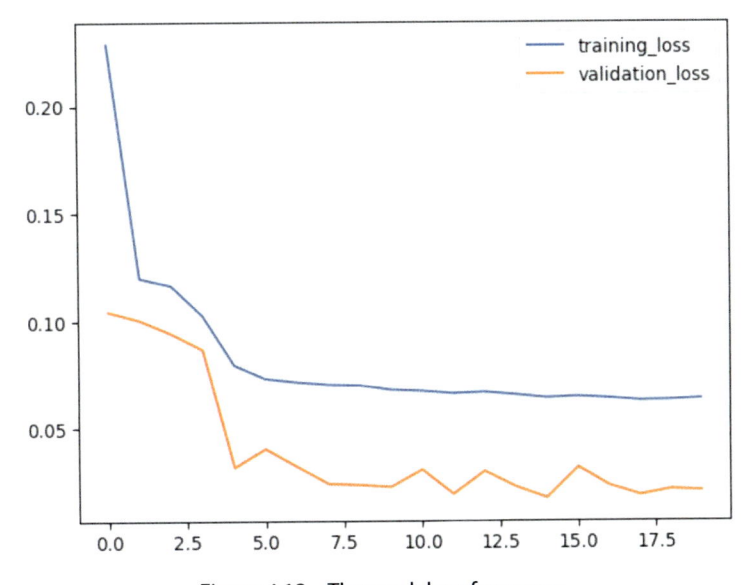

    Figure 4.12 – The model performance

13. Calculate reconstruction error in the training dataset:

    ```
    reconstructed = model.predict(train_x)
    train_mae_loss = np.mean(np.abs(reconstructed - train_x),
    axis=1)
    ```

14. Set a percentile threshold based on reconstruction error to determine anomalies. We are setting the 80th percentile or 0.03 as the reconstruction error threshold in this case:

    ```
    THRESHOLD = np.percentile(train_mae_loss, 80)
    print(f'Reconstruction error threshold: {THRESHOLD}')
    ```

Figure 4.13 shows the 80th percentile reconstruction error threshold.:

```
Reconstruction error threshold: 0.033567614035417116
```

Figure 4.13 – Reconstruction error threshold

15. Visualize the train MAE loss distribution:

    ```
    sns.histplot(train_mae_loss[:,0], kde=True,
    stat='density', linewidth=0).set_xlabel('train_mae_loss')
    plt.show()
    ```

Figure 4.14 shows the MAE distribution to assess reconstruction error for train data:

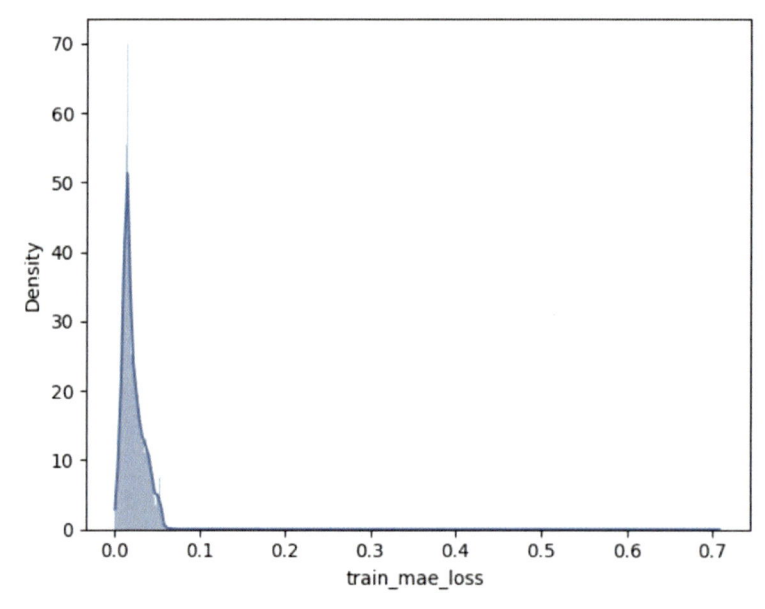

Figure 4.14 – The train MAE distribution

16. Calculate the reconstruction error for test data. A test data point will be labeled as an anomaly if it returns a reconstruction error higher than the train data point:

    ```
    test_reconstruction = model.predict(test_x)
    test_mae_loss = np.mean(np.abs(test_x - test_
    reconstruction), axis=1)
    ```

17. Let us now test the MAE loss distribution:

```
sns.histplot(test_mae_loss[:,0], kde=True,
stat='density', linewidth=0).set_xlabel('test_mae_loss')
plt.show()
```

Figure 4.15 shows the test MAE loss distribution. Note that a test data point with an MAE higher than the 80th percentile of the train MAE or 0.03 that we configured previously as the reconstruction error threshold will be labeled as an anomaly.

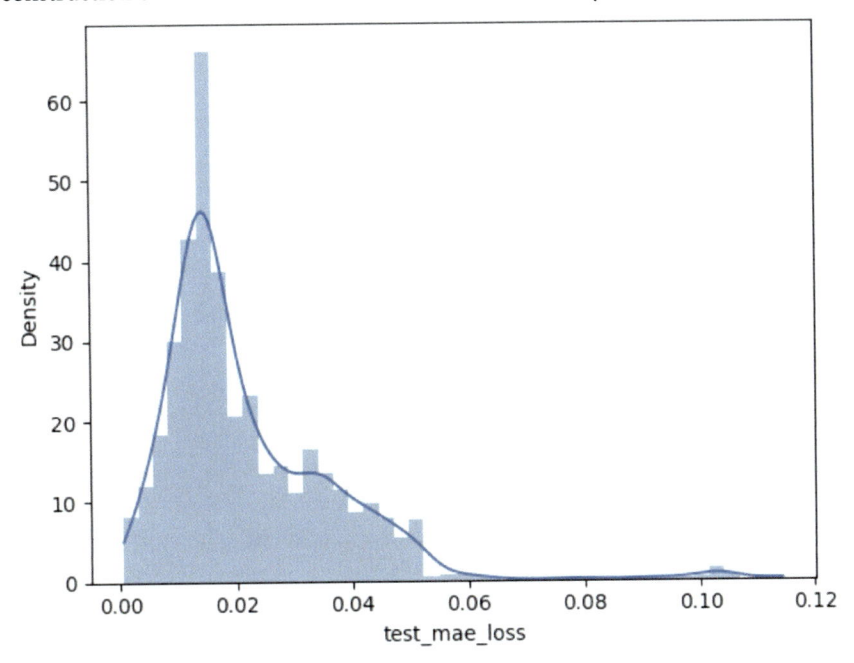

Figure 4.15 – The test MAE distribution

18. Filter the identified anomalies:

```
anomaly_results_df = test_data[TIMESTEPS:][['value',
'scaled_value']].copy()
anomaly_results_df.index = test_data[TIMESTEPS:].index

anomaly_results_df['date'] = test_data['date']
anomaly_results_df['deviation'] = test_mae_loss
anomaly_results_df['threshold'] = THRESHOLD
anomaly_results_df['anomaly'] = anomaly_results_
df['deviation'].apply(lambda dev: 1 if dev > THRESHOLD
```

```
    else 0)

anomalies = anomaly_results_df[anomaly_results_
df['anomaly'] == 1]
not_anomalies = anomaly_results_df[anomaly_results_
df['anomaly'] == 0]

print(f'Total normal: {not_anomalies.shape[0]}')
print(f'Total anomalies: {anomalies.shape[0]}')
```

Figure 4.16 shows a preview of observations flagged as anomalies:

```
Total normal: 1639
Total anomalies: 423
```

Figure 4.16 – Predicted normal and abnormal observations

19. Preview the identified anomalies:

    ```
    anomalies.head(5)
    ```

    Figure 4.17 shows a preview of observations flagged as anomalies:

	value	scaled_value	date	deviation	threshold	anomaly
8258	22993	1.132044	2014-12-20 01:00:00	0.034212	0.033568	1
8294	25685	1.519987	2014-12-20 19:00:00	0.037085	0.033568	1
8295	25252	1.457587	2014-12-20 19:30:00	0.044607	0.033568	1
8296	23238	1.167350	2014-12-20 20:00:00	0.039972	0.033568	1
8301	24614	1.365645	2014-12-20 22:30:00	0.034693	0.033568	1

    Figure 4.17 – The preview of the identified anomalies

20. The following is the code to view the detected anomalies distribution:

    ```
    distribution:anomaly_results_df['anomaly'].
    plot(kind='hist')
    plt.show()
    ```

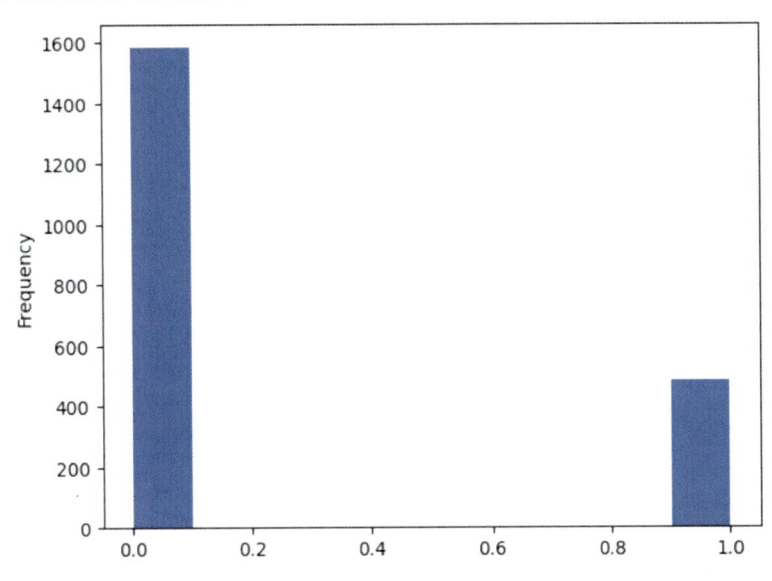

Figure 4.18 shows the detected anomalies distribution:

Figure 4.18 – The anomalies distribution

21. Visualize deviation versus threshold. The result is shown in *Figure 4.19*:

```
anomaly_results_df[['deviation', 'threshold']].
plot(figsize=(14, 6))
plt.xlabel('Index')
plt.show()
```

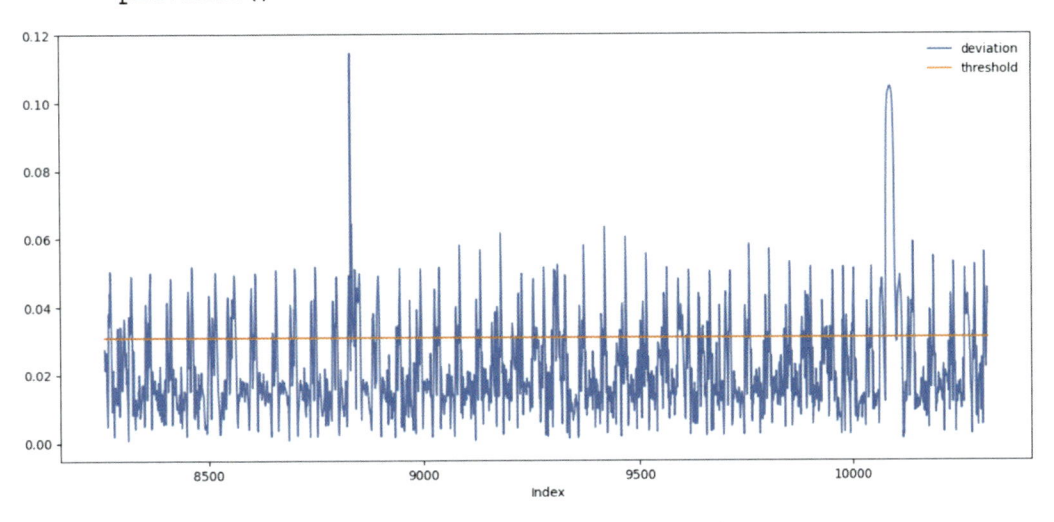

Figure 4.19 – Deviation versus threshold

22. Next, we will see the distribution of the detected layers:

```
sns.set(rc={'figure.figsize':(20,10)})
sns.lineplot(x=anomaly_results_df.date, y=anomaly_
results_df.value, label='Total passengers',alpha=0.6)
sns.scatterplot(x=anomalies.date, y=anomalies.value,
color='r', label='Anomalies')
plt.ylabel('Count')
fig.autofmt_xdate()
plt.savefig('anomalies_vs_total.png', bbox_
inches='tight')
plt.show()
```

Figure 4.20 shows the distribution of the detected outliers. Note that the outliers that occurred during New Year's Day 2015, and the drop toward the end of January that was detected coincided with the 2015 snowstorm around the New York area.

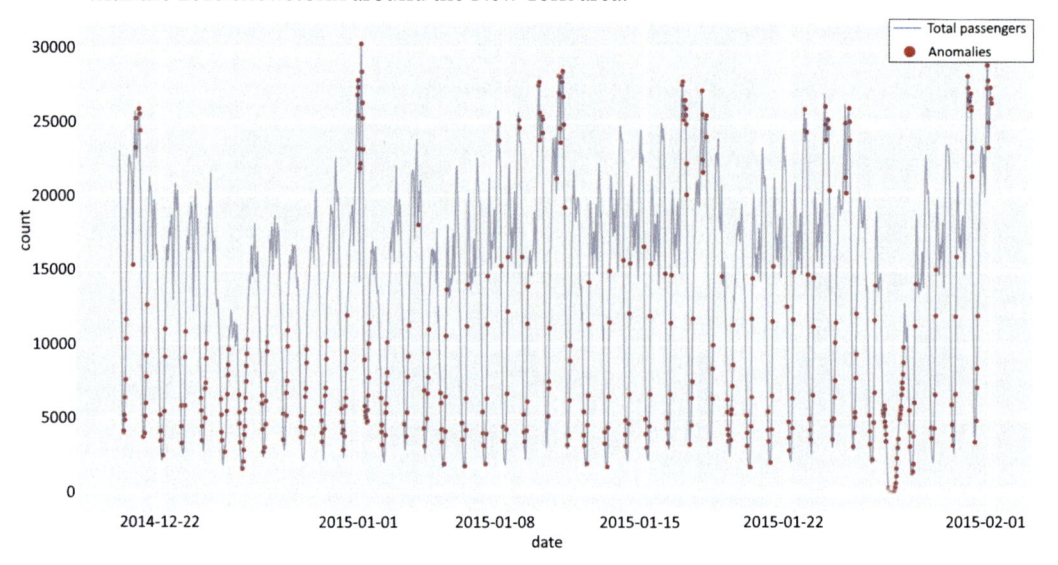

Figure 4.20 – The detected anomalies

23. Now, we are ready to assess the explainability of this LSTM-based anomaly detector. Import the OmniXAI libraries:

```
from omnixai.data.timeseries import Timeseries
from omnixai.explainers.timeseries import
TimeseriesExplainer
from omnixai.explainers.timeseries import ShapTimeseries
```

24. Load the NYC Taxi Traffic time series dataset:

    ```
    df = pd.read_csv('nyc.csv')
    df = df[['date', 'value']]
    df['date'] = pd.to_datetime(df['date'], infer_datetime_
    format=True)
    df = df.set_index('date')
    ```

25. Create a training and test dataset. You can modify the sample range to assess different local explainability:

    ```
    train_df = df.iloc[:8600]
    test_df = df.iloc[8600:9000]
    ```

26. Set an anomaly threshold of the 80th percentile for detecting outliers:

    ```
    threshold = np.percentile(train_df['value'].values, 80)
    ```

27. Create a function to determine whether a time series window is anomalous:

    ```
    def detector(ts: Timeseries):
        anomaly_scores = np.sum((ts.values > threshold).
    astype(int))
        return anomaly_scores / ts.shape[0]
    ```

28. To initialize a SHAP explainer, set the training dataset as `training_data`, the model as `predict_function`, and `anomaly_detection` as mode. `predict_function` generates anomaly scores where higher scores mean more anomalous:

    ```
    explainer = ShapTimeseries(
        training_data=Timeseries.from_pd(train_df),
        predict_function=detector,
        mode='anomaly_detection'
    )
    test_x = Timeseries.from_pd(test_df)
    ```

29. SHAP generates local explanations by calling the explainer to explain the test instances. The parameter index indicates the position of a data instance in `test_x`. For example, `index = 0` refers to the first instance in `test_x`. When working with a large dataset, you can sample the dataset for shorter runtime using the `nsamples` parameter:

    ```
    explanations = explainer.explain(
        test_x
    ```

```
                #params={'shap': {'nsamples': 500}}
    )
    explanations.ipython_plot()
```

Figure 4.21 compares the number of taxi passengers and the calculated anomaly scores in dashed lines for selected test instances. OmniXAI's SHAP explainer provides post hoc local explainability for the detected anomalies using anomaly scores, correlating the spike in the total number of taxi passengers with New Year's Day 2015 in this case:

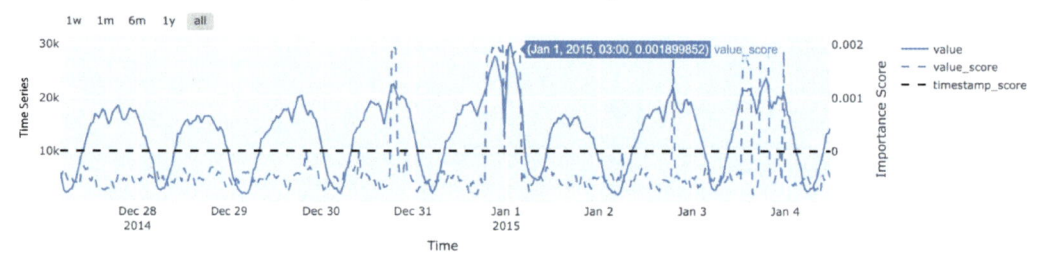

Figure 4.21 – OmniXAI SHAP local explainability

Congratulations! You have completed end-to-end time series anomaly detection with deep learning. You transformed the dataset, created an LSTM-based anomaly detector, and analyzed the post hoc local explainability using the SHAP explainer by OmniXAI. In the following section, let's discuss how you can practice time series deep learning anomaly detection with a different dataset.

Exercise

To practice what we learned in this chapter, I recommend exploring the **Numenta Anomaly Benchmark** (**NAB**) for any hidden anomalous trend: `https://www.kaggle.com/datasets/julienjta/twitter-mentions-volumes`. This time series dataset contains a collection of Twitter mentions for large companies, including Apple, Amazon, Salesforce, CVS, Facebook, Google, IBM, Coca-Cola, Pfizer, and UPS. The data is aggregated at a 5-minute interval between February and April 2015. For example, can your model detect the unusual spike of Twitter mentions for Apple in March? Can you explain the detected time series anomalies with an XAI method? Be sure to check for imbalance distribution and missing values in the dataset.

Summary

Explaining the logic behind a machine learning model's decision is crucial to increasing transparency and interpretability to earn users' trust and meet regulatory compliance. In contrast, demonstrating failures in an AI model is equally important to improve model performance and avoid detrimental impacts in high-stakes settings.

Finding anomalies can be tedious, since there are various anomalies in time series data, such as seasonal and quantile anomalies. In this chapter, you learned about detecting and explaining anomalies for time series data with deep learning. I hope you can apply what you have learned about time series anomaly explainability to identify actionable insights.

The next chapter will cover computer vision anomaly explainability.

5
Computer Vision Anomaly Explainability

Computer vision anomaly detection has broad applications, such as industrial manufacturing, medical imaging analysis, and autonomous driving. Detecting anomalies in image data is challenging yet crucial to identifying abnormal events, safety risks, and quality defects that may cause financial and brand damage to many companies.

According to the American Society for Quality at `https://asq.org/quality-resources/cost-of-quality`, organizations can incur 15-20% quality-related costs from their sales revenue. Besides financial loss, quality-related activities can result in poor customer satisfaction, potential lawsuits, and productivity impact. Hence, research for visual anomaly detection plays a critical role in theory and applications. For example, the adoption of robotics is expected to increase by 50% in the next 5 years, according to a survey by **Material Handling Institute** (**MHI**) at `https://www.nytimes.com/2022/07/12/business/warehouse-technology-robotics.html`. However, a broader adoption of self-driving vehicles on public roads still faces technical challenges and legal scrutiny.

We reviewed anomaly explainability for **natural language processing** (NLP) in *Chapter 3* and time series in *Chapter 4*. In this chapter, we will explore the following topics to understand **Explainable AI** (**XAI**) aspects of deep learning anomaly detection for computer vision, also known as visual anomaly detection.

More specifically, in this chapter, we will cover the following topics:

- Reviewing visual anomaly detection
- Integrating deep visual anomaly detection with XAI
- Problem and solution walkthrough

For the example walkthrough, you will experiment with a visual anomaly detection problem using a chest X-ray dataset to detect images with pneumonia. Then, you will visualize the model's **Class Activation Map (CAM)** and **Gradient-weighted Class Activation Mapping (Grad-CAM)** to interpret discriminative image regions that a **convolutional neural network (CNN)** uses to identify a target image class.

The following section reviews the taxonomy of visual anomaly detection.

Reviewing visual anomaly detection

Anomaly detection extracts non-conforming patterns based on expected behavior to create a reasonable model for observing unseen data. Visual anomaly detection refers to identifying and localizing anomalous regions in imagery data using **machine learning** (**ML**) approaches, such as supervised, semi-supervised, and unsupervised techniques to surface anomalies through visual inspection. Please refer to *Chapter 1* for comparisons of these techniques.

There are two approaches for assessing visual anomalies:

- **Image-level**: This approach evaluates whether the whole image is normal or abnormal.
- **Pixel-level**: This approach detects abnormal regions in an image to determine whether an image is normal or abnormal. The pixel-level method is widely used in industrial fault detection and medical diagnosis. However, this approach can be challenging for mission-critical applications due to large variations and ambiguous boundaries.

Generally, most computer vision XAI methods explain an ML model's decisions by producing values based on output probabilities, heatmap generation, or scatter plots to reveal the contributions of input features. Examples include CAM and Grad-CAM, which we will review in this chapter, saliency maps in *Chapter 7*, and **Guided Integrated Gradients** (**Guided IG**) in *Chapter 8*.

The following section reviews various image-level and pixel-level techniques.

Reviewing image-level visual anomaly detection

Traditional ML methods typically compare the output distribution of image features with a reference distribution model. These methods evaluate differences in the distribution model to determine whether anomalies exist. Deep learning algorithms such as CNNs enhance traditional methods with powerful representation capability using high-dimensional data. The following are examples of image-level visual anomaly detection:

- **Density estimation**: This method estimates and compares the probability distribution model between a normal and an unseen image to determine deviations for anomaly detection. Density estimation methods such as **k-nearest neighbors** (**KNN**) require a large dataset. Furthermore, feature dimensions become increasingly complex as the dataset grows. Deep learning models can enhance density estimation by establishing probability distribution for high-dimensional imagery data.

- **One-class classification** (OCC): This method classifies the normal class by constructing a decision boundary in the feature space. Estimating concrete probability for each data point is optional for OCC. Deep neural networks enhance OCC by applying feature extraction. For example, **One-Class Convolutional Neural Network (OC-CNN)**, `https://arxiv.org/pdf/1901.08688.pdf`, is a CNN-based OCC. Many anomaly detection applications employ OCC since anomalies are rare and the learning process focuses only on one target class.

- **Image reconstruction**: This method maps an input image to a low-dimensional vector representation to reconstruct the original image through inverse mapping. Image reconstruction assumes normal images produce small reconstruction errors, whereas anomalous data should yield higher reconstruction errors. Image reconstruction methods such as autoencoder, which we reviewed in *Chapter 1*, is an unsupervised neural network that compresses the input data through a hidden middle layer to reconstruct the original image. The intuition is that compressing information will be difficult if the input features are independent or non-redundant. Conversely, compressing redundant information should be straightforward if the data has a similar structure.

- **Self-supervised classification**: This method uses large-scale unsupervised data to learn visual representations such as color, texture, location, shape, position, and direction from available self-constructed supervision information for downstream tasks such as anomaly detection.

Reviewing pixel-level visual anomaly detection

Although image-level algorithms can be used for deriving pixel-level anomaly detection by segmenting the whole image into patches, semantic information may be lacking. Hence, the following unsupervised pixel-level approaches are ideal:

- **Image reconstruction**: Assuming convolutional neural networks are only trained with normal images, the pixel-level image reconstruction method reconstructs the input image. Then, it evaluates the pixel difference between the input and reconstructed image to determine anomalous regions. Creating high-quality images from sharp edges and complex textures is challenging for pixel-level anomaly detection, leading to a higher probability of false positives in detecting abnormalities.

- **Feature modeling**: Unlike image reconstruction, feature-based methods focus on detecting anomalies using curated local region feature representations of the whole image. Deviations in feature distribution between a regional feature and the test image's local region determine whether the target region should be labeled as an anomaly.

Having provided an overview of anomaly detection techniques for computer vision, let's explore what a deep learning model looks for when finding visual anomalies in the following section.

Integrating deep visual anomaly detection with XAI

Deep learning presents enormous opportunities in computer vision anomaly detection by teaching computers to mimic human visual systems. For example, CNNs are designed to replicate the structure of the human visual cortex for computer vision tasks such as object detection, image classification, and semantic segmentation. *Figure 5.1* shows a high-level architecture of a CNN:

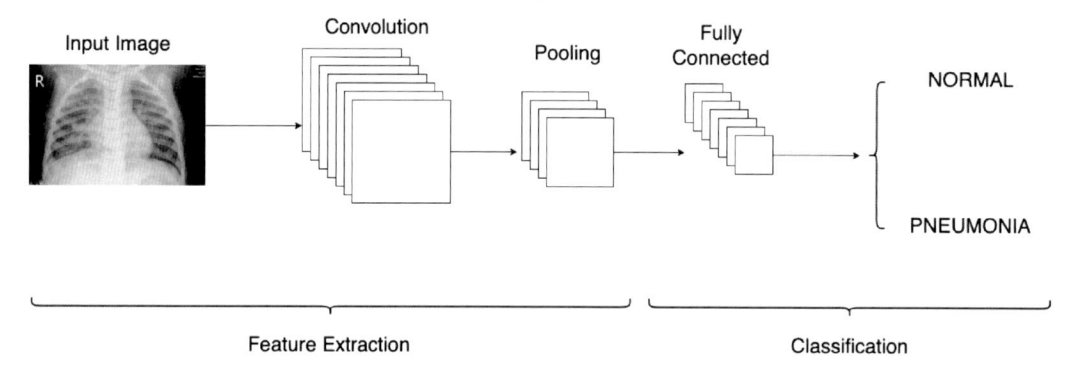

Figure 5.1 – A simple CNN architecture

As you can see in the preceding image, the high-level architecture of a CNN is shown with the following main layers. You can learn more about CNNs from this paper, https://ieeexplore.ieee.org/document/8308186. The layers in this architecture are as follows:

- **Convolutional layer**: This is the first layer that extracts various features from an input image. When the convolutional layer receives an input image, it produces a 2D activation map by convolving each filter across the spatial dimensionality. The network learns a specific feature at a particular spatial position by gliding through the input using these filters.

- **Pooling layer**: This layer processes each activation map from the input using max pooling or average pooling operations to reduce the number of parameters and downsample the spatial dimensionality of a given input image for activations.

- **Fully-connected layer**: This is the last layer that receives outputs from the pooling layer and predicts the best possible target label by producing scores based on activations for classification.

You are probably wondering, can humans understand how deep learning thinks? It is not feasible for humans to figure out the complex mapping and millions of weights that a neural network uses to predict a given input. Hence, XAI methods such as CAM and Grad-CAM are essential to facilitate interpretability.

CAM, http://cnnlocalization.csail.mit.edu/, helps users interpret how a CNN predicts a specific image label by localizing the relevant regions in an image to this class. Visualizing what the model sees using heatmaps allows users to identify potential biases influencing a model's decision-making and debug the model before deploying it to production. While CAM provides heatmaps to interpret a CNN model, it can be noisy and suffer a loss of spatial information. Alternatively, Grad-CAM can improve CAM's accuracy by retaining important spatial information to capture more accurate activation maps.

Grad-CAM, `https://arxiv.org/abs/1610.02391`, is a technique that generalizes CAM to produce visual explanations for CNN-based models. Grad-CAM exploits spatial information captured across convolutional layers to identify features that influence a model's prediction. Then, it uses gradients at the final convolutional activation maps to highlight important regions in the image. Grad-CAM is a post hoc attention mechanism for visualization. Unlike CAM, Grad-CAM does not have specific CNN architecture requirements.

Now that you understand XAI approaches for visual anomaly detection using deep learning, let's discuss what you will need for the example walkthrough.

Technical requirements

You will need the following technical requirements to experiment with the example:

- **OpenCV-Python**: An open source Python library for image processing and computer vision tasks such as face detection and object tracking
- **Keras**: An open source library for building neural networks
- **Matplotlib**: A plotting library for creating data visualizations
- **NumPy**: An open source library that provides mathematical functions when working with arrays
- **pandas**: A library that offers data analysis and manipulation tools
- **SciPy**: An open source Python library for scientific and technical computing
- **Sklearn**: An ML tool library for predictive data analysis
- **TensorFlow**: An open source framework for building deep learning applications

A sample Jupyter notebook and requirements file for package dependencies discussed in this chapter are available at `https://github.com/PacktPublishing/Deep-Learning-and-XAI-Techniques-for-Anomaly-Detection/tree/main/Chapter5`.

You can experiment with this example on Amazon SageMaker Studio Lab at `https://aws.amazon.com/sagemaker/studio-lab/`, a free notebook development environment that provides up to 12 hours of CPU or 4 hours of GPU per user session and 15 GiB storage at no cost. Alternatively, you can try this on your preferred **integrated development environment** (IDE).

Next, let's explore the dataset for this example.

Problem

Pneumonia is an acute respiratory infection caused by viruses, bacteria, or fungi where the air sacs fill with pus or fluid. Symptoms of pneumonia include a cough with phlegm, fever, chills, and difficulty breathing. Pneumonia can be life-threatening if left untreated, especially in vulnerable groups such as infants, young children, and the elderly. Almost 2.5 million people died from pneumonia in 2019, according to Our World in Data, https://ourworldindata.org/pneumonia. Viral pneumonia in the United States is commonly caused by influenza viruses, **respiratory syncytial virus** (**RSV**), and SARS-CoV-2 (COVID-19).

Chest X-rays are commonly used in diagnosing pneumonia in addition to clinical examination and medical history records. The continuous advancement in AI has shown promising results in finding abnormal patterns in chest X-rays, addressing the concern of needing more experts to screen radiographs.

This section reviews an example of visual anomaly detection using the chest X-ray image dataset, which is available for download at: https://www.kaggle.com/datasets/paultimothymooney/chest-xray-pneumonia. You will learn about detecting visual anomalies with a pre-trained VGG16 model. Then, you will localize abnormal regions in the image using standard activation maps and Grad-CAM to explain the model's prediction.

The chest X-ray image dataset contains 5,864 images organized in three main folders (`train`, `test`, `val`) and two subfolders (`PNEUMONIA`, `NORMAL`). These images were collected from patients' routine clinical care and graded by expert physicians for AI use.

The following section provides a step-by-step walkthrough for this example.

Solution walkthrough

This section provides a detailed review of the visual anomaly detection example to interpret anomalies identified by a pre-trained VGG16 model. The sample notebook, `chapter5_gradcam_cv.ipynb`, can be found in the book's GitHub repo:

1. First, let's install the required packages using the `requirements.txt` file:

   ```
   import sys
   !{sys.executable} -m pip install -qr requirements.txt
   ```

2. Load the essential libraries:

   ```
   import cv2
   import os
   import re
   import glob
   import random
   ```

```
import warnings
import numpy as np
import pandas as pd
import scipy as sp
import matplotlib.pyplot as plt
import matplotlib.cm as cm
import matplotlib.image as mpimg
from platform import python_version
from IPython.display import Image, display
from sklearn.model_selection import train_test_split
from sklearn.metrics import classification_report,
accuracy_score, confusion_matrix, ConfusionMatrixDisplay
import tensorflow as tf
from tensorflow import keras
from tensorflow.keras.models import *
from tensorflow.keras.layers import *
from tensorflow.keras.optimizers import *
from tensorflow.keras.applications import vgg16
from tensorflow.keras.preprocessing.image import img_to_
array, array_to_img, ImageDataGenerator
warnings.simplefilter(action='ignore',
category=FutureWarning)
os.environ['TF_CPP_MIN_LOG_LEVEL'] = '3'


print(f'TensorFlow version: {tf.__version__}')
print(f'Python version: {python_version()}')
```

Figure 5.2 shows the Python and TensorFlow package dependencies:

```
TensorFlow version: 2.11.0
Python version: 3.9.10
```

Figure 5.2 – Package dependencies

3. Set variables for the image dataset path, desired input shape, and batch size:

```
%matplotlib inline
base_path = "images/chest_xray/"
train_path = base_path + "train/"
test_path = base_path + "test/"
```

```
val_path = base_path + "val/"

SHAPE = (224,224,3)
batch_size = 256
classes = ["NORMAL", "PNEUMONIA"]

print(f'train_path: {train_path}')
print(f'test_path: {test_path}')
print(f'val_path: {val_path}')
```

Figure 5.3 shows the image paths for train, test, and validation:

```
train_path: images/chest_xray/train/
test_path: images/chest_xray/test/
val_path: images/chest_xray/val/
```

Figure 5.3 – Image paths

4. Create a function to load the raw images:

```
def load_image_data(path, label):
    images = []
    for img_path in glob.glob(path + label + '/*.jpeg'):
        images.append(mpimg.imread(img_path))
        if len(images)>4:
            break

    fig = plt.figure(figsize=(25, 10))
    columns = 5
    for i, image in enumerate(images):
        plt.subplot(round(len(images) / columns + 1), columns, i + 1)
        plt.imshow(image, cmap='gray', aspect='auto')
        plt.title(label)
```

5. Load a preview of sample images classified as the PNEUMONIA class:

   ```
   load_image_data(train_path, classes[1])
   ```

   Figure 5.4 shows a preview of sample images classified as the PNEUMONIA class. Typically, white opacity areas in chest X-rays indicate lung inflammation and pneumonia:

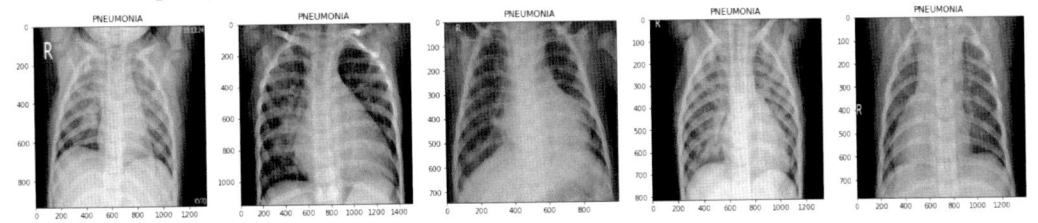

   Figure 5.4 – Pneumonia chest X-rays

6. Load a preview of sample images classified as the NORMAL class:

   ```
   load_image_data(train_path, classes[0])
   ```

   Figure 5.5 shows some sample images classified as the NORMAL class:

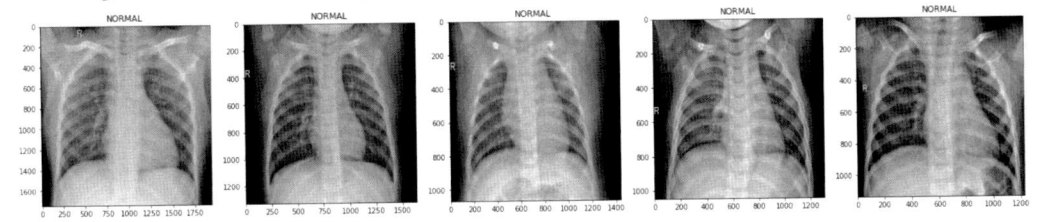

   Figure 5.5 – Normal chest X-rays

7. Next, we will load the VGG16 pre-trained model and prepare for training:

   ```
   def set_seed(seed):
       tf.random.set_seed(seed)
       os.environ['PYTHONHASHSEED'] = str(seed)
       np.random.seed(seed)
       random.seed(seed)


   def get_model():
       set_seed(33)

       vgg = vgg16.VGG16(weights='imagenet', include_top=False, input_shape = SHAPE)
   ```

```python
    for layer in vgg.layers[:-8]:
        layer.trainable = False

    x = vgg.output
    x = GlobalAveragePooling2D()(x)
    x = Dense(2, activation="softmax")(x)

    model = Model(vgg.input, x)
    model.compile(loss = "categorical_crossentropy",
                            optimizer
= SGD(learning_rate=0.0001, momentum=0.9),
metrics=["accuracy"])
    return model
```

8. Generate batches of tensor image data with real-time augmentation to rescale the images:

```python
train_datagen = ImageDataGenerator(
        rescale=1/255
)

test_datagen = ImageDataGenerator(
        rescale=1/255
)

val_datagen = ImageDataGenerator(
        rescale=1/255
)
```

9. Read images from a directory and augment them while the neural network is learning on the training data:

```python
train_generator = train_datagen.flow_from_directory(
                train_path,
                target_size = (SHAPE[0],
SHAPE[1]),
                batch_size = batch_size,
                class_mode = 'categorical',
                shuffle = True,
                subset = None,
```

```
                        seed = 33
)

test_generator = test_datagen.flow_from_directory(
                        test_path,
                        target_size = (SHAPE[0],
SHAPE[1]),
                        batch_size = batch_size,
                        class_mode = 'categorical',
                        shuffle = True,
                        subset = None,
                        seed = 33
)

val_generator = val_datagen.flow_from_directory(
                        val_path,
                        target_size = (SHAPE[0],
SHAPE[1]),
                        batch_size = batch_size,
                        class_mode = 'categorical',
                        shuffle = True,
                        subset = None,
                        seed = 33
)
```

10. Retrieve test labels from the generator:

```
test_num = test_generator.samples

label_test = []
for i in range((test_num // test_generator.batch_
size)+1):
        X,y = test_generator.next()
        label_test.append(y)

label_test = np.argmax(np.vstack(label_test), axis=1)

label_test.shape
```

11. Load the VGG16 model and view the model summary, as shown in *Figure 5.6*:

```
model = get_model()
model.summary()
```

```
Model: "model"
_____
Layer (type)                 Output Shape              Param #
=================================================================
input_1 (InputLayer)         [(None, 224, 224, 3)]     0
block1_conv1 (Conv2D)        (None, 224, 224, 64)      1792
block1_conv2 (Conv2D)        (None, 224, 224, 64)      36928
block1_pool (MaxPooling2D)   (None, 112, 112, 64)      0
block2_conv1 (Conv2D)        (None, 112, 112, 128)     73856
block2_conv2 (Conv2D)        (None, 112, 112, 128)     147584
block2_pool (MaxPooling2D)   (None, 56, 56, 128)       0
block3_conv1 (Conv2D)        (None, 56, 56, 256)       295168
block3_conv2 (Conv2D)        (None, 56, 56, 256)       590080
block3_conv3 (Conv2D)        (None, 56, 56, 256)       590080
block3_pool (MaxPooling2D)   (None, 28, 28, 256)       0
block4_conv1 (Conv2D)        (None, 28, 28, 512)       1180160
block4_conv2 (Conv2D)        (None, 28, 28, 512)       2359808
block4_conv3 (Conv2D)        (None, 28, 28, 512)       2359808
block4_pool (MaxPooling2D)   (None, 14, 14, 512)       0
block5_conv1 (Conv2D)        (None, 14, 14, 512)       2359808
block5_conv2 (Conv2D)        (None, 14, 14, 512)       2359808
block5_conv3 (Conv2D)        (None, 14, 14, 512)       2359808
block5_pool (MaxPooling2D)   (None, 7, 7, 512)         0
global_average_pooling2d (G  (None, 512)               0
lobalAveragePooling2D)
dense (Dense)                (None, 2)                 1026
=================================================================
Total params: 14,715,714
Trainable params: 12,980,226
Non-trainable params: 1,735,488
_____
```

Figure 5.6 – The VGG16 model summary

12. Train the model with 8 epochs:

    ```
    model.fit(
            train_generator,
            steps_per_epoch=train_generator.samples/train_generator.batch_size,
            epochs=8
    )
    ```

    The result is as follows:

    ```
    Epoch 1/8
    20/20 [==============================] - 244s 12s/step - loss: 0.5509 - accuracy: 0.7429
    Epoch 2/8
    20/20 [==============================] - 243s 12s/step - loss: 0.5010 - accuracy: 0.7429
    Epoch 3/8
    20/20 [==============================] - 242s 12s/step - loss: 0.4415 - accuracy: 0.7500
    Epoch 4/8
    20/20 [==============================] - 244s 12s/step - loss: 0.3763 - accuracy: 0.8202
    Epoch 5/8
    20/20 [==============================] - 243s 12s/step - loss: 0.3097 - accuracy: 0.8921
    Epoch 6/8
    20/20 [==============================] - 244s 12s/step - loss: 0.2551 - accuracy: 0.9112
    Epoch 7/8
    20/20 [==============================] - 243s 12s/step - loss: 0.2152 - accuracy: 0.9220
    Epoch 8/8
    20/20 [==============================] - 244s 12s/step - loss: 0.1901 - accuracy: 0.9293
    ```

    Figure 5.7 – Result of training with 8 epochs

13. Once the training completes, let's evaluate the model performance by creating a classification report:

    ```
    print(classification_report(label_test, np.argmax(model.predict(test_generator),axis=1)))
    ```

    Figure 5.8 shows the classification report:

    ```
    3/3 [==============================] - 16s 4s/step
                  precision    recall  f1-score   support

               0       0.93      0.51      0.66       234
               1       0.77      0.98      0.86       390

        accuracy                           0.80       624
       macro avg       0.85      0.74      0.76       624
    weighted avg       0.83      0.80      0.78       624
    ```

    Figure 5.8 – The classification report

14. Obtain predictions for the test data:

    ```
    y_preds = np.argmax(model.predict(test_generator),axis=1)
    ```

15. Let's create a confusion matrix to assess model performance:

    ```
    cm = confusion_matrix(label_test, y_preds)
    cmp = ConfusionMatrixDisplay(cm, display_labels=classes)

    fig, ax = plt.subplots(figsize=(5,5))
    cmp.plot(ax=ax)

    plt.xlabel('Predicted Class')
    plt.ylabel('True Class')
    plt.savefig("pneumonia_confusion_matrix.png", bbox_inches='tight')
    ```

    Figure 5.9 shows the confusion matrix:

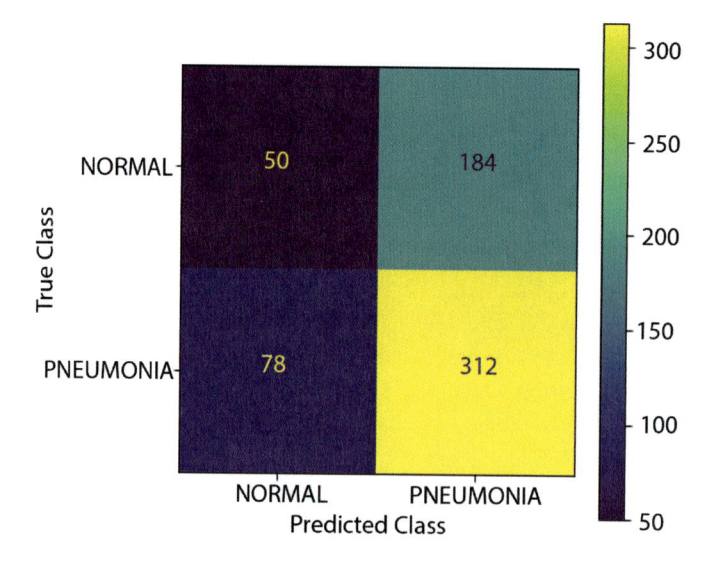

    Figure 5.9 – The confusion matrix

16. Now, we are ready to generate CAM. Create a function to plot activations:

    ```
    def plot_activation(img):
        pred = model.predict(img[np.newaxis,:,:,:])
        pred_class = np.argmax(pred)
    ```

```
            weights = model.layers[-1].get_weights()[0]
            class_weights = weights[:, pred_class]

            intermediate = Model(model.input, model.get_
layer("block5_conv3").output)
            conv_output = intermediate.predict(img[np.
newaxis,:,:,:])
            conv_output = np.squeeze(conv_output)

            h = int(img.shape[0]/conv_output.shape[0])
            w = int(img.shape[1]/conv_output.shape[1])

            activation_maps = sp.ndimage.zoom(conv_output,
(h, w, 1), order=1)
            out = np.dot(activation_maps.reshape((img.
shape[0]*img.shape[1], 512)), class_weights).reshape(
                img.shape[0],img.shape[1])

    plt.imshow(img.astype('float32').reshape(img.
shape[0],img.shape[1],3), aspect='auto')
            plt.imshow(out, cmap='jet', alpha=0.35,
aspect='auto')
            plt.title('Pneumonia' if pred_class == 1 else
'Normal')
```

17. Call the `plot_activation` function to visualize a few test images and their labels:

```
fig = plt.figure(figsize=(25, 5))

rows = 1
columns = 5

for i in range(5):
        fig.add_subplot(rows, columns, i+1)
        plot_activation(X[i])
```

As shown in *Figure 5.10*, CAM helps visualize discriminative image regions that CNN uses to identify the target image label:

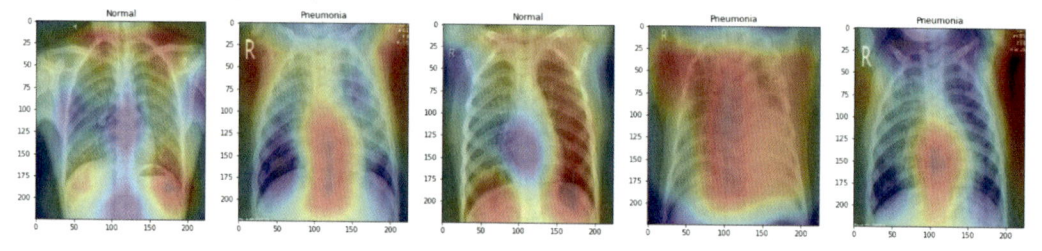

Figure 5.10 – CAM

18. Let's try a different visualization of activations using Grad-CAM. We will first load some test images:

    ```
    pneumonia_data_dir = test_path + classes[1]
    normal_data_dir = test_path + classes[0]

    gradcam_test_pneumonia = []
    gradcam_test_normal = []

    def load_gradcam_images(data_dir, output_list):
        for x in os.listdir(data_dir):
            if x.endswith(".jpeg"):
                filename = os.path.join(data_dir, x)
                output_list.append(filename)

    load_gradcam_images(pneumonia_data_dir, gradcam_test_pneumonia)
    load_gradcam_images(normal_data_dir, gradcam_test_normal)
    ```

19. Set image size, last convolutional layer, and preprocessing variable:

    ```
    img_size = SHAPE
    last_conv_layer_name = "block5_conv3"
    preprocess_input = keras.applications.vgg16.preprocess_input
    ```

20. Create functions to get the image array. Map the input image to the last convolutional layer and compute gradients to show activation corresponding to the last convolutional layer's feature map:

```
def get_img_array(img_path, size):
    img = keras.preprocessing.image.load_img(img_path, target_size=size)
    array = keras.preprocessing.image.img_to_array(img)
    array = np.expand_dims(array, axis=0)
    return array

def make_gradcam_heatmap(img_array, model, last_conv_layer_name, pred_index=None):

    grad_model = tf.keras.models.Model(
        [model.inputs], [model.get_layer(last_conv_layer_name).output, model.output]
    )

    with tf.GradientTape() as tape:
        last_conv_layer_output, preds = grad_model(img_array)
        if pred_index is None:
            pred_index = tf.argmax(preds[0])
        class_channel = preds[:, pred_index]

    grads = tape.gradient(class_channel, last_conv_layer_output)

    pooled_grads = tf.reduce_mean(grads, axis=(0, 1, 2))

    last_conv_layer_output = last_conv_layer_output[0]
    heatmap = last_conv_layer_output @ pooled_grads[..., tf.newaxis]
    heatmap = tf.squeeze(heatmap)

    heatmap = tf.maximum(heatmap, 0) / tf.math.
```

```
        reduce_max(heatmap)
    return heatmap.numpy()
```

21. Generate heatmaps to surface activations:

```
model = model

heatmaps_pneumonia = []
heatmaps_normal = []

def create_heatmap(images, heatmap_path):
    img_array = preprocess_input(get_img_array(images, size=img_size))
    model.layers[-1].activation = None
    heatmap = make_gradcam_heatmap(img_array, model, last_conv_layer_name)
    heatmap_path.append(heatmap)
```

22. Rescale the heatmaps between 0 and 255 to superimpose over the original test images:

```
import matplotlib.cm as cm
gradcam_pneumonia_images = []
gradcam_normal_images = []

def save_and_display_gradcam(img_path, heatmap, output_path, alpha=0.4):
    img = keras.preprocessing.image.load_img(img_path)
    img = keras.preprocessing.image.img_to_array(img)

    heatmap = np.uint8(255 * heatmap)

    jet = cm.get_cmap("jet")

    jet_colors = jet(np.arange(256))[:, :3]
    jet_heatmap = jet_colors[heatmap]

    jet_heatmap = keras.preprocessing.image.array_to_img(jet_heatmap)
```

```
            jet_heatmap = jet_heatmap.resize((img.shape[1],
img.shape[0]))
            jet_heatmap = keras.preprocessing.image.img_to_
array(jet_heatmap)

            superimposed_img = jet_heatmap * alpha + img
            superimposed_img = keras.preprocessing.image.
array_to_img(superimposed_img)
            output_path.append(superimposed_img)
```

23. Using Grad-CAM, we can localize anomalous regions and pinpoint a more specific area of interest within an input image:

```
fig = plt.figure(figsize=(25, 5))

for i in range(3):
        create_heatmap(gradcam_test_pneumonia[i],
heatmaps_pneumonia)
        fig.add_subplot(rows, columns, i+1)
        plt.imshow(heatmaps_pneumonia[i], aspect='auto')
        plt.title(re.sub(pneumonia_data_dir, " ",gradcam_
test_pneumonia[i]))

fig = plt.figure(figsize=(25, 5))

for i in range(3):
        save_and_display_gradcam(gradcam_test_
pneumonia[i], heatmaps_pneumonia[i], gradcam_pneumonia_
images)
        fig.add_subplot(rows, columns, i+1)
        plt.imshow(gradcam_pneumonia_images[i],
aspect='auto')
        plt.title(re.sub(pneumonia_data_dir, " ",gradcam_
test_pneumonia[i]))
```

The result is shown in *Figure 5.11*:

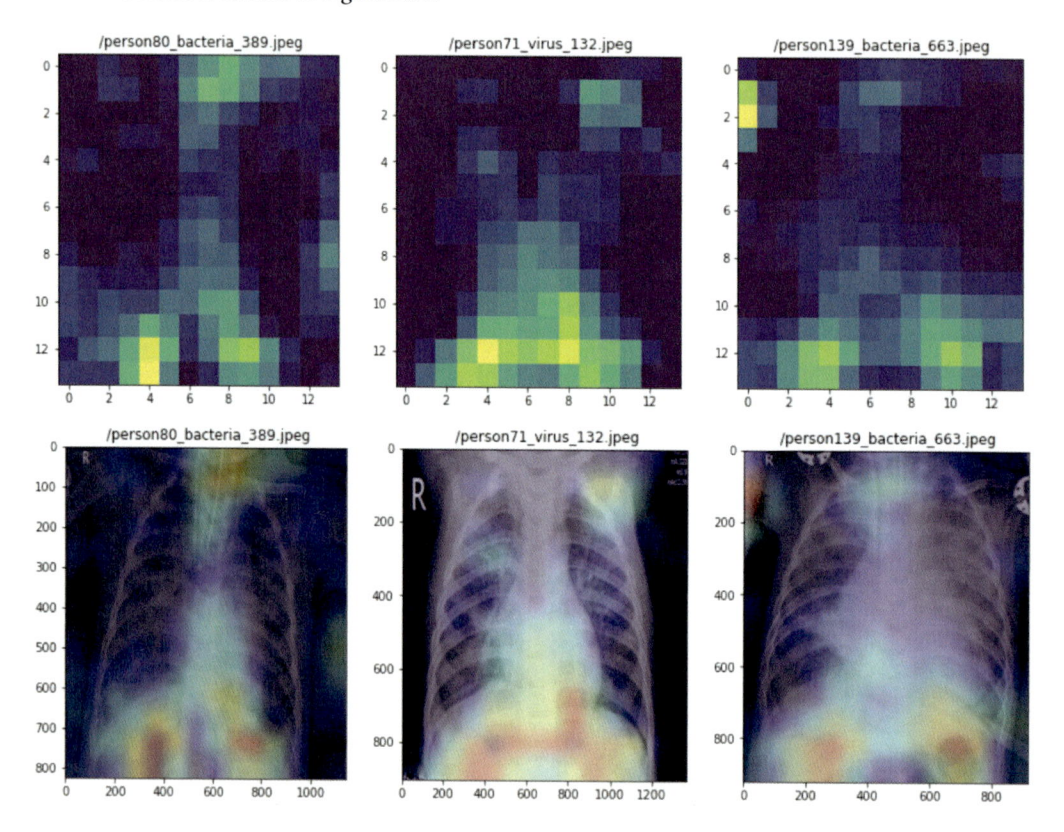

Figure 5.11 – The Grad-CAM PNEUMONIA class

24. Repeat the heatmap visualization for the NORMAL class using Grad-CAM:

```
fig = plt.figure(figsize=(25, 5))

for i in range(3):
        create_heatmap(gradcam_test_normal[i], heatmaps_
normal)
        fig.add_subplot(rows, columns, i+1)
        plt.imshow(heatmaps_normal[i], aspect='auto')
        plt.title(re.sub(normal_data_dir, " ",gradcam_
test_normal[i]))

fig = plt.figure(figsize=(25, 5))
```

Solution walkthrough | 119

```
for i in range(3):
        save_and_display_gradcam(gradcam_test_normal[i],
heatmaps_normal[i], gradcam_normal_images)
        fig.add_subplot(rows, columns, i+1)
        plt.imshow(gradcam_normal_images[i],
aspect='auto')
        plt.title(re.sub(normal_data_dir, " ",gradcam_
test_normal[i]))
```

The result is pictured in *Figure 5.12*:

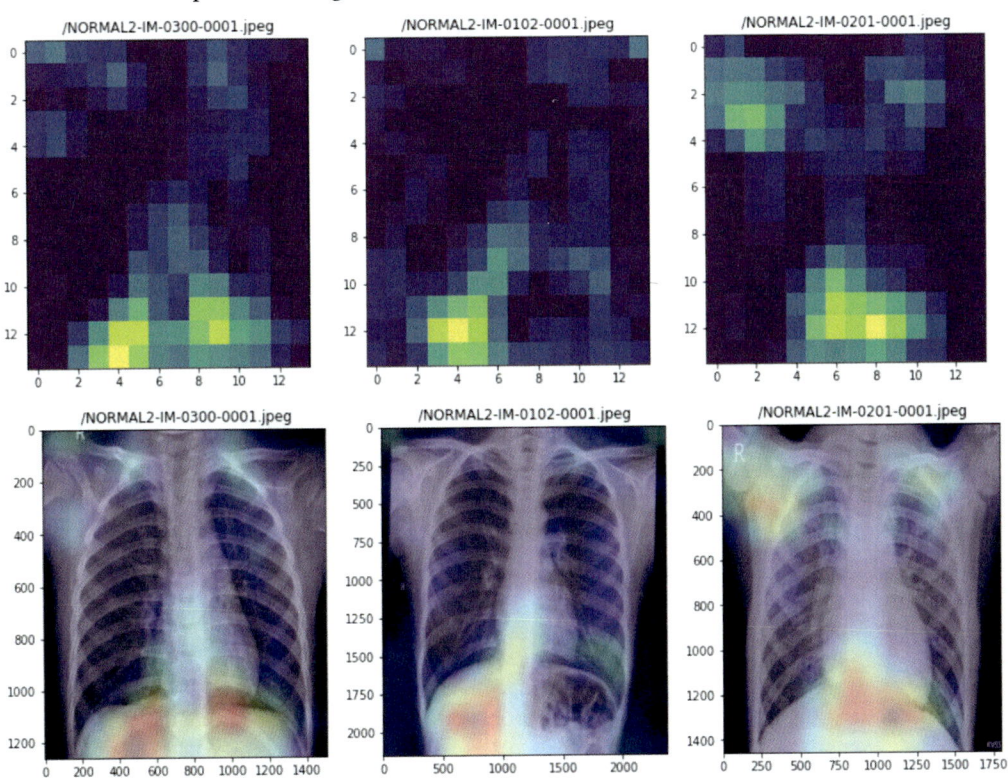

Figure 5.12 – The Grad-CAM NORMAL class

Can you distinguish the two classes simply by looking at the images? According to the dataset description, normal chest X-ray images typically show clear lungs without opacification or cloudiness. Bacteria pneumonia displays a focal lobar consolidation in one of the lobes of the lung. Viral pneumonia shows a more diffuse interstitial pattern surrounding both lungs. By superimposing heatmaps over images, you localize the discriminative image regions to understand how the VGG16 model decides on the target predicted class.

Great work! You have completed an end-to-end walkthrough of visual anomaly detection in this section. Let's discuss how you can apply what you have learned in the following section.

Exercise

To practice what we learned in this chapter, I recommend exploring the *Marble Surface Anomaly Detection* dataset for detecting dots and cracked marble. This dataset is available for download at: `https://www.kaggle.com/datasets/wardaddy24/marble-surface-anomaly-detection`. It contains images with two classes, good and defect. Note that the joints in the good category are not defects.

Summary

This chapter showed you how CAM and Grad-CAM provide anomaly localization by identifying class discriminative activation maps. In addition, you learned how to provide transparency and build user trust by adding visual explanations into a CNN for computer vision anomaly detection. In the next chapter, we will explore intrinsic versus post hoc explainability.

Part 3 – Evaluating an Explainable Deep Learning Anomaly Detector

Part 3 further elaborates on the different dimensions of these XAI techniques. By the end of *Part 3*, you will have enhanced your skills by analyzing XAI approaches, gauging the extent of interpretability, and evaluating the quality of explanations based on four fundamental principles for XAI systems by the **National Institute of Standards and Technology (NIST)**.

This part comprises the following chapters:

- *Chapter 6, Differentiating Intrinsic versus Post Hoc Explainability*
- *Chapter 7, Backpropagation versus Perturbation Explainability*
- *Chapter 8, Model-Agnostic versus Model-Specific Explainability*
- *Chapter 9, Explainability Evaluation Schemes*

6
Differentiating Intrinsic and Post Hoc Explainability

Artificial intelligence (**AI**) continues to develop at an unprecedented rate and transform our lives across various fields, from finding cancer cures to tackling climate change and exploring space. According to PwC's 2022 annual business survey, `https://www.pwc.com/us/en/tech-effect/ai-analytics/ai-business-survey.html`, 41% of surveyed companies indicated they used AI to enhance decision-making.

While the potential for autonomous learning using **machine learning** (**ML**) models is promising, demand for explanations as to how algorithms make decisions is emerging. The research community and end users want to understand AI systems' influence on real-life scenarios, hidden risks, and consequences for people's lives as AI proliferates and becomes a mainstream technology. Hence, explainability and explainability are indispensable elements of ML models.

We discussed the differences between explainability and explainability in *Chapter 2*. Without understanding the rationale for how decisions are made and justified, it may be risky to deploy ML models to production that could potentially cause negative business and social impacts.

Interpretable ML refers to tools that enable ML models to explain their behaviors in human-understandable terms. Many interpretable ML techniques have been proposed, yet a consensus is lacking for standards. Generally, interpretable ML is grouped into two main categories depending on when explainability is measured:

- **Intrinsic explainability** – Limiting the complexity and dimensionality of ML models during the initial design phase
- **Post hoc explainability** – Applying explainability methods to analyze the model after training

Intrinsic explainable models are intentionally designed and constructed with simple structures to be self-explanatory. Examples of interpretable ML models include **linear regression**, **generalized additive models** (**GAMs**), **decision trees**, and **k-nearest neighbors**. In contrast, ML models that require additional models or post-processing to provide explanations are known as having post hoc explainability.

This chapter covers existing **explainable AI (XAI)** techniques by reviewing intrinsic versus post hoc explainability. We will explore local and global explainability for each category. Local explainability refers to understanding an individual model prediction and tracing how a model arrives at a decision. In contrast, global explainability focuses on the overall model structure for decision-making.

The following are the main topics of this chapter:

- Understanding intrinsic explainability
- Understanding post hoc explainability
- Considering intrinsic versus post hoc explainability

By the end of this chapter, you will understand the differences between intrinsic and post hoc explainability and future considerations for these techniques. We will also have an example walk-through to explain an image classifier's outputs using **Local Interpretable Model-agnostic Explanations (LIME)**, `https://arxiv.org/abs/1602.04938`. Now, let's review the technical requirements for this chapter.

Technical requirements

Here are the packages you will need for the example walk-through:

- **Lime** – An open source Python library to explain ML models
- **scikit-image** – An open source Python image-processing library
- **Matplotlib** – A plotting library for creating data visualizations
- **NumPy** – An open source library that provides mathematical functions when working with arrays
- **pandas** – A library that offers data analysis and manipulation tools
- **Keras** – An open source library that provides an API interface for neural networks
- **TensorFlow** – An open source framework for building deep learning applications

A sample Jupyter notebook and a requirements file for the package dependencies discussed in this chapter are available at `https://github.com/PacktPublishing/Deep-Learning-and-XAI-Techniques-for-Anomaly-Detection/tree/main/Chapter6`.

You can experiment with this example on Amazon SageMaker Studio Lab, `https://aws.amazon.com/sagemaker/studio-lab/`, a free ML development environment that provides up to 12 hours of CPU or 4 hours of GPU per user session and 15 GiB storage at no cost. Alternatively, you can try this on your preferred **integrated development environment (IDE)**.

In the following section, we will cover intrinsic explainability in more depth.

Understanding intrinsic explainability

Interpretable ML aims to address the challenge of incomprehensible ML models and predictions by humans. Models with explainability incorporated directly into the structures are locally and globally interpretable, requiring no further processing to interpret their predictions. We can determine the marginal influence of a specific feature on its target variable by reviewing coefficients with intrinsic explainable models such as linear or logistic regression. This section discusses how to achieve intrinsic explainability locally and globally.

Intrinsic global explainability

In this paper, `https://arxiv.org/pdf/1808.00033.pdf`, the authors stated that intrinsic models could achieve global explainability by enforcing sparsity terms or semantic monotonicity constraints:

- **Sparsity** refers to using fewer features for model prediction, which increases model explainability by highlighting influential features. For example, the **Least Absolute Shrinkage and Selection Operator** (**LASSO regression or L1 regularization**) helps build sparsity when dealing with many features in the dataset. Reducing the coefficients of less important features to zero enables LASSO regression to select subsets of features with less collinearity and thus remove related features, making **generalized linear models** (**GLMs**) more interpretable.
- **Semantic monotonicity constraints** ensure certain features and target predictions are progressing in the same direction. Creating interactions intentionally between features simplifies relationship correlation, leading to increased explainability. For example, adding regularization loss allows a **convolutional neural network** (**CNN**) to learn more effectively.

Alternatively, approximating outputs of a complex model with a more straightforward approach such as decision trees can also achieve global intrinsic explainability. This technique is known as **knowledge distillation**, `https://arxiv.org/pdf/2006.05525.pdf`, where information is transferred from a large or ensemble model to a small model without performance compromise. In this case, decision trees are interpretable because they closely resemble the human thought process by asking clarifying questions until gaining sufficient information to reach a final prediction. However, decision trees are prone to overfitting and lose explainability as the depth increases. Applying active learning with decision trees avoids overfitting while achieving comparable performance to complex models and better explainability.

Intrinsic local explainability

Unlike intrinsic global explainability, local intrinsic models provide explanations for individual predictions. Attention-based neural networks, such as transformers used in **neural machine translation** (**NMT**), provide intrinsic local explainability. For example, NMT encompasses an encoder to compute representation for source sentences and a decoder to translate words sequentially. Different weights added to the hidden layers of the decoder enable NMT to focus selectively on various parts of input sentences when generating translations. Users can interpret important elements utilized by an attention-based model by visualizing the weight matrix and attention scores for individual predictions.

You learned about intrinsic explainability in this section. Next, let's explore post hoc explainability.

Understanding post hoc explainability

Post hoc explainability refers to applying explainability techniques after model training. Generally, post hoc explainability methods approximate model behavior by correlating features and predictions. Hence, assessing the quality of explanations, such as **faithfulness** and **monotonicity**, which we will review in *Chapter 9*, is crucial when using these methods. This section discusses how to achieve post hoc explainability locally and globally. We will walk through an example of explaining an image classifier using LIME.

Post hoc global explainability

ML models learn by training with a large amount of data to derive knowledge into structure and parameters. Traditional pipelines use feature engineering to transform raw data into features. ML models then map the learned representation to outputs.

Post hoc global explainability generally focuses on feature importance by assessing how model accuracy deviates after permuting the values of a specific feature, which is an iterative process using a modified dataset to obtain prediction scores for all features.

Generally, learned representations from **deep neural network** (**DNN**) models are not human-interpretable. Hence, deep learning explanations rely on understanding the inner layer representations. For instance, the activation maximization framework helps identify preferred inputs for specific layers of neurons for CNNs by evaluating the quality of generated images corresponding to neuron activations, thus providing the context of global structure.

Post hoc local explainability

Post hoc local explainability aims to provide explanations for individual predictions by identifying input features attributing to model behavior. Popular post hoc local explainability methods include local approximation-based and perturbation-based explanation frameworks.

The local approximation-based explanation framework uses if-then rules to reproduce individual predictions within the range of inputs using an interpretable model. In contrast, a perturbation-based explanation determines feature attribution by measuring how prediction scores change when the feature is altered through omission or occlusion, resulting in counterfactual explanations. However, omitting a feature might not be practical in some cases, and occlusion might introduce new information leading to an undesirable outcome.

LIME is a popular local approximation and perturbation-based framework that provides post hoc explanations for individual predictions. It performs perturbations on a local neighborhood of an instance to learn interpretable sparse linear models as explanations. LIME also provides qualitative explanations for a model's prediction by highlighting relationships between an instance's elements in textual and visual artifacts.

Let's review an example of how to explain an image classifier using LIME. You can access the sample notebook, `chapter6_LIME.ipynb`, from the book's GitHub repo:

1. First, let's install the required packages:

    ```
    import sys
    !{sys.executable} -m pip install -qr requirements.txt
    ```

2. Load the essential libraries:

    ```
    %matplotlib inline

    from tensorflow import keras
    from tensorflow.keras.preprocessing import image
    from tensorflow.keras.applications import inception_v3 as incv3
    from tensorflow.keras.applications.imagenet_utils import decode_predictions

    import tensorflow as tf
    from skimage.io import imread
    import os
    import matplotlib.pyplot as plt
    import numpy as np
    import lime
    from lime import lime_image
    from skimage.segmentation import mark_boundaries
    from platform import python_version

    os.environ["TF_CPP_MIN_LOG_LEVEL"] = "3"

    print(f'TensorFlow version: {tf.__version__}')
    print(f'Python version: {python_version()}')
    ```

Figure 6.1 shows the TensorFlow and Python dependencies:

```
TensorFlow version: 2.11.0
Python version: 3.8.2
```

Figure 6.1 – Package dependencies

3. Load an Inception V3 pre-trained model. The default input image size is 299x299:

```
model = incv3.InceptionV3()

def load_process_img(path):
    images = []
    for img_path in path:
        img = image.load_img(img_path, target_size=(299, 299))
        m = image.img_to_array(img)
        m = np.expand_dims(m, axis=0)
        m = incv3.preprocess_input(m)
        images.append(m)
    return np.vstack(images)

images = load_process_img([os.path.join('./','pets.jpg')])

plt.imshow(images[0] / 2 + 0.5)
plt.axis('off')
plt.title("Original Image", fontsize=12)
```

Figure 6.2 shows the original input image:

Original Image

Figure 6.2 – Original image

4. Obtain predictions from the Inception V3 model and view the top five classes:

```
preds = model.predict(images)
print('Top 5 classes:')
for im in decode_predictions(preds)[0]:
    print(im)
```

Figure 6.3 shows the top five predicted classes:

```
Top 5 classes:
('n02113023', 'Pembroke', 0.28453475)
('n02342885', 'hamster', 0.09641102)
('n04399382', 'teddy', 0.020572951)
('n02113186', 'Cardigan', 0.011049673)
('n02094258', 'Norwich_terrier', 0.010510642)
```

Figure 6.3 – Top 5 predicted classes

5. We are ready to call `LimeImageExplainer` to explain predictions from the Inception V3 image classification model:

```
explainer = lime_image.LimeImageExplainer()
explanation = explainer.explain_instance(images[0],
```

```
        model.predict, top_labels=5, hide_color=0, num_
samples=1000)
```

6. Let's visualize superpixels that positively contribute to the top three predicted classes while hiding the rest of the image:

   ```
   fig = plt.figure(figsize=(30, 30))

   rows = 1
   columns = 3

   top3_classes = ['Pembroke', 'Hamster', 'Teddy']

   for i in range(3):
       fig.add_subplot(rows, columns, i+1)
       tmp, mask = explanation.get_image_and_
   mask(explanation.top_labels[i], positive_only=True, num_
   features=5, hide_rest=True)
       plt.imshow(mark_boundaries(tmp / 2 + 0.5, mask))
       plt.axis('off')
       plt.title(f'Predicted: {top3_classes[i]}',
   fontsize=18)
   ```

Figure 6.4 highlights superpixels that influenced the top three class predictions:

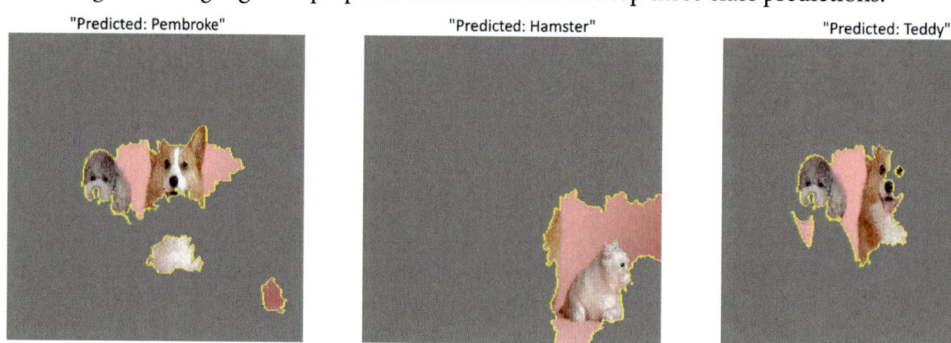

Figure 6.4 – Superpixels for the top three class predictions

7. Visualize the boundary of superpixels that positively contribute to the top three class predictions with the rest of the image present:

   ```
   fig = plt.figure(figsize=(30, 30))
   rows = 1
   ```

```
columns = 3

for i in range(3):
    fig.add_subplot(rows, columns, i+1)
    tmp, mask = explanation.get_image_and_
mask(explanation.top_labels[i], positive_only=True, num_
features=5, hide_rest=False)
    plt.imshow(mark_boundaries(tmp / 2 + 0.5, mask))
    plt.axis('off')
plt.title(f'Predicted: {top3_classes[i]}', fontsize=18)
```

Figure 6.5 shows the boundary of superpixels that influenced the top three predicted classes:

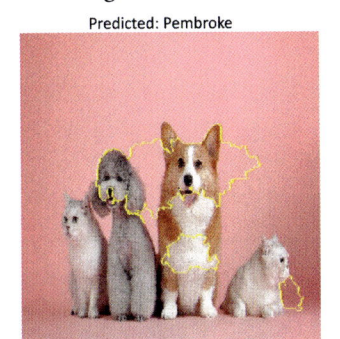

Figure 6.5 – Boundary of superpixels

8. We can view superpixels that positively and negatively influenced the top three class predictions by setting `positive_only` to False:

```
fig = plt.figure(figsize=(30, 30))
rows = 1
columns = 3

for i in range(3):
    fig.add_subplot(rows, columns, i+1)
    tmp, mask = explanation.get_image_and_
mask(explanation.top_labels[i], positive_only=False, num_
features=5, hide_rest=True)
    plt.imshow(mark_boundaries(tmp / 2 + 0.5, mask))
    plt.axis('off')
plt.title(f'Predicted: {top3_classes[i]}', fontsize=18)
```

Figure 6.6 shows superpixels that positively and negatively contribute to the predicted classes. If you are viewing the output in a Jupyter notebook or your local IDE, superpixels with positive influence are in green and negative in red:

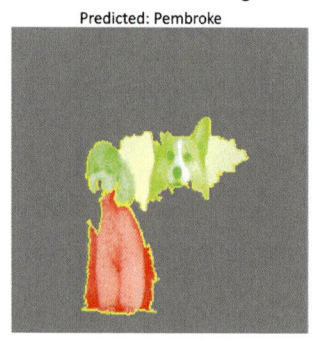

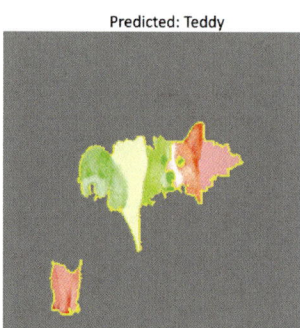

Figure 6.6 – Positive and negative superpixels

9. Lastly, we can filter superpixels with a minimum weight of 0.1 that positively impact the predicted classes. Only the predicted Pembroke class has explanations with more than 0.1 minimum weights in this case. You can adjust min_weight to visualize variations in the model's explanations:

```
fig = plt.figure(figsize=(30, 30))

rows = 1
columns = 3
min_weight = 0.1

for i in range(3):
    fig.add_subplot(rows, columns, i+1)
    tmp, mask = explanation.get_image_and_mask(explanation.top_labels[i], positive_only=False, num_features=5, hide_rest=False, min_weight=min_weight)
    plt.imshow(mark_boundaries(tmp / 2 + 0.5, mask))
    plt.axis('off')
    plt.title(f'Predicted: {top3_classes[i]}', fontsize=18)
```

Figure 6.7 highlights superpixels with at least `0.1` minimum weight:

Figure 6.7 – Superpixels with more than a defined minimum weight

Deep learning models are excellent in extracting low-level features for images, such as corners, edges, and stripes. However, these low-level features are not interpretable by humans. The `LimeImageExplainer` method from the `lime_image` module provides high-level explanations for an image classifier by highlighting the **regions of interest** (**ROIs**) or superpixels that contribute positively or negatively to the model's predictions. Consequently, LIME helps assess whether the provided explanations are sensible and prevent a model from making accurate predictions for the wrong reasons.

In this section, you built an image classifier using an Inception V3 pre-trained model and explained the output using LIME. Next, let's discuss best practices when considering intrinsic versus post hoc explainability.

Considering intrinsic versus post hoc explainability

Can we ignore explainability and just trust state-of-the-art models? The short answer is no. A correct prediction does not adequately solve real-world problems. Users will not adopt an AI system unless it is trustworthy. Knowing why predictions are made is important to show how much an AI system can be trusted and provide insights into the best course of action when combined with domain expertise.

There are no hard-and-fast rules when choosing intrinsic versus post hoc explainability. For explainability's sake, an intrinsic explainable model with adequate accuracy is always preferable over a complex model. Otherwise, post-processing explanation methods are alternatives to provide post hoc explainability after model training.

Inevitably, humans trust explanations selectively with unconscious bias based on profession, domain knowledge, and personal experience. Often, humans seek contrastive and interactive explanations since they are easier to understand. Hence, partial information might be lost when producing explanations. Therefore, judicious explanations faithful to the model are essential to increase user trust by focusing on important aspects rather than every detail.

Summary

Explainability will be indispensable as ML becomes mainstream. Interpretable ML helps validate models, prevents correct predictions for the wrong reasons, and increases user trust, resulting in broader adoption. For example, we do not want a credit application to deny unqualified applicants based on gender instead of poor payment history.

Interpretable ML uncovers new insights by helping humans comprehend the model's decision-making process. Today, users demand information about causal links in addition to probabilities based on statistical relationships. Despite the lack of consensus on design standards, interpretable ML techniques face challenges with benchmarking methods. In the next chapter, we will explore backpropagation and perturbation XAI techniques.

7
Backpropagation versus Perturbation Explainability

Researchers discovered that the human brain can process and interpret images the eye sees in 13 milliseconds. The human visual process begins when light reaches the retina, which converts light into neural signals for sending information, such as shape, hue, and orientation, to the brain. Based on past experiences, the human brain extracts information that influences visual perception.

Figure 7.1 shows how the computer sees images in a grid of pixel values ranging between **0** and **255** without inherent knowledge of shapes and colors. Deep neural networks, such as **convolutional neural networks** (**CNNs**), resemble the human brain, containing nonlinear structures and layers of artificial neurons to learn features from the input image.

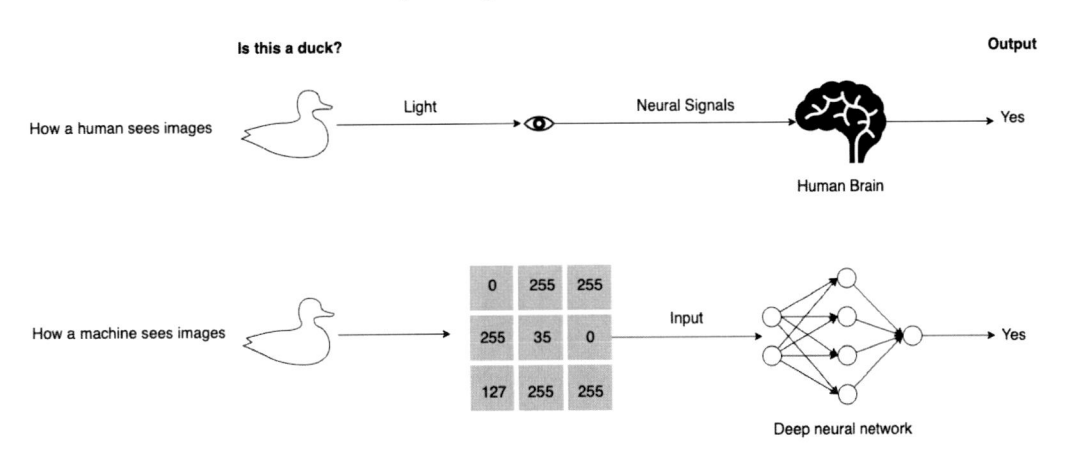

Figure 7.1 – Human visual perception versus computer vision

Despite promising results in recent years, these state-of-the-art models have yet to gain broad adoption due to uncertainty with their opaque characteristics. Explainable neural networks provide a mechanism to visualize how networks learn and explain the relationship between training input and predictions.

There are many **explainable artificial intelligence** (**XAI**) techniques to study the inner workings of neural networks. In *Chapter 6*, we reviewed the scope of local and global interpretability and how they are applied in intrinsic and post hoc explainability models. This chapter covers two popular XAI approaches: backpropagation and perturbations. The main topics covered in this chapter are the following:

- Reviewing backpropagation explainability
- Reviewing perturbation explainability
- Comparing backpropagation and perturbation XAI

By the end of this chapter, you will have learned more about backpropagation and perturbation methods to choose the appropriate approach for your use case.

Reviewing backpropagation explainability

Feature attribution methods generally encompass two steps to determine inference results through a forward pass, followed by a backpropagation to assign relevance scores for input features on a trained model.

Backpropagation is a gradient-based XAI method that evaluates feature attributions by generating partial derivatives of output in multiple forward and backward passes through neural networks. Unlike neural network training, backpropagation in the context of feature attribution does not require gradient computation for weight updates on model parameters. Instead of beginning with the input layer, backpropagation feature attribution starts by assigning importance scores at the final output layer, then calculating local activation gradients inversely across each intermediate layer until it reaches the input layer, as shown in *Figure 7.2*:

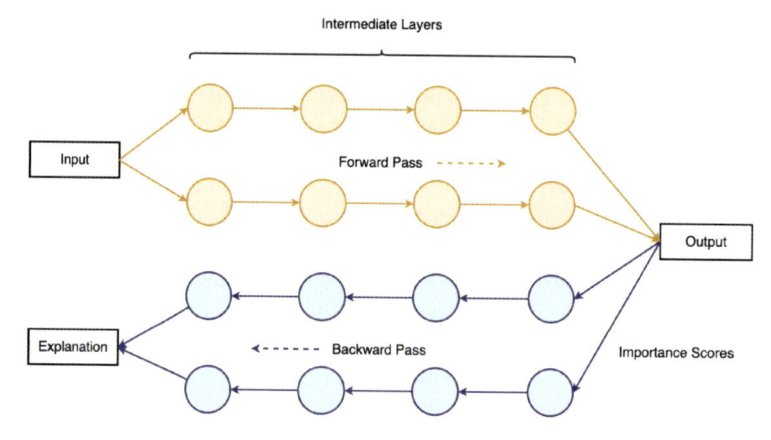

Figure 7.2 – Backpropagation XAI

This section provides a walkthrough of saliency maps, a backpropagation-based XAI technique.

Saliency maps

Saliency maps are one of the most frequently used XAI methods for interpreting images with CNNs. It applies to most deep learning networks and provides an intuitive way to investigate hidden layers within CNNs.

Saliency maps use backpropagation to probe a trained neural network for spatial information about a particular class – for example, identifying the location of an object without explicitly labeling the image with such information. Saliency maps assume the weight of gradients to reflect or approximate relevant parts of an input image. Users can visualize important regions that stand out from the input image. Saliency maps only require one backpropagation pass since it focuses on the highest-scoring class.

There are three ways to obtain saliency maps:

- Using **deconvolutional networks (DeconvNet)** by inverting a specific activated input layer with unpooling and inverse ReLU techniques
- Using **gradient-based backpropagation** by highlighting contributing pixels based on computed gradients to the input network
- Using **guided backpropagation** by combining DeconvNet and gradient-based backpropagation

Let's look at an example of how saliency maps work using the gradient-based backpropagation approach. A sample Jupyter notebook (*chapter7_saliency_maps.ipynb*) and requirements file for package dependencies discussed in this chapter are available at https://github.com/PacktPublishing/Deep-Learning-and-XAI-Techniques-for-Anomaly-Detection/tree/main/Chapter7.

You can experiment with this example on Amazon SageMaker Studio Lab, https://aws.amazon.com/sagemaker/studio-lab/, a free ML development environment that provides up to 12 hours of CPU or 4 hours of GPU per user session and 15 GiB storage at no cost. Alternatively, you can try this on your preferred Integrated Development Environment (IDE). Alternatively, you can try this on your preferred IDE:

1. First, let's load the essential libraries:

    ```
    import tensorflow as tf
    import numpy as np
    import matplotlib.pyplot as plt
    from platform import python_version
    import os
    import warnings

    warnings.filterwarnings("ignore")
    os.environ["TF_CPP_MIN_LOG_LEVEL"] = "3"
    ```

```
print(f'TensorFlow version: {tf.__version__}')
print(f'Python version: {python_version()}')
%matplotlib inline
```

2. Load a VGG16 image classification model pre-trained with weights on ImageNet:

```
model = tf.keras.applications.VGG16(weights='imagenet')
model.summary()
```

Figure 7.3 shows a summary of the VGG16 model architecture:

```
Model: "vgg16"
_____
Layer (type)                 Output Shape              Param #
=================================================================
input_1 (InputLayer)         [(None, 224, 224, 3)]     0
block1_conv1 (Conv2D)        (None, 224, 224, 64)      1792
block1_conv2 (Conv2D)        (None, 224, 224, 64)      36928
block1_pool (MaxPooling2D)   (None, 112, 112, 64)      0
block2_conv1 (Conv2D)        (None, 112, 112, 128)     73856
block2_conv2 (Conv2D)        (None, 112, 112, 128)     147584
block2_pool (MaxPooling2D)   (None, 56, 56, 128)       0
block3_conv1 (Conv2D)        (None, 56, 56, 256)       295168
block3_conv2 (Conv2D)        (None, 56, 56, 256)       590080
block3_conv3 (Conv2D)        (None, 56, 56, 256)       590080
block3_pool (MaxPooling2D)   (None, 28, 28, 256)       0
block4_conv1 (Conv2D)        (None, 28, 28, 512)       1180160
block4_conv2 (Conv2D)        (None, 28, 28, 512)       2359808
block4_conv3 (Conv2D)        (None, 28, 28, 512)       2359808
block4_pool (MaxPooling2D)   (None, 14, 14, 512)       0
block5_conv1 (Conv2D)        (None, 14, 14, 512)       2359808
block5_conv2 (Conv2D)        (None, 14, 14, 512)       2359808
block5_conv3 (Conv2D)        (None, 14, 14, 512)       2359808
block5_pool (MaxPooling2D)   (None, 7, 7, 512)         0
flatten (Flatten)            (None, 25088)             0
fc1 (Dense)                  (None, 4096)              102764544
fc2 (Dense)                  (None, 4096)              16781312
predictions (Dense)          (None, 1000)              4097000
=================================================================
Total params: 138,357,544
Trainable params: 138,357,544
Non-trainable params: 0
_____
```

Figure 7.3 – The VGG16 model summary

3. Load an image file and set the expected target input size for VGG16:

   ```
   img_path = 'panda.jpeg'
   image = tf.keras.utils.load_img(img_path, target_size=(224,224))
   plt.imshow(image)
   plt.axis('off')
   plt.show()
   ```

   Figure 7.4 shows the original image:

   Figure 7.4 – The original image

4. Preprocess the image before obtaining a prediction for the top five classes:

   ```
   img = tf.keras.utils.img_to_array(image)
   img = img.reshape((1, *img.shape))
   y_pred = model.predict(img)
   top5 = tf.keras.applications.vgg16.decode_predictions(y_pred, top=5)
   print('Top 5 classes:')
   top5
   ```

Figure 7.5 shows the top five predicted classes, with the highest predicted probability as a giant panda:

```
1/1 [==============================] - 1s 540ms/step
Top 5 classes:
[[('n02510455', 'giant_panda', 0.9559301),
  ('n02509815', 'lesser_panda', 0.039848775),
  ('n02483362', 'gibbon', 0.0019217625),
  ('n02443114', 'polecat', 0.000856469),
  ('n02488702', 'colobus', 0.0003992283)]]
```

Figure 7.5 – The top five predicted classes

5. Let's identify the **region of interest** (**ROI**) for such predictions by finding the absolute and maximum values of the gradients. We will normalize the gradients:

```
images = tf.Variable(img, dtype=float)
with tf.GradientTape() as tape:
    pred = model(images, training=False)
    sorted_class = np.argsort(pred.numpy().flatten())[::-1]
    loss = pred[0][sorted_class[0]]
grads = tape.gradient(loss, images)
grads_abs = tf.math.abs(grads)
grads_max = np.max(grads_abs, axis=3)[0]
gmin, gmax  = np.min(grads_max), np.max(grads_max)
grads_eval = (grads_max - gmin) / (gmax - gmin + 1e-18)
```

6. *Figure 7.6* shows the saliency maps for this input image, where the panda's eyes and nose contribute to the feature importance score to its predicted class as a giant panda. The `colorbar` function highlights the ROI with a range of intensity:

```
fig, axes = plt.subplots(1,2,figsize=(20,7))
axes[0].imshow(image)
fig.colorbar(axes[1].imshow(grads_eval,cmap="turbo",
alpha=0.9))
plt.savefig('panda_saliency_maps.png')
```

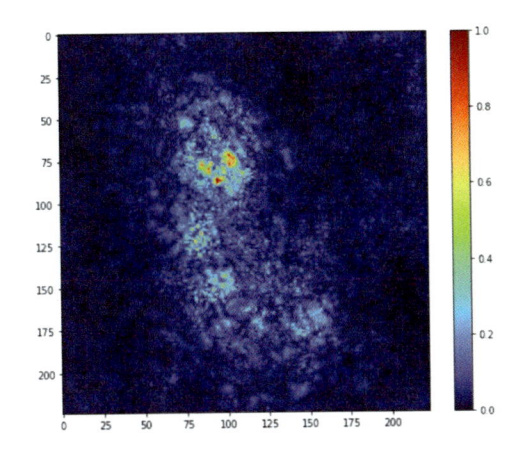

Figure 7.6 – Saliency maps

The preceding example shows how saliency maps extract contributing pixels using gradient-based backpropagation to find contributing pixels. Now, let's explore perturbation explainability in the next section.

Reviewing perturbation explainability

Perturbation-based methods investigate neural network properties by perturbing the training input, either partially occluding pixels in an image or substituting words in textual data to observe how they influence a model's prediction. Domain experts and users can evaluate the quality of explanations by analyzing saliency representations based on natural intuition to correlate features that stand out in the images.

Measuring the level of changes in output based on the presence or absence of a feature indicates its importance to the overall model prediction. This section explores a perturbation-based explainability example using **local interpretable model-agnostic explanations** (**LIME**).

LIME

We discussed LIME as a local approximation post hoc explainability framework in *Chapter 6*. In this section, let's explore how LIME provides local explainability using interpretable representations through perturbations. LIME defines interpretable explanations as human-understandable representations using numerical, visual, or textual artifacts. There are three types of LIME explainers:

- **LimeTabularExplainer**: Explains predictions by classifiers that use tabular data based on weighted columns
- **LimeImageExplainer**: Explains an image classifier's predictions based on the presence or absence of superpixels or grouping of pixels with common characteristics

- **LimeTextExplainer**: Explains a text classifier's predictions based on the presence or absence of words. For example, LIME perturbs a given sentence, *"The cake is delicious,"* to come up with variations such as *"The cake delicious,"* *"The is delicious,"* or *"cake is delicious,"* and identify the relevant word of *"delicious."*

Let's look at an example of how LIME provides local explainability for a text classifier using the Amazon Product Reviews dataset, https://www.kaggle.com/datasets/arhamrumi/amazon-product-reviews. A sample Jupyter notebook (*chapter7_lime_nlp.ipynb*) and requirements file for package dependencies discussed in this chapter are available at https://github.com/PacktPublishing/Deep-Learning-and-XAI-Techniques-for-Anomaly-Detection/tree/main/Chapter7. Alternatively, you can try this on your preferred IDE:

1. First, let's install and load the essential libraries:

    ```
    !pip install lime nltk wordcloud
    import pandas as pd
    import numpy as np
    import matplotlib.pyplot as plt
    import lime
    import tensorflow as tf
    from tensorflow import keras
    from platform import python_version
    import os
    import warnings
    warnings.filterwarnings("ignore")
    os.environ["TF_CPP_MIN_LOG_LEVEL"] = "3"
    print(f'TensorFlow version: {tf.__version__}')
    print(f'Python version: {python_version()}')
    %matplotlib inline
    ```

2. Next, load and preview the dataset, as shown in *Figure 7.7*:

    ```
    df = pd.read_csv('reviews.csv')
    df.head()
    ```

Reviewing perturbation explainability   143

	Id	ProductId	UserId	ProfileName	HelpfulnessNumerator	HelpfulnessDenominator	Score	Time	Summary	Text
0	1	B001E4KFG0	A3SGXH7AUHU8GW	delmartian	1	1	5	1303862400	Good Quality Dog Food	I have bought several of the Vitality canned d...
1	2	B00813GRG4	A1D87F6ZCVE5NK	dll pa	0	0	1	1346976000	Not as Advertised	Product arrived labeled as Jumbo Salted Peanut...
2	3	B000LQOCH0	ABXLMWJIXXAIN	Natalia Corres "Natalia Corres"	1	1	4	1219017600	"Delight" says it all	This is a confection that has been around a fe...
3	4	B000UA0QIQ	A395BORC6FGVXV	Karl	3	3	2	1307923200	Cough Medicine	If you are looking for the secret ingredient i...

Figure 7.7 – Preview dataset

3. *Figure 7.8* shows the feature and target columns we will use for text classification:

   ```
   df = df[['Text','Score']]
   df.head()
   ```

	Text	Score
0	I have bought several of the Vitality canned d...	5
1	Product arrived labeled as Jumbo Salted Peanut...	1
2	This is a confection that has been around a fe...	4
3	If you are looking for the secret ingredient i...	2
4	Great taffy at a great price. There was a wid...	5

   Figure 7.8 – The feature and target columns

4. View the unique target classes:

   ```
   df['Score'].unique()
   ```

5. Drop rows with missing values:

   ```
   df = df.dropna().reset_index(drop=True)
   df.info()
   ```

Figure 7.9 shows that the dataset contains 568,454 samples with 2 columns, `Text` and `Score`:

```
<class 'pandas.core.frame.DataFrame'>
RangeIndex: 568454 entries, 0 to 568453
Data columns (total 2 columns):
 #   Column  Non-Null Count   Dtype
---  ------  --------------   -----
 0   Text    568454 non-null  object
 1   Score   568454 non-null  int64
dtypes: int64(1), object(1)
memory usage: 8.7+ MB
```

Figure 7.9 – Information about the dataset

6. We will sample the dataset for demo purposes. You can try to increase this number:

   ```
   subsample_size = 3000
   df = df.sample(n=subsample_size, random_state=1)
   ```

7. We will generate a word cloud for this dataset:

   ```
   from nltk.corpus import stopwords
   from wordcloud import WordCloud
   import re

   def clean_text(s):
       s = re.sub(r'http\S+', '', s)
       s = re.sub('(RT|via)((?:\\b\\W*@\\w+)+)', ' ', s)
       s = re.sub(r'@\S+', '', s)
       s = re.sub('&amp', ' ', s)
       return s

   df['clean_text'] = df['Text'].apply(clean_text)
   text = df['clean_text'].to_string().lower()

   wordcloud = WordCloud(
       collocations = False,
       relative_scaling = 0.2,
       stopwords=set(stopwords.words('english'))).
   generate(text)

   plt.figure(figsize=(15,15))
   ```

```
plt.imshow(wordcloud)
plt.axis("off")
plt.savefig('review_wordcloud.png', bbox_inches='tight')
plt.show()
```

Figure 7.10 shows the post-text cleaning word cloud for this dataset:

Figure 7.10 – Word cloud

8. Assign model features and targets to variables:

   ```
   X = df['clean_text']
   y = df['Score']
   y.value_counts()
   ```

9. Set a random seed for reproducibility. Split the dataset with 80% for training and 20% for testing. You should have 2,400 training samples and 600 test samples:

   ```
   seed = 42
   np.random.seed(seed)

   from sklearn.model_selection import train_test_split
   X_train, X_test, y_train, y_test = train_test_split(X, y,
   test_size=0.2, stratify=y, random_state=42)
   print(f'X_train count: {X_train.shape[0]}')
   print(f'y_train count: {y_train.shape[0]}')
   ```

```
           print(f'X_test count: {X_test.shape[0]}')
           print(f'y_test count: {y_test.shape[0]}')
```

10. Set a maximum number of unique words to train and a maximum number of words to keep for each product review:

    ```
    vocab_size = 20000
    maxlen = 80
    ```

11. Tokenize and pad the sequences to have the same length:

    ```
    from keras.preprocessing.text import Tokenizer
    from keras_preprocessing.sequence import pad_sequences
    from sklearn.pipeline import TransformerMixin
    from sklearn.base import BaseEstimator

    class TextsToSequences(Tokenizer, BaseEstimator,
    TransformerMixin):
        def __init__(self, **kwargs):
            super().__init__(**kwargs)

        def fit(self, texts, y=None):
            self.fit_on_texts(texts)
            return self

        def transform(self, texts, y=None):
            return np.array(self.texts_to_sequences(texts))

    sequencer = TextsToSequences(num_words=vocab_size)

    class Padder(BaseEstimator, TransformerMixin):
        def __init__(self, maxlen=500):
            self.maxlen = maxlen
            self.max_index = None

        def fit(self, X, y=None):
            self.max_index = pad_sequences(X, maxlen=self.maxlen).max()
            return self
    ```

```
        def transform(self, X, y=None):
            X = pad_sequences(X, maxlen=self.maxlen)
            X[X > self.max_index] = 0
            return X

    padder = Padder(maxlen)
```

12. Create an LSTM model:

    ```
    from keras.models import Sequential
    from keras.layers import Dense, Embedding, LSTM
    from keras.wrappers.scikit_learn import KerasClassifier
    from sklearn.pipeline import make_pipeline

    batch_size = 128
    max_features = vocab_size + 1

    import tensorflow as tf
    tf.random.set_seed(seed)

    def create_model(max_features):
        model = Sequential()
        model.add(Embedding(max_features, 128))
        model.add(LSTM(100, dropout=0.2, recurrent_dropout=0.2))
        model.add(Dense(5, activation='softmax'))
        model.compile(loss='categorical_crossentropy', optimizer='adam', metrics=['accuracy'])
    return model
    ```

13. Create a sklearn pipeline for training:

    ```
    pipeline = KerasClassifier(build_fn=create_model, epochs=10, batch_size=batch_size, max_features=max_features, verbose=1)
    pipeline = make_pipeline(sequencer, padder, pipeline)
    pipeline.fit(X_train, y_train)
    ```

14. Make predictions on the test set:

    ```
    y_preds = pipeline.predict(X_test)
    ```

15. Generate the model's accuracy score and classification report, as shown in *Figure 7.11*:

    ```
    from sklearn.metrics import accuracy_score, confusion_
    matrix, classification_report, ConfusionMatrixDisplay

    print(f'Test Accuracy: {accuracy_score(y_test,y_
    preds)*100:.2f}%')
    print(f'Classification Report:\n {classification_
    report(y_test, y_preds)}')
    ```

    ```
    Test Accuracy: 55.67%
    Classification Report:
                   precision    recall  f1-score   support

                1       0.44      0.27      0.34        59
                2       0.00      0.00      0.00        29
                3       0.24      0.25      0.24        48
                4       0.20      0.38      0.26        85
                5       0.78      0.72      0.75       379

         accuracy                           0.56       600
        macro avg       0.33      0.32      0.32       600
     weighted avg       0.58      0.56      0.56       600
    ```

    Figure 7.11 – Test accuracy and classification report

16. Let us use the confusion matrix to summarize the predicted versus actual class:

    ```
    labels = [1,2,3,4,5]
    cm = confusion_matrix(y_test, y_preds)
    ConfusionMatrixDisplay(cm, display_labels=labels).
    plot(cmap=plt.cm.Blues)
    plt.xlabel('Predicted Rating')
    plt.ylabel('True Rating')
    plt.savefig("confusion_matrix.png", bbox_inches='tight')
    ```

Figure 7.12 shows the results:

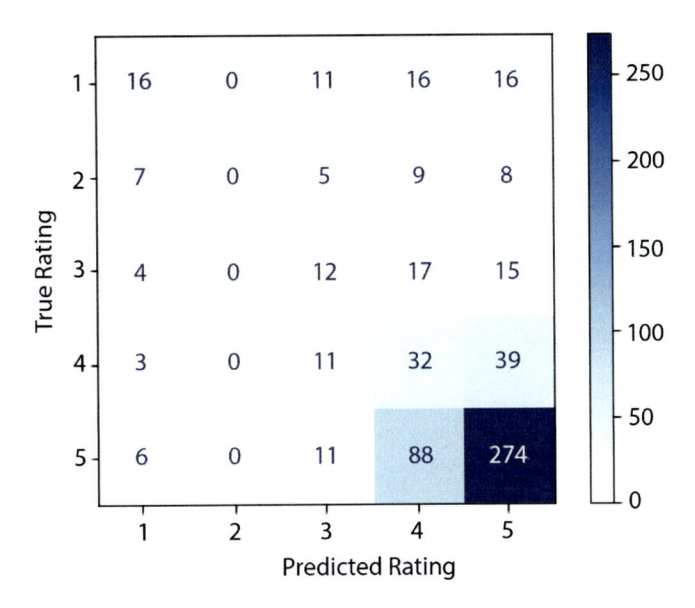

Figure 7.12 – Confusion matrix

17. *Figure 7.13* shows the correct predicted class of 5 for this sample text:

    ```
    idx = 599
    test_text = np.array(X_test)
    test_class = np.array(y_test)
    text_sample = test_text[idx]

    class_names = [1,2,3,4,5]
    print(f'Sample Text:\n{text_sample}\n')
    print(f'Probability: {pipeline.predict_proba([text_
    sample]).round(3)}')
    print(f'True class: {class_names[test_class[idx]]}')
    ```

    ```
    Sample Text:
    This nutritious bar is great for before or after workouts.  Low in sugar, high in protein makes this a perfect snack for Diabetics too.
    1/1 [==============================] - 0s 30ms/step
    Probability: [[0.   0.   0.   0.002 0.998]]
    True class: 5
    ```

    Figure 7.13 – Sample text and predicted probabilities

18. Instantiate `LimeTextExplainer` to produce local explanations, as shown in *Figure 7.14*:

```
from lime.lime_text import LimeTextExplainer
explainer = LimeTextExplainer(class_names=class_names)
exp = explainer.explain_instance(text_sample, pipeline.
predict_proba, num_features=10, top_labels=1)
exp.show_in_notebook(text=text_sample)
```

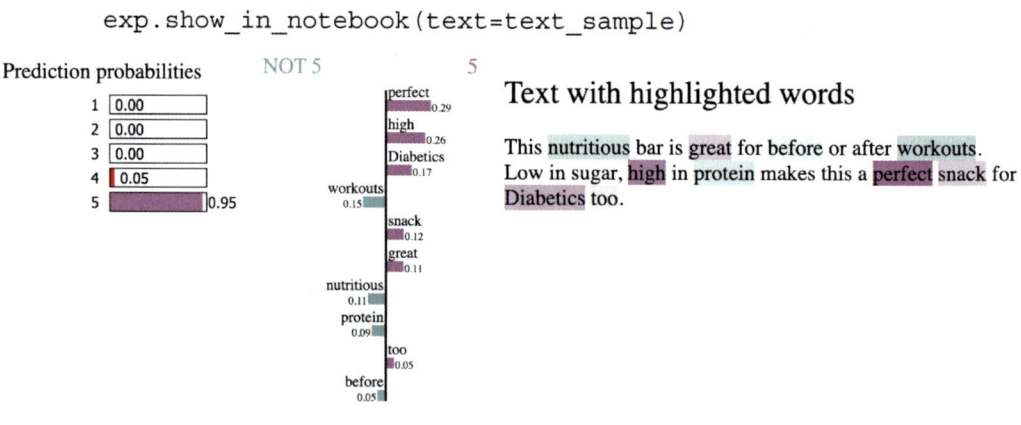

Figure 7.14 – Local explanations by LimeTextExplainer

19. *Figure 7.15* shows the modified text after removing important words identified by `LimeTextExplainer` and reassessing the predicted probabilities:

```
text_sample_modified = re.sub('perfect|high|great|makes',
' ', text_sample)
print(f'Modified Sample Text:\n{text_sample_modified}\n')
print(f'Probability: {pipeline.predict_proba([text_
sample_modified]).round(3)}')
```

```
Modified Sample Text:
This nutritious bar is   for before or after workouts. Low in sugar,   in protein   this a   snack for Diabetics too.

1/1 [==============================] - 0s 37ms/step
Probability: [[0.071 0.05  0.164 0.22  0.495]]
```

Figure 7.15 – Modified text with new predicted probabilities

We can see the predicted probability change after removing important words from the text. You can try a different sample text and swap out different words to evaluate the impact.

After reviewing examples of backpropagation and perturbation methods, the following section will summarize the pros and cons of these XAI techniques.

Comparing backpropagation and perturbation XAI

After reviewing backpropagation and perturbation, let's compare the pros and cons of these XAI techniques.

Generally, backpropagation is more efficient than perturbation-based XAI methods in generating importance scores for all input features in a single backward pass through the network. However, backpropagation-based XAI methods are typically prone to noise and require internal information about the model. While feature attributions associated with an area of input image seem intuitive, neighboring individual pixels can experience a high variant of attribution assignments, which is a shortcoming of backpropagation-based methods. Furthermore, a lack of granular description of a model's characteristics might result in inconsistent correlation to its output variation, resulting in less faithful explanations.

In contrast, perturbation-based methods are widely applicable to any deep learning model, regardless of its architecture. They experience less noise compared to backpropagation-based methods. Instead of creating variant objects, perturbation-based methods assess a model's explainability through incremental evaluations. Nevertheless, despite broad applicability, perturbation-based XAI methods often depend on input modality, which fails to capture the general neural network characteristics. Furthermore, evaluating all plausible feature sets can be time-consuming and resource intensive.

Perturbations of static images tend to be more straightforward than textual data with unique characteristics and videos with temporal dimensions. Hence, the advancement of perturbation-based methods has been around image classification, leaving room for future research on perturbations with other data types. Perturbation methods can be sensitive to minor modifications to instances resulting in a drastic output deviation.

Building a reliable XAI system takes beyond interpreting the model's predictions. Mission- and safety-critical applications require faithful explanations aligning with their original model. For example, an XAI system must produce accurate and faithful explanations when classifying a pathology image as malignant so that a clinician can confidently focus on investigating the ROI.

Can we unify the backpropagation and perturbation-based methods to get the best of both worlds in post hoc explanations for complex black-box models? For continuous efforts to achieve interpretability beyond prediction accuracy, there is an emerging desire to unify both approaches, such as DeepExplain, `https://github.com/marcoancona/DeepExplain`.

Explainability drives interpretability. However, interpretability is not equivalent to causality. Besides considering computation efficiency and generalization ability, involving domain experts when designing an XAI system is crucial for detecting potential bias, assuring model behaviors, and validating the quality of predictions.

Summary

This chapter has covered an in-depth overview of backpropagation and perturbation XAI methods, including practical examples, advantages, and limitations. In the next chapter, we will explore model-agnostic versus model-specific explainability XAI techniques.

8
Model-Agnostic versus Model-Specific Explainability

Creating a **machine learning** (**ML**) model for high-stake decisions requires considerations for accuracy and interpretability throughout the ML life cycle. In healthcare, physicians must provide vital information to educate patients on the potential risks and benefits of a medical procedure, treatment, or clinical trial through an informed consent process.

Similarly, when **artificial intelligence** (**AI**) is incorporated into the medical diagnosis process, physicians must be able to clarify important ML model-related information to derive a prediction, including the type of input data and training process.

With such a diverse landscape of **explainable artificial intelligence** (**XAI**) methods, you might wonder which XAI method to choose. In this chapter, we will explore the following topics to understand the differences between model-agnostic and model-specific XAI methods:

- Reviewing model-agnostic explainability
- Reviewing model-specific explainability
- Choosing an XAI method

By the end of this chapter, you will have a better understanding of these two approaches and hands-on experience. Let's review the technical requirements for this chapter in the following section.

Technical requirements

You will need the following Python packages for the example walkthrough:

- Matplotlib – A plotting library for creating data visualizations
- NumPy – An open source library that provides mathematical functions when working with arrays
- pandas – A library that offers data analysis and manipulation tools
- MXNet – An open source deep learning framework
- Keras – An open source library that provides an API interface for neural networks
- TensorFlow – An open source framework for building deep learning applications
- AutoGluon – An open source AutoML library that automates ML tasks
- MoveColumn – A package to move columns in a Python DataFrame
- Scikit-learn – An ML library for predictive data analysis
- SHAP – A Python library that explains an ML output using Shapley values
- Saliency – A Python library that provides the implementation for saliency techniques
- Pillow – An open source Python image-processing library

Sample Jupyter notebooks and requirements files for package dependencies discussed in this chapter are available at https://github.com/PacktPublishing/Deep-Learning-and-XAI-Techniques-for-Anomaly-Detection/tree/main/Chapter8.

You can experiment with these notebooks on Amazon SageMaker Studio Lab, https://aws.amazon.com/sagemaker/studio-lab/, a free ML development environment that provides up to 12 hours of CPU or 4 hours of GPU per user session and 15 GiB storage at no cost. Alternatively, you can try this on your preferred **integrated development environment** (IDE).

In the following section, we will discuss model-agnostic explainability in more depth.

Reviewing model-agnostic explainability

Model-agnostic XAI methods are universal regardless of the model type. They are often used as post hoc explainability after a model is trained. Their goal is to produce explanations faithful to the original models without the need to understand the internal network structure, which provides flexibility in model selection. Hence, model-agnostic methods are more relevant for complex and opaque models where it is difficult to extract the inner workings of the network. Model-agnostic methods are also suitable for comparing model performance since they can be applied to various models.

In *Chapter 6* and *Chapter 7*, we reviewed **local interpretable model-agnostic explanations** (**LIME**), a local approximation post hoc perturbation explainability technique. In *Chapter 3*, you learned how to build an NLP multiclassification model using **AutoGluon**. This section reviews **Kernel SHAP**, a popular model-agnostic method that uses LIME and Shapley values. You will learn how to create a binary classification model using AutoGluon and the Breast Cancer dataset, which you can download from this link, `https://www.kaggle.com/datasets/yasserh/breast-cancer-dataset`. Finally, you will assess the model's interpretability using Kernel SHAP.

Explaining AutoGluon with Kernel SHAP

Shapley values have gained popularity in XAI methods based on the cooperative game theory concept, where individual features in the dataset represent individual players, and the target prediction is viewed as a payout to players based on the weighted average of their marginal contribution. Breaking down the additive contribution of each feature by Shapley values provides an intuitive measurement to assess feature importance in the overall trained model. Note that Shapley values merely highlight how features can influence a prediction and do not provide causality.

In contrast, LIME, covered in *Chapter 7*, provides local explanations by training interpretable linear models using perturbation techniques. LIME evaluates feature importance based on the presence or absence of sampled features in the model's prediction.

Kernel SHAP, `https://proceedings.neurips.cc/paper/2017/file/8a20a8621978632d76c43dfd28b67767-Paper.pdf`, is a model-agnostic XAI method that combines LIME and SHAP to measure feature importance using weighted linear regression. Extending LIME using linear regression models without regularization allows Kernel SHAP to achieve improved computation efficiency for Shapley values. However, estimating Shapley values can still be computationally expensive and time-consuming as the number of features grows to calculate all possible permutations of feature sets.

In the following example walkthrough, we will build a binary classifier using AutoGluon, `https://github.com/autogluon/autogluon`, to analyze the Breast Cancer dataset and classify tumors into malignant (cancerous) or benign (non-cancerous) categories. Then, we will use Kernel SHAP to assess the model's interpretability.

According to the American Cancer Society, `https://www.cancer.org/cancer/breast-cancer/about/how-common-is-breast-cancer.html`, breast cancer is the second leading cause of cancer death among women after lung cancer. A woman in the United States has an average risk of 13% of being diagnosed with breast cancer, meaning there is a 1 in 8 chance of developing it. Let's review how Kernel SHAP works using this example. A sample notebook, `chapter8_KernelSHAP.ipynb`, is available in the book's GitHub repo:

1. First, install the required packages using the provided requirements file:

    ```
    import sys
    !{sys.executable} -m pip install -qr requirements.txt
    ```

2. Load the essential libraries:

```
%matplotlib inline

import tensorflow as tf
from tensorflow import keras
from sklearn.model_selection import train_test_split
import matplotlib.pyplot as plt
import pandas as pd
import numpy as np
import sklearn
import shap
import os
import re
import string
from platform import python_version
import warnings
import movecolumn as mc
from sklearn import preprocessing
from autogluon.tabular.version import __version__
from autogluon.tabular import TabularDataset, TabularPredictor

warnings.filterwarnings("ignore")

os.environ["TF_CPP_MIN_LOG_LEVEL"] = "3"

print(f'TensorFlow version: {tf.__version__}')
print(f'Python version: {python_version()}')
print(f'AutoGluon version: {__version__}')
```

Figure 8.1 shows the package dependencies:

```
TensorFlow version: 2.11.0
Python version: 3.9.10
AutoGluon version: 0.6.2
```

Figure 8.1 – Package dependencies

3. Load the Breast Cancer dataset:

```
df = pd.read_csv('breast-cancer.csv')
df.head(5)
```

Figure 8.2 shows a preview of the Breast Cancer dataset:

	id	diagnosis	radius_mean	texture_mean	perimeter_mean	area_mean	smoothness_mean	compactness_mean	concavity_mean	concave points_mean
0	842302	M	17.99	10.38	122.80	1001.0	0.11840	0.27760	0.3001	0.14710
1	842517	M	20.57	17.77	132.90	1326.0	0.08474	0.07864	0.0869	0.07017
2	84300903	M	19.69	21.25	130.00	1203.0	0.10960	0.15990	0.1974	0.12790
3	84348301	M	11.42	20.38	77.58	386.1	0.14250	0.28390	0.2414	0.10520
4	84358402	M	20.29	14.34	135.10	1297.0	0.10030	0.13280	0.1980	0.10430

5 rows × 32 columns

Figure 8.2 – Load the Breast Cancer dataset

4. View the class distribution for the target `diagnosis` column:

```
df['diagnosis'].value_counts().plot(kind = 'bar')
```

Figure 8.3 shows the frequency distribution between the benign (**B**) and malignant (**M**) classes:

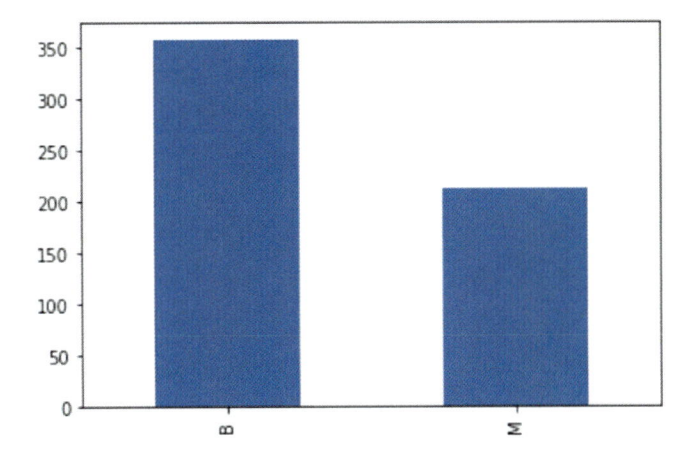

Figure 8.3 – B and M class distribution

5. Review information about the dataset:

```
df.info()
```

Figure 8.4 shows some dataset information:

```
<class 'pandas.core.frame.DataFrame'>
RangeIndex: 569 entries, 0 to 568
Data columns (total 32 columns):
 #   Column                   Non-Null Count  Dtype
---  ------                   --------------  -----
 0   id                       569 non-null    int64
 1   diagnosis                569 non-null    object
 2   radius_mean              569 non-null    float64
 3   texture_mean             569 non-null    float64
 4   perimeter_mean           569 non-null    float64
 5   area_mean                569 non-null    float64
 6   smoothness_mean          569 non-null    float64
 7   compactness_mean         569 non-null    float64
 8   concavity_mean           569 non-null    float64
 9   concave points_mean      569 non-null    float64
 10  symmetry_mean            569 non-null    float64
 11  fractal_dimension_mean   569 non-null    float64
 12  radius_se                569 non-null    float64
 13  texture_se               569 non-null    float64
 14  perimeter_se             569 non-null    float64
 15  area_se                  569 non-null    float64
 16  smoothness_se            569 non-null    float64
 17  compactness_se           569 non-null    float64
 18  concavity_se             569 non-null    float64
 19  concave points_se        569 non-null    float64
 20  symmetry_se              569 non-null    float64
 21  fractal_dimension_se     569 non-null    float64
 22  radius_worst             569 non-null    float64
 23  texture_worst            569 non-null    float64
 24  perimeter_worst          569 non-null    float64
 25  area_worst               569 non-null    float64
 26  smoothness_worst         569 non-null    float64
 27  compactness_worst        569 non-null    float64
 28  concavity_worst          569 non-null    float64
 29  concave points_worst     569 non-null    float64
 30  symmetry_worst           569 non-null    float64
 31  fractal_dimension_worst  569 non-null    float64
dtypes: float64(30), int64(1), object(1)
memory usage: 142.4+ KB
```

Figure 8.4 – Dataset information

6. AutoGluon infers the target label as the last column. Therefore, we will move the `diagnosis` column to the end:

    ```
    mc.MoveToLast(df,'diagnosis')
    df.head(3)
    ```

    Figure 8.5 shows the label column has been moved to the end:

perimeter_worst	area_worst	smoothness_worst	compactness_worst	concavity_worst	concave points_worst	symmetry_worst	fractal_dimension_worst	diagnosis
184.6	2019.0	0.1622	0.6656	0.7119	0.2654	0.4601	0.11890	M
158.8	1956.0	0.1238	0.1866	0.2416	0.1860	0.2750	0.08902	M
152.5	1709.0	0.1444	0.4245	0.4504	0.2430	0.3613	0.08758	M

    Figure 8.5 – Move the target label to the last column

7. List all columns from the dataset:

    ```
    df.columns
    ```

    Figure 8.6 lists all features from the dataset:

    ```
    Index(['id', 'radius_mean', 'texture_mean', 'perimeter_mean', 'area_mean',
           'smoothness_mean', 'compactness_mean', 'concavity_mean',
           'concave points_mean', 'symmetry_mean', 'fractal_dimension_mean',
           'radius_se', 'texture_se', 'perimeter_se', 'area_se', 'smoothness_se',
           'compactness_se', 'concavity_se', 'concave points_se', 'symmetry_se',
           'fractal_dimension_se', 'radius_worst', 'texture_worst',
           'perimeter_worst', 'area_worst', 'smoothness_worst',
           'compactness_worst', 'concavity_worst', 'concave points_worst',
           'symmetry_worst', 'fractal_dimension_worst', 'diagnosis'],
          dtype='object')
    ```

    Figure 8.6 – Dataset features

8. Encode the categorical columns to numerical values using `LabelEncoder` and view the class frequency distribution. `0` means benign, and `1` means malignant:

    ```
    le = preprocessing.LabelEncoder()
    le.fit(df['diagnosis'])
    df['diagnosis'] = le.transform(df['diagnosis'])

    df['diagnosis'].value_counts().plot(kind = 'bar')
    ```

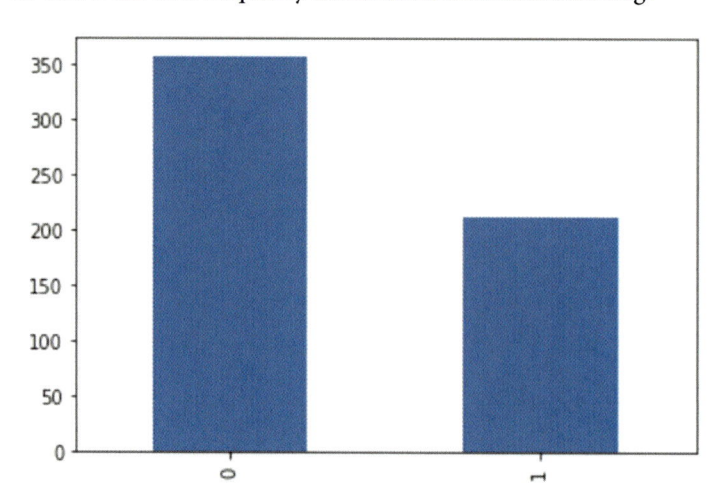

Figure 8.7 shows the class frequency distribution after label encoding:

Figure 8.7 – Encoded class distribution

9. Split the dataset into an 80:20 ratio for training and testing:

    ```
    train_data,test_data = train_test_split(df, test_
    size=0.2, random_state = 42)

    print(f'Train data: {train_data.shape[0]}')
    print(f'Test data: {test_data.shape[0]}')
    ```

    Figure 8.8 shows the dataset split:

    ```
    Train data: 455
    Test data: 114
    ```

    Figure 8.8 - Train and test split

10. We are now ready to build a binary classifier using AutoGluon. Define the output folder for AutoGluon to save the trained models. We will remove any existing folder a with the same folder name:

    ```
    save_path = 'ag_breast_cancer'

    DO_DELETE = True

    if DO_DELETE:
    ```

```
try:
    tf.compat.v1.gfile.DeleteRecursively(OUTPUT_DIR)
except:
    pass

tf.io.gfile.makedirs(save_path)
print(f'Model output directory: {save_path}')
```

11. Assign the target column to predict:

    ```
    label = 'diagnosis'
    print("Class variable summary: \n", train_data[label].describe())
    ```

    Figure 8.9 shows the summary of class variables:

    ```
    Class variable summary:
     count    455.000000
     mean       0.371429
     std        0.483719
     min        0.000000
     25%        0.000000
     50%        0.000000
     75%        1.000000
     max        1.000000
    Name: diagnosis, dtype: float64
    ```

    Figure 8.9 – Class variable summary

12. Set the target label, output directory, and evaluation metric to fit the model. Here, we set `time_limit` to 120 seconds for efficiency. You can remove this setting to train at full duration if needed, for example, `predictor = TabularPredictor(label=label, path=save_path, eval_metric='accuracy').fit(train_data, presets='best_quality')`. AutoGluon automatically infers the type of problem task as a binary classification based on the type of target column values:

    ```
    predictor = TabularPredictor(label=label, path=save_path,
    eval_metric='accuracy').fit(train_data, time_limit=120,
    presets='best_quality')
    ```

Model-Specific Explainability

Figure 8.10 shows the details of AutoGluon fitting:

```
Presets specified: ['best_quality']
Stack configuration (auto_stack=True): num_stack_levels=0, num_bag_folds=5, num_bag_sets=20
Beginning AutoGluon training ... Time limit = 120s
AutoGluon will save models to "ag_breast_cancer/"
AutoGluon Version:  0.6.2
Python Version:     3.9.10
Operating System:   Linux
Platform Machine:   x86_64
Platform Version:   #1 SMP Wed Oct 26 20:36:53 UTC 2022
Train Data Rows:    455
Train Data Columns: 31
Label Column: diagnosis
Preprocessing data ...
AutoGluon infers your prediction problem is: 'binary' (because only two unique label-values observed).
        2 unique label values: [0, 1]
```

Figure 8.10 – AutoGluon fitting

13. We can get the individual model performance using the `leaderboard` function:

    `predictor.leaderboard(test_data, silent=True)`

    Figure 8.11 shows the AutoGluon leaderboard predictive performance:

	model	score_test	score_val	pred_time_test	pred_time_val	fit_time	pred_time_test_marginal	pred_time_val_marginal	fit_time_marginal	stack_level	can_infer	fit_order
0	LightGBMLarge_BAG_L1	0.973684	0.962637	0.035319	0.009481	5.607196	0.035319	0.009481	5.607196	1	True	13
1	ExtraTreesGini_BAG_L1	0.973684	0.969231	0.080204	0.115706	0.529064	0.080204	0.115706	0.529064	1	True	8
2	ExtraTreesEntr_BAG_L1	0.973684	0.973626	0.080616	0.129573	0.552604	0.080616	0.129573	0.552604	1	True	9
3	NeuralNetTorch_BAG_L1	0.973684	0.980220	0.126236	0.159303	7.019799	0.126236	0.159303	7.019799	1	True	12
4	CatBoost_BAG_L1	0.964912	0.967033	0.065612	0.007055	10.603860	0.065612	0.007055	10.603860	1	True	7
5	RandomForestEntr_BAG_L1	0.964912	0.964835	0.073206	0.113540	0.588865	0.073206	0.113540	0.588865	1	True	6
6	RandomForestGini_BAG_L1	0.964912	0.967033	0.074253	0.114979	0.545684	0.074253	0.114979	0.545684	1	True	5
7	NeuralNetFastAI_BAG_L1	0.964912	0.986813	0.230629	0.180764	6.781015	0.230629	0.180764	6.781015	1	True	10
8	WeightedEnsemble_L2	0.964912	0.986813	0.234094	0.182042	7.373578	0.003464	0.001278	0.592562	2	True	14
9	LightGBMXT_BAG_L1	0.964912	0.982418	0.390843	0.009857	4.205060	0.390843	0.009857	4.205060	1	True	3
10	LightGBM_BAG_L1	0.956140	0.969231	0.025051	0.009724	4.470727	0.025051	0.009724	4.470727	1	True	4
11	XGBoost_BAG_L1	0.956140	0.971429	0.055231	0.020815	3.006829	0.055231	0.020815	3.006829	1	True	11
12	KNeighborsDist_BAG_L1	0.789474	0.806593	0.028558	0.020687	0.009137	0.028558	0.020687	0.009137	1	True	2
13	KNeighborsUnif_BAG_L1	0.754386	0.771429	0.023936	0.011761	0.007596	0.023936	0.011761	0.007596	1	True	1

Figure 8.11 – AutoGluon leaderboard

14. To evaluate the model performance, let's prepare new test data without the target label:

    ```
    y_test = test_data[label]

    test_data_nolabel = test_data.drop(columns=[label])
    test_data_nolabel.head()
    ```

15. Obtain predictions on the test data using the trained model. Our model achieved a `0.96` accuracy score and a `0.95` F1_score:

    ```
    y_pred = predictor.predict(test_data_nolabel)
    print("Predictions: \n", y_pred)
    perf = predictor.evaluate_predictions(y_true=y_test, y_pred=y_pred, auxiliary_metrics=True)
    ```

    Figure 8.12 shows the evaluation metrics:

    ```
    Evaluation: accuracy on test data: 0.9649122807017544
    Evaluations on test data:
    {
        "accuracy": 0.9649122807017544,
        "balanced_accuracy": 0.9626596790042581,
        "mcc": 0.9253193580085162,
        "f1": 0.9534883720930233,
        "precision": 0.9534883720930233,
        "recall": 0.9534883720930233
    }
    Predictions:
     204    0
     70     1
     131    1
     431    0
     540    0
            ..
     486    0
     75     1
     249    0
     238    0
     265    1
    Name: diagnosis, Length: 114, dtype: int64
    ```

    Figure 8.12 – Evaluation metrics

16. We can get the predicted class probabilities by calling `predict_probs`:

    ```
    pred_probs = predictor.predict_proba(test_data_nolabel)
    pred_probs.head(5)
    ```

164   Model-Specific Explainability

Figure 8.13 shows the predicted class probabilities:

	0	1
204	0.950747	0.049253
70	0.001357	0.998643
131	0.017722	0.982278
431	0.985273	0.014727
540	0.991829	0.008171

Figure 8.13 – Predicted class probabilities

17. Here, we can review a complete summary of the training process, including the number and type of models trained, evaluation metrics, and processing time:

```
results = predictor.fit_summary(show_plot=True)
```

Figure 8.14 shows the complete summary of the AutoGluon training:

```
*** Summary of fit() ***
Estimated performance of each model:
                      model  score_val  pred_time_val   fit_time  pred_time_val_marginal  fit_time_marginal  stack_level  can_infer  fit_order
0       NeuralNetFastAI_BAG_L1   0.986813       0.151035   6.893745                0.151035           6.893745            1       True         10
1          WeightedEnsemble_L2   0.986813       0.152269   7.472078                0.001234           0.578334            2       True         14
2              LightGBMXT_BAG_L1   0.982418       0.010299   4.088349                0.010299           4.088349            1       True          3
3        NeuralNetTorch_BAG_L1   0.980220       0.126647   7.163876                0.126647           7.163876            1       True         12
4         ExtraTreesEntr_BAG_L1   0.973626       0.122370   0.581059                0.122370           0.581059            1       True          9
5                XGBoost_BAG_L1   0.971429       0.019473   3.023371                0.019473           3.023371            1       True         11
6                LightGBM_BAG_L1   0.969231       0.009121   4.655586                0.009121           4.655586            1       True          4
7         ExtraTreesGini_BAG_L1   0.969231       0.113346   0.517663                0.113346           0.517663            1       True          8
8                CatBoost_BAG_L1   0.967033       0.007781  10.785936                0.007781          10.785936            1       True          7
9        RandomForestGini_BAG_L1   0.967033       0.112606   0.536492                0.112606           0.536492            1       True          5
10       RandomForestEntr_BAG_L1   0.964835       0.112577   0.573340                0.112577           0.573340            1       True          6
11           LightGBMLarge_BAG_L1   0.962637       0.009531   5.738750                0.009531           5.738750            1       True         13
12          KNeighborsDist_BAG_L1   0.806593       0.016240   0.005436                0.016240           0.005436            1       True          2
13          KNeighborsUnif_BAG_L1   0.771429       0.018518   0.006104                0.018518           0.006104            1       True          1
Number of models trained: 14
Types of models trained:
{'StackerEnsembleModel_RF', 'StackerEnsembleModel_LGB', 'StackerEnsembleModel_XT', 'StackerEnsembleModel_TabularNeuralNetTorch', 'StackerEnsembleModel_CatBoost', 'StackerEnsembleModel_XGBoost', 'WeightedEnsembleModel', 'StackerEnsembleModel_NNFastAiTabular', 'StackerEnsembleModel_KNN'}
Bagging used: True  (with 5 folds)
Multi-layer stack-ensembling used: False
Feature Metadata (Processed):
(raw dtype, special dtypes):
('float', [])  : 30 | ['radius_mean', 'texture_mean', 'perimeter_mean', 'area_mean', 'smoothness_mean', ...]
('int', [])    :  1 | ['id']
Plot summary of models saved to file: ag_breast_cancer/SummaryOfModels.html
*** End of fit() summary ***
```

Figure 8.14 – Full AutoGluon training summary

18. Review the problem type and features inferred by AutoGluon:

```
print("AutoGluon infers problem type is: ", predictor.problem_type)
print("AutoGluon identified the following types of features:")
print(predictor.feature_metadata)
```

Figure 8.15 shows the inferred problem and feature types:

```
AutoGluon infers problem type is:  binary
AutoGluon identified the following types of features:
('float', []) : 30 | ['radius_mean', 'texture_mean', 'perimeter_mean', 'area_mean', 'smoothness_mean', ...]
('int', [])   :  1 | ['id']
```

Figure 8.15 – Inferred problem and feature types

19. We are ready to assess the model's prediction using Kernel SHAP. First, let's load the previously saved trained model from AutoGluon's `save_path`:

    ```
    loaded_predictor = TabularPredictor.load('ag_breast_cancer/')
    ```

20. Create a function to get the predictions on the test data and pass them to `KernelExplainer`:

    ```
    columns = train_data.columns

    def get_predictions(input):
        df = pd.DataFrame(input, columns=columns)
        return predictor.predict(df)

    data = np.array(train_data.values.tolist())

    explainer = shap.KernelExplainer(get_predictions, data)
    ```

21. Calculate the SHAP values. For efficiency, we set a value for `nsamples` to limit the number of times SHAP re-evaluates the model when explaining each prediction. You can change it to a lower value to reduce computation time:

    ```
    shap_values = explainer.shap_values(test_data, nsamples=20)
    ```

22. View the SHAP values length:

    ```
    print(f'SHAP values length: {len(shap_values)}')
    ```

    Figure 8.16 shows the SHAP values length:

    ```
    SHAP values length: 114
    ```

    Figure 8.16 – SHAP values length

SHAP provides various visualizations to interpret feature importance based on SHAP values. Let's see a few examples:

1. A SHAP force plot shows which features influenced the model's prediction for a single observation. We will call `shap.initjs` to load the JS visualization code, followed by explaining a specific data instance. A force plot shows a baseline or average prediction. Each feature value is represented in an arrow that pushes the outcome toward a positive or negative prediction. The increment or decrement of each feature leads us to the final prediction. This sample is predicted to be class 1 as a malignant tumor is influenced by the increments of the `area_worst`, `radius_mean`, `fractal_dimension_se`, and `concave points_mean` features:

   ```
   shap.initjs()

   shap.force_plot(explainer.expected_value, shap_
   values=shap_values[5], features=test_data.iloc[1,:])
   ```

   Figure 8.17 shows a SHAP force plot of class 1 prediction:

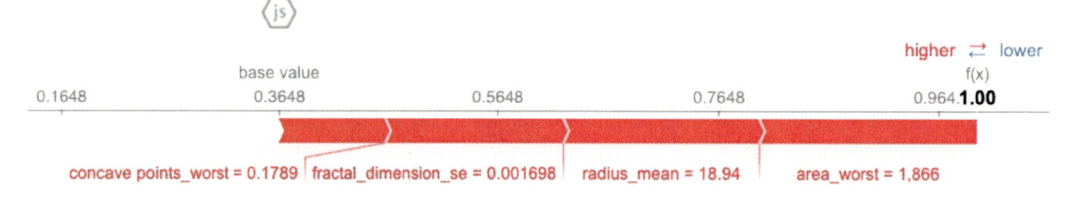

   Figure 8.17 – A force plot of class 1 prediction

2. Let's view a different sample using a force plot. This sample is predicted to be class 0 as a benign tumor is influenced by the decrements of the `radius_mean`, `concavity_se`, `concave points_worst`, `area_worst`, and `concavity_mean` features. The increments of `fractal_dimension_worst` and `perimenter_worst` also influenced the final prediction:

   ```
   shap.force_plot(explainer.expected_value, shap_
   values=shap_values[0], features=test_data.iloc[1,:])
   ```

   Figure 8.18 shows a force plot of class 0 prediction:

   Figure 8.18 – A force plot of class 0 prediction

3. We can aggregate and visualize SHAP values using a decision plot to understand the overall model behavior in decision-making. The features are ordered by descending importance, and the lines move upward from the bottom at a base value to their final prediction. The x axis represents SHAP values for each feature on the y axis. Let's visualize the decision plots using the same test samples:

```
shap.decision_plot(explainer.expected_value, shap_
values[5], test_data)
```

Figure 8.19 shows a decision plot of class 1 prediction:

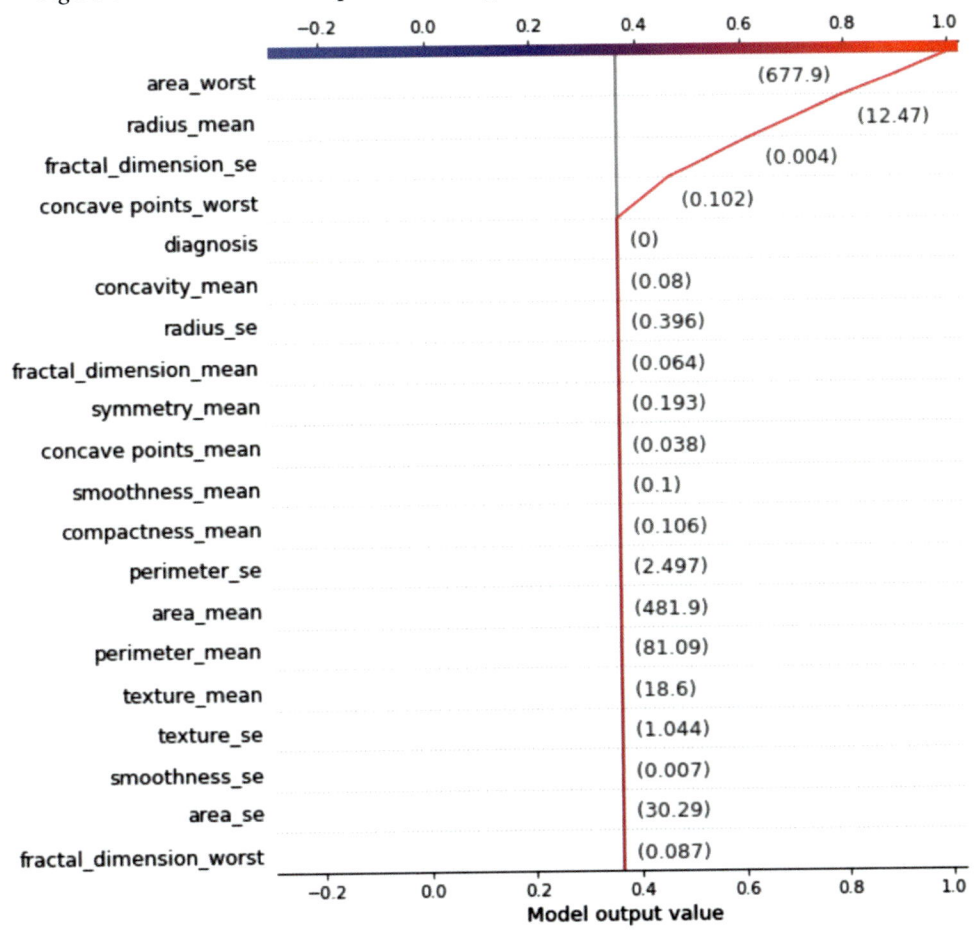

Figure 8.19 – A decision plot of class 1 prediction

4. Here is the decision plot for the second test sample:

```
shap.decision_plot(explainer.expected_value, shap_
values[0], test_data)
```

Figure 8.20 shows a decision plot of class 0 prediction:

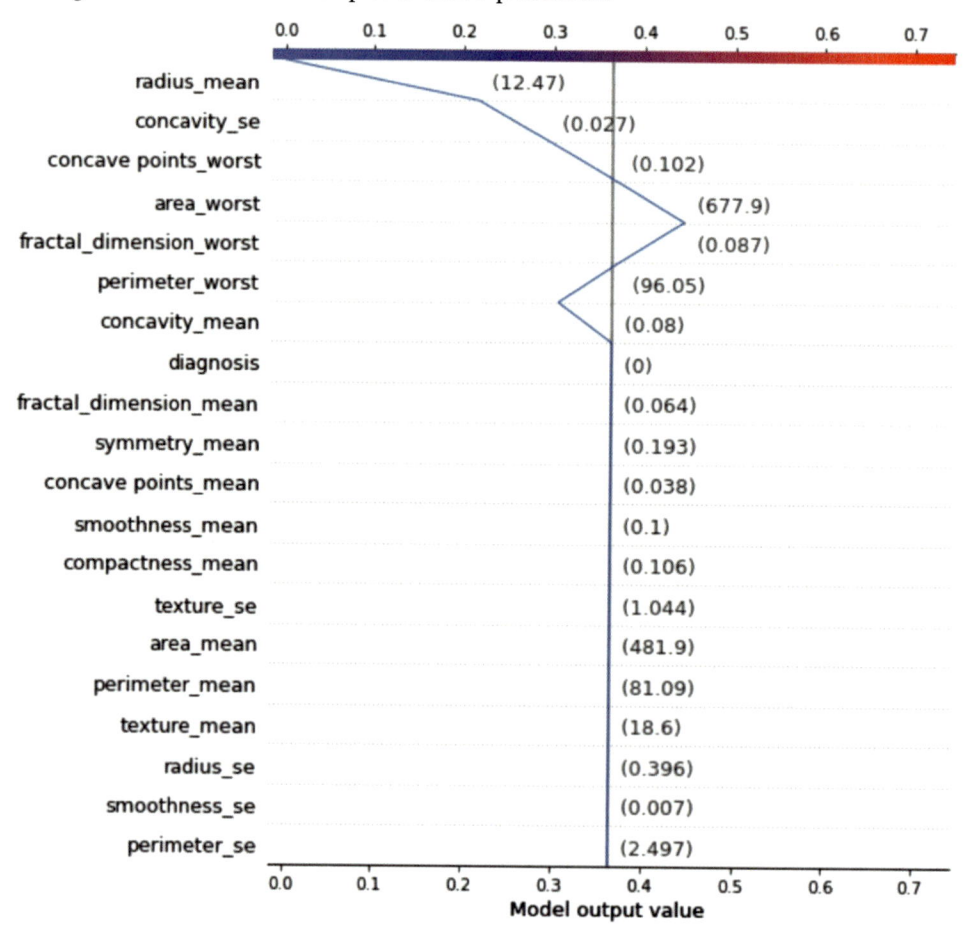

radius_mean	(12.47)
concavity_se	(0.027)
concave points_worst	(0.102)
area_worst	(677.9)
fractal_dimension_worst	(0.087)
perimeter_worst	(96.05)
concavity_mean	(0.08)
diagnosis	(0)
fractal_dimension_mean	(0.064)
symmetry_mean	(0.193)
concave points_mean	(0.038)
smoothness_mean	(0.1)
compactness_mean	(0.106)
texture_se	(1.044)
area_mean	(481.9)
perimeter_mean	(81.09)
texture_mean	(18.6)
radius_se	(0.396)
smoothness_se	(0.007)
perimeter_se	(2.497)

Figure 8.20 – A decision plot of class 0 prediction

5. The summary bar plot shows the mean absolute SHAP values for each feature across all observations, which is useful for analyzing the global effect of the features:

```
shap.summary_plot(shap_values, test_data, plot_type="bar")
```

Figure 8.21 shows a summary plot aggregated across all predictions:

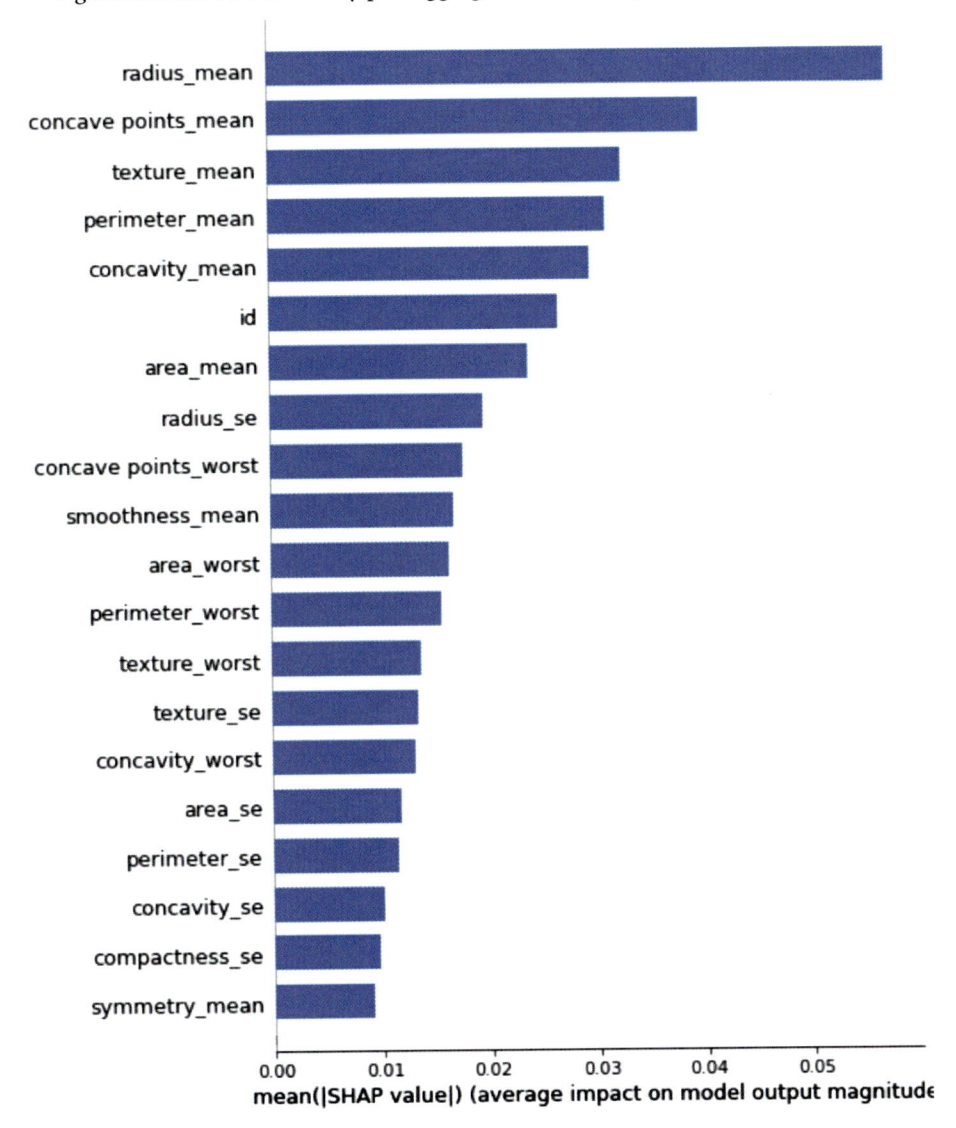

Figure 8.21 – Summary plot

6. Here is a summary plot with default dot visualization:

   ```
   shap.summary_plot(shap_values, test_data)
   ```

   Figure 8.22 shows a default dot summary plot:

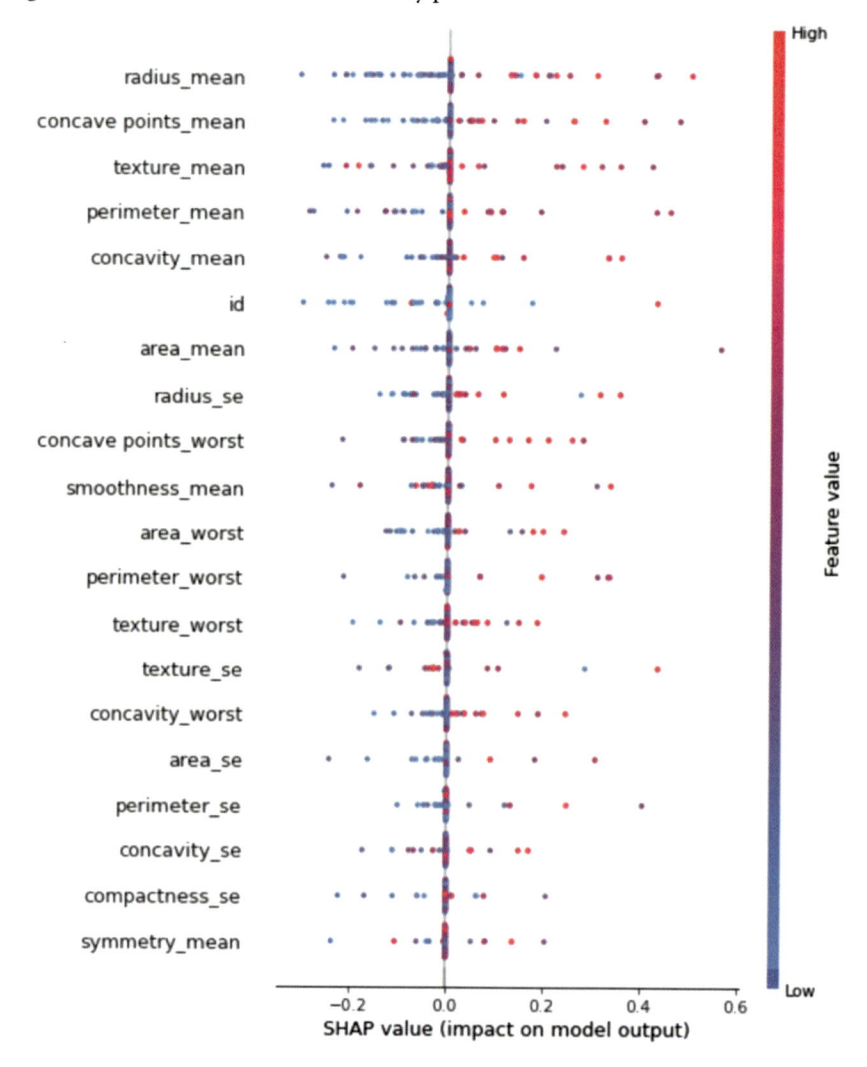

   Figure 8.22 – Summary plot with dot visualization

7. A dependence plot shows a single feature attribution on the model predictions. For each data point, the feature value is on the *x* axis, whereas the corresponding SHAP value is on the *y* axis. The `compactness_mean` feature is chosen by default for coloring:

   ```
   shap.dependence_plot(2, shap_values, test_data)
   ```

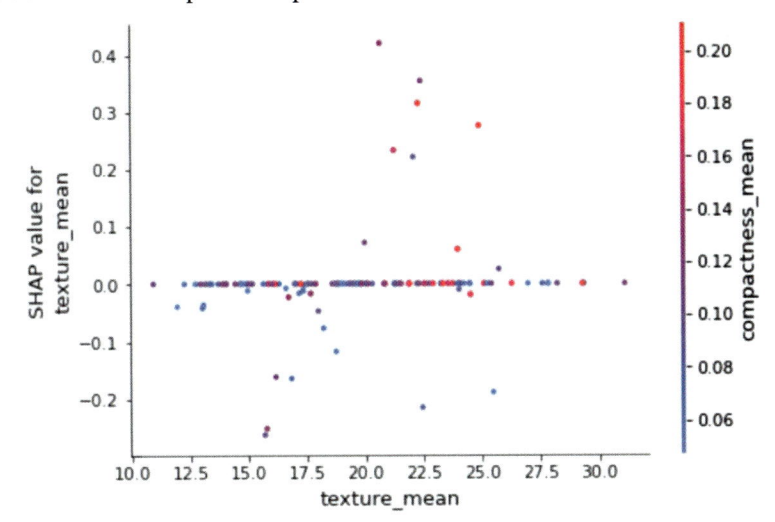

Figure 8.23 shows a dependence plot between two features:

Figure 8.23 – Dependence plot

8. Alternatively, in this case, you can specify a different feature for coloring, such as `texture_mean`:

```
shap.dependence_plot('radius_worst', shap_values, test_
data, interaction_index="texture_mean")
```

Figure 8.24 shows a dependence plot with a specified second feature:

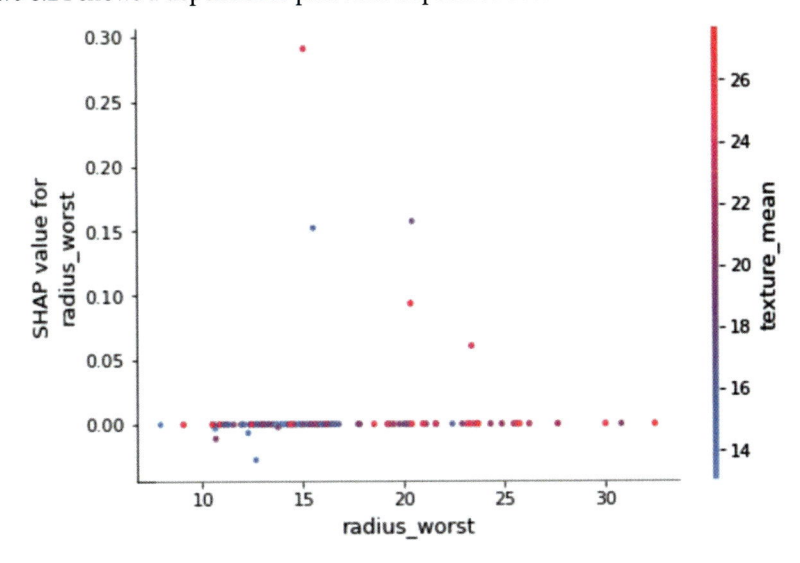

Figure 8.24 – Dependence plot with a specified second feature

Kernel SHAP is model agnostic. Hence it has wide applicability to interpret predictions for a broad range of ML models. However, calculating Shapley values with large datasets using Kernel SHAP can be time-consuming and computationally intensive. We used the `nsamples` setting in this example to limit the number of SHAP evaluations for each prediction as an alternative.

In contrast, Amazon SageMaker Clarify, `https://aws.amazon.com/sagemaker/clarify`, improves Kernel SHAP runtime significantly and enhances scalability by parallelizing SHAP computation. Refer to *Amazon SageMaker Clarify: Machine Learning Bias Detection and Explainability in the Cloud*, `https://assets.amazon.science/45/76/30bab4f14ccab96cfe8067ed2b4a/amazon-sagemaker-clarify-machine-learning-bias-detection-and-explainability-in-the-cloud.pdf`, for more info on Amazon SageMaker Clarify's implementation of Kernel SHAP.

In this section, you completed an end-to-end walkthrough of building and explaining a deep learning model to detect breast cancer by classifying a benign or malignant tumor. The following section explores model-specific explainability in more depth.

Reviewing model-specific explainability

Unlike model-agnostic techniques, **model-specific XAI** methods depend on the choice of model class and require knowledge of the inner workings of a model. Hence, model-specific methods are applicable for inherently interpretable models or when we explicitly understand internal network representation. Gaining insights into the underlying model structure allows us to reverse engineer the rationale through deductive reasoning to justify the decisions made by the model.

While providing a deeper understanding of a specific model, implementing model-specific XAI methods such as backpropagation approaches involves recreating the model in reverse order to unfold the inner logic and complexity. This section will discuss a model-specific example using **Guided Integrated Gradients** (**Guided IG**).

Interpreting saliency with Guided IG

Integrated Gradient (IG), `https://arxiv.org/abs/1703.01365`, is an XAI technique that evaluates feature attribution by computing gradients of a model's prediction. IG is more scalable and works independently from the number of features within a network. However, IG is slower than the other backpropagation-based methods, requiring between 50 and 200 backward passes for gradient evaluations.

Guided IG is an enhanced feature attribution method based on IG for deep learning models. Guided IG minimizes irrelevant attributions by introducing an **adaptive path method** (**APM**) to calculate an alternate integration path than IG.

This section covers an image classification task using Guided IG. A sample notebook, `chapter8_GuidedIG.ipynb`, is available in the book's GitHub repo:

1. First, install the required packages using the provided requirements file:

   ```
   import sys
   !{sys.executable} -m pip install -r requirements.txt
   ```

2. Load the essential libraries:

   ```
   import numpy as np
   import PIL.Image as Image
   import matplotlib.pylab as plt
   import tensorflow.compat.v1 as tf
   import tensorflow_hub as hub
   import saliency.tf1 as saliency
   import os
   from platform import python_version
   import warnings

   warnings.filterwarnings("ignore")
   os.environ["TF_CPP_MIN_LOG_LEVEL"] = "3"
   print(f'TensorFlow version: {tf.__version__}')
   print(f'Python version: {python_version()}')
   %matplotlib inline
   ```

   Figure 8.25 shows the package dependencies for this example:

   ```
   TensorFlow version: 2.11.0
   Python version: 3.9.10
   ```

   Figure 8.25 – Package dependencies

3. Load a sample image and the pre-trained InceptionV3 model for image classification:

   ```
   IMAGE_SHAPE = (224, 224)
   im = Image.open("gsdog.jpeg").resize(IMAGE_SHAPE)
   im
   ```

Figure 8.26 shows the original input image:

Figure 8.26 – Original input image

4. Download a pre-trained `Inception V3` model:

   ```
   classifier_model = "https://tfhub.dev/google/imagenet/inception_v3/classification/3"

   classifier = tf.keras.Sequential([
       hub.KerasLayer(classifier_model,
       input_shape=IMAGE_SHAPE+(3,))
   ])
   ```

5. Convert the input image to a NumPy array and add a dimension:

   ```
   im = np.array(im)/255.0
   im.shape
   ```

6. Obtain the predicted class and identify the top predicted classes:

   ```
   result = classifier.predict(im[np.newaxis, ...])
   result.shape
   predicted_class = tf.math.argmax(result[0], axis=-1)
   ```

7. Read the `ImageNetLabels` file to decode the model's prediction. Preview the image classes:

   ```
   labels_path = tf.keras.utils.get_file('ImageNetLabels.txt','https://storage.googleapis.com/download.tensorflow.org/data/ImageNetLabels.txt')
   ```

```
imagelist = []
with open(labels_path, "r") as file:
    for line in file:
        line = line.strip()
        line = line.strip('"')
        if line:
            imagelist.append(line)
imagelist[:10]
```

8. View the top predicted class:

```
plt.imshow(im)
plt.axis('off')
predicted_class_name = imagelist[predicted_class]
predicted_class_index = imagelist.index(predicted_class_name)
_ = plt.title(f'Prediction: {predicted_class_name.title()} \n Class: {str(predicted_class_index)}')
plt.savefig('guidedIG_gs.png', bbox_inches='tight')
```

Figure 8.27 shows the predicted class ID of 236 and the German Shepherd category:

Figure 8.27 – Predicted class ID of 236 and category as German Shepherd

9. We are ready to compare saliency maps for IG and Guided IG. Define `Graph` and `Session` for computation:

```
graph = tf.Graph()
sess = tf.Session(graph=graph)
with graph.as_default():
  hub.Module(classifier_model)
  sess.run(tf.global_variables_initializer())
  sess.run(tf.tables_initializer())
with graph.as_default():
  images = graph.get_tensor_by_name('module/hub_input/
images:0')
  logits = graph.get_tensor_by_name('module/InceptionV3/
Logits/SpatialSqueeze:0')
  neuron_selector = tf.placeholder(tf.int32)
  y = logits[:,neuron_selector]
  prediction = tf.argmax(logits, 1)
```

10. Create saliency objects and a black image baseline for Guided IG:

```
ig = saliency.IntegratedGradients(graph, sess, y, images)
guided_ig = saliency.GuidedIG(graph, sess, y, images)
baseline = np.zeros(im.shape)
```

11. Compute the attribution mask for IG and Guided IG:

```
ig_mask_3d = ig.GetMask(
  im, feed_dict = {neuron_selector:
  predicted_class_index}, x_steps=25,
  x_baseline=baseline, batch_size=20)
guided_ig_mask_3d = guided_ig.GetMask(
  im, feed_dict = {neuron_selector:
    predicted_class_index}, x_steps=25,
  x_baseline=baseline, max_dist=0.2, fraction=0.5)
```

12. Convert 3D tensors to 2D grayscale:

```
ig_grayscale =
    saliency.VisualizeImageGrayscale(ig_mask_3d)
```

```
    guided_ig_grayscale = 
        saliency.VisualizeImageGrayscale(guided_ig_mask_3d)
```

13. Visualize and compare saliency maps for IG and Guided IG. We can see Guided IG is less noisy than IG:

```
fig = plt.figure(figsize=(20, 20))
rows = 1
columns = 3
fig.add_subplot(rows, columns, 1)
plt.imshow(im)
plt.axis('off')
plt.title("Original Image", fontsize=24)

fig.add_subplot(rows, columns, 2)
plt.imshow(ig_grayscale, cmap="gray")
plt.axis('off')
plt.title("Integrated Gradients", fontsize=24)

fig.add_subplot(rows, columns, 3)
plt.imshow(guided_ig_grayscale, cmap="gray")
plt.axis('off')
plt.title("Guided Integrated Gradients", fontsize=24)
```

Figure 8.28 shows the visual comparisons between IG and Guided IG:

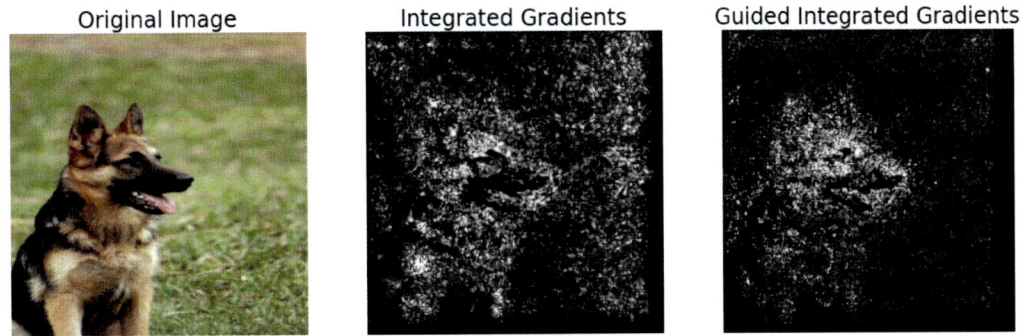

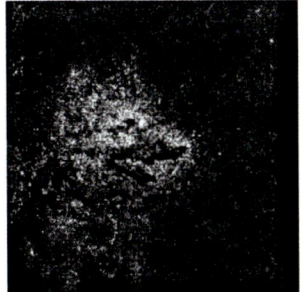

Figure 8.28 – Comparisons of IG and Guided IG

In this section, you completed a walk-through of evaluating saliency techniques by comparing IG and Guided IG. Traditionally, backpropagation methods evaluate gradients corresponding to the input image to identify pixel attribution and produce a saliency map using weighted gradients in a specific neural network. The path in IG starts with a black baseline and ends at the input image by following a fixed direction where all pixels increment at the same rate, hence capturing irrelevant pixels along the way. Although IG detected most attributions, Guided IG demonstrated less noise and better visual saliency.

Guided IG applies APMs to generalize the attribution path for both the image and model to create more realistic saliency maps that are true to the predicted class. Selectively filtering subsets of pixels with the lowest absolute value and adapting the integration path to the input, baseline, and model allows Guided IG to avoid picking up noisy signals.

After reviewing model-agnostic and model-specific XAI examples, you might wonder which method to choose. The following section provides a general guideline for selecting an XAI method.

Choosing an XAI method

With a shift in public awareness and regulatory compliance, explainability is now essential for organizations that leverage automated decision-making. This paper, https://arxiv.org/abs/2107.04427, proposes a methodology containing the following properties to bridge the gap between stakeholder needs and explainability methods based on human-centered AI:

- **Explanation method properties**: XAI should consist of compatibility properties, explanation properties, method usage, and process properties. Compatibility properties refer to elements that determine the feasibility of an XAI method for a problem type or use case. In contrast, explanation properties must define the scope of explanations, including language type and the context of an explanation. Furthermore, method usage should provide information on using an XAI method with process properties to identify a mechanism for producing explanations.

- **Explainability needs**: It is essential to identify the right target stakeholders and capture stakeholder needs through questionnaires, including use case context, constraints, and functional and non-functional requirements.

- **Information collection**: Once the identification of stakeholders is finalized, curate a list of questionnaires to obtain details for each requirement need.

- **Matching stakeholder needs with explanation method properties**: After a thorough requirements analysis, you should integrate XAI technical knowledge and present the extent of explainability that will be addressed and any known limitations with existing XAI techniques to stakeholders.

Once you gain clarity on stakeholder needs, the next step is to decide which XAI method to choose. Generally, you should determine whether the internal structure for an ML model is interpretable and has a clear representation. For example, decision trees are more interpretable than deep learning neural networks. You can interpret a decision tree by extracting decision rules and measuring the quality of the decision split using the Gini impurity metric to identify potential misclassification. However, the complexity of decision trees increases as the number of terminal nodes grows. In contrast, neural networks combine layers of neurons with non-linear mathematical operations, making them difficult to interpret.

Figure 8.29 summarizes what we have covered for model-agnostic and model-specific XAI methods in this chapter and how you should consider what's best for your use case:

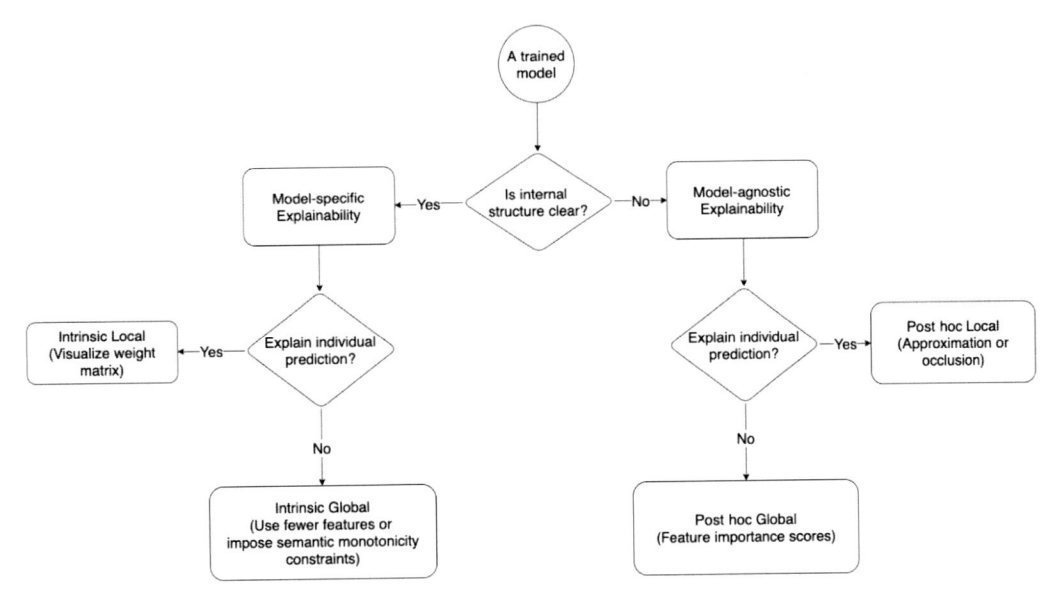

Figure 8.29 – Choosing model-agnostic versus model-specific XAI methods

As shown in the preceding diagram, starting with a trained model, if you can obtain the inner network structure, such as coefficient weights or the frequency of a feature used in an ensemble tree model, you should explore a model-specific framework for better explainability performance. Otherwise, you should evaluate a model-agnostic framework since it does not rely on an internal model structure and focuses on correlating the relationship between the input and output. Subsequently, consider the scope of explainability, whether you will provide local explanations for individual predictions or global explanations for the overall model behavior.

Summary

Awareness of explainability with AI systems is not limited to technological advancement in XAI techniques. Instead, it involves a multi-disciplinary collaboration to review legal, ethical, and societal questions comprehensively. You should be aware that the guiding explanations facilitate further model behavioral probing and debugging.

So, why can't we just use model-agnostic methods for everything? Although model-agnostic methods have broad applicability, they often have a lower efficiency than model-specific methods. If you need targeted explanations and the internal model structure is known, choose model-specific methods for efficiency. Otherwise, model-agnostic models are a good starting point. Combining model-agnostic and model-specific techniques is recommended when you need to provide a comprehensive evaluation of the model's prediction.

You gained deeper insights into model-agnostic and model-specific XAI techniques in this chapter. Coupled with two practical examples, you learned that model-agnostic methods explain a model's predictions regardless of the ML algorithm, whereas model-specific methods are designed to efficiently explain a specific model type. So, here is food for thought, can we trust AI-generated explanations? In the next chapter, we will explore XAI benchmarking schemes and evaluation methodologies to discuss this topic further.

9
Explainability Evaluation Schemes

According to the World Economic Forum, https://www.weforum.org/agenda/2022/01/artificial-intelligence-ai-technology-trust-survey/, approximately 60% of adults believe **artificial intelligence** (**AI**) systems will transform their daily life. In contrast, only 50% said they trust AI technology firms. Advances in AI systems and calibrating trust require a balancing act between speed, transparency, and fairness.

Generally, **Explainable AI** (**XAI**) systems provide explainability by generating explanations for individual predicted instances or describing how a model derives a prediction. Existing XAI approaches fall into two main categories: they favor interpretable models or assess change in output through model manipulation.

The **National Institute of Standards and Technology** (**NIST**), in their paper, *Four Principles of Explainable Artificial Intelligence*, identifies four fundamental principles for XAI systems (https://www.nist.gov/publications/four-principles-explainable-artificial-intelligence):

- **Explanation**: An XAI system must produce evidence to justify **machine learning** (**ML**) outputs
- **Meaningful**: Evidence produced by an XAI system must be comprehensible by the target audience
- **Explanation accuracy**: Explanations demonstrate correct reasoning that preserves the justification of an ML output
- **Knowledge limits**: An XAI system operates within design boundaries and confidence limits

Paper citation
Phillips, P., Hahn, C., Fontana, P., Yates, A., Greene, K., Broniatowski, D. and Przybocki, M. (2021), *Four Principles of Explainable Artificial Intelligence*, NIST Interagency/Internal Report (NISTIR), National Institute of Standards and Technology, Gaithersburg, MD, [online], `https://doi.org/10.6028/NIST.IR.8312`, `https://tsapps.nist.gov/publication/get_pdf.cfm?pub_id=933399` (Accessed December 12, 2022).

Hence, firms must define an AI governance model that provides guardrails without slowing innovation and adoption. The goal is to achieve optimal confidence in AI systems and avoid distrust between humans and machines. *Figure 9.1* summarizes key design considerations for XAI systems.

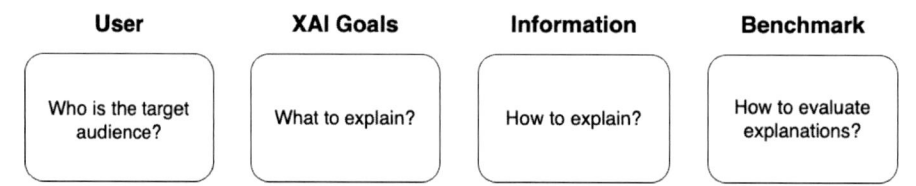

User	XAI Goals	Information	Benchmark
Who is the target audience?	What to explain?	How to explain?	How to evaluate explanations?

Figure 9.1 – XAI system design considerations

So far, you have learned and experimented with various XAI techniques throughout the book. In this chapter, we will cover the following evaluation schemes based on NIST's fundamental principles to measure the quality of explanations for XAI systems:

- Reviewing the **System Causability Scale (SCS)**
- Exploring **Benchmarking Attribution Methods (BAM)**
- Faithfulness and monotonicity
- Human-grounded evaluation framework

In this chapter, you will learn about the existing XAI evaluation and benchmarking landscape and get a sense of which approach to consider for your applications.

Reviewing the System Causability Scale (SCS)

Created in 1986 by John Brooke, the **System Usability Scale (SUS)** provides a simple tool to measure the usability of a system's user interface. It consists of a 10-item questionnaire with 5 response options, allowing respondents to evaluate the quality of products and services from *strongly agree* to *strongly disagree*.

Inspired by SUS, SCS, available at `https://doi.org/10.1007/s13218-020-00636-z`, focuses on measuring the qualitative aspect of XAI systems. SCS meets the XAI principle of meaningfulness by NIST to determine end user perception against explanations provided by XAI systems.

SCS assesses the effectiveness of an XAI user interface in providing explanations to the target audience using a Likert scale questionnaire covering the following scopes:

- A given explanation offers accurate causal factors with relevant granularity
- The context of a given explanation makes sense to the user
- Users can tune the level of granularity of the provided explanations
- Users need guidance to interpret explanations
- Users understand the causality of the generated explanations without support
- Users can apply the causality of the generated explanations with domain knowledge
- An XAI system produces consistent explanations
- Users agree that the generated explanations are easy to follow
- Users need references or documentation to interpret the generated explanations
- An XAI system generates explanations promptly and efficiently

SCS aims to provide a straightforward methodology to evaluate the effectiveness of an XAI user interface and the quality of explanations provided by XAI systems. Unlike the SUS score, which measures usability between 0 and 100 percent, SCS normalizes the scores to produce a percentile ranking. Suppose the SCS scale ranges between 1 and 5 points for *strongly disagree, disagree, neutral, agree,* and *strongly agree* ratings. A perfect score of 50 is given if an XAI system meets all 10 requirements. For example, if the sum of the ratings of an XAI system is 44 based on the preceding requirements, dividing by 50 gives us a normalized 0.88 SCS score.

The purpose of SCS is to provide a rapid evaluation framework to assess the quality of an XAI interface based on end user experience. One caveat with SCS is that the Likert scales follow ordinal measurement where the difference between each response category is not well-defined. Assuming the interval between response categories is equal can be misleading and may result in an erroneous conclusion. For example, the variations in the magnitude of emotional responses between strongly agree and agree could differ with other consecutive categories, such as strongly disagree and disagree. Furthermore, subjective user ratings on the explanation quality could misrepresent an explanation's effectiveness in simulation tests.

After learning how to obtain qualitative feedback from users with SCS, the following section explores a quantitative approach to identify false positive explanations using benchmarking attribution methods.

Exploring Benchmarking Attribution Methods (BAM)

With various feature attribution XAI methods available today, it can be challenging to quantify which inputs are indeed important to a model due to a lack of ground truth data. Relying solely on visual assessment can be misleading. XAI methods that compute gradients insensitive to the input data fail to produce relevant explanations for desired target outputs, which can be detrimental in ML tasks, such as anomaly detection. For instance, research has shown that some XAI saliency methods are unable to demonstrate true feature importance and produce identical visual explanations or saliency maps despite randomizing a trained model's parameters. For AI-assisted medical diagnosis, this can be risky and concerning when there is no change in explanations to a model's prediction after randomizing a trained model's data and parameters.

There is no value in providing false positive explanations to the target audience. A common approach to address this gap involves using *human-in-the-loop assessment* to evaluate the quality of explainability, which can be expensive with large datasets. Hence, XAI evaluation metrics should demonstrate the rationale of a model's prediction by capturing false positives.

BAM, `https://doi.org/10.48550/arXiv.1907.09701`, aims to tackle false positive explanations. BAM evaluates the accuracy of feature attributions using semi-synthetic datasets with trained models on known relative feature importance. BAM's approach meets the NIST's XAI principle to achieve explanation accuracy.

BAM trains two classifiers for detecting a target object class and background scene from an input image. The expectation is that adding irrelevant pixels to the input image should not impact the model's ability to predict the expected target object or background scene class.

For example, an input image of a desert with a random inclusion of fish, as shown in *Figure 9.2*, should result in the expected target background scene as a desert class. Explanations that assign higher attributions to fish as the background scene class should be false positives. Such a false positive prediction can mislead the target audience because the fish is considered semantically more meaningful than the desert in this input image.

Figure 9.2 – Input image with random object inclusion

BAM evaluates feature attribution methods using the following metrics:

- **Model contrast score** (**MCS**): Given the same input, measure the difference in attribution between two models
- **Input dependence rate** (**IDR**): Given two different inputs to the same model, calculate the difference in attribution
- **Input independence rate** (**IIR**): Given two functionally similar inputs to the same model, measure the difference in attribution

MCS and IDR only apply to BAM datasets and models, `https://github.com/google-research-datasets/bam`, whereas IIR applies to any models and inputs. According to BAM's observation, **vanilla gradient descent** and **Gradient-weighted Class Activation Mapping (Grad-CAM)** are less likely to produce false positive explanations. In contrast, **guided backpropagation** seems to assign similar attributions regardless of evolution in feature importance.

As discussed in *Chapter 7*, perturbation-based methods provide explainability by evaluating changes in model performance based on removing a subset of pre-determined, highly attributed features from input data. Contrary to perturbation-based methods, BAM evaluates false positives by identifying unimportant features with their expected zero attributions. BAM does not make assumptions on pre-determined feature importance. Instead, BAM's approach focuses on assessing the significance of a feature relative to two different models by adjusting the frequency to introduce this feature in the dataset.

Thus far, this section has reviewed how BAM can enhance explainability by analyzing relative feature importance. Next, let's discuss the significance of faithfulness and monotonicity in benchmarking explainability.

Understanding faithfulness and monotonicity

Faithfulness in XAI refers to evaluating the correlation between feature importance scores to the actual individual feature's performance effect on a correct prediction. Measuring faithfulness is typically done by removing pre-determined important features incrementally, observing changes in model performance, and validating feature relevance to a model's prediction. In other words, are the identified important features genuinely relevant to the final model output?

Besides feature importance correlation, researchers identified additional properties such as polarity consistency for evaluating the faithfulness of explanations, `https://doi.org/10.48550/arXiv.2201.12114`. **Polarity** in ML refers to positive and negative analysis – for example, the amount of positive and negative phrases for sentiment analysis. Polarity consistency validates faithfulness by measuring explanation weight based on their contribution and suppression effects on the model's predictions.

Evaluating faithfulness meets the NIST's XAI principles in assessing an XAI system's ability to produce justifiable explanations and uncover knowledge limits. An explanation is considered faithful if the identified important features genuinely contribute to a model's prediction.

Figure 9.3 is a Venn diagram of faithfulness, encompassing feature importance correlation and polarity consistency:

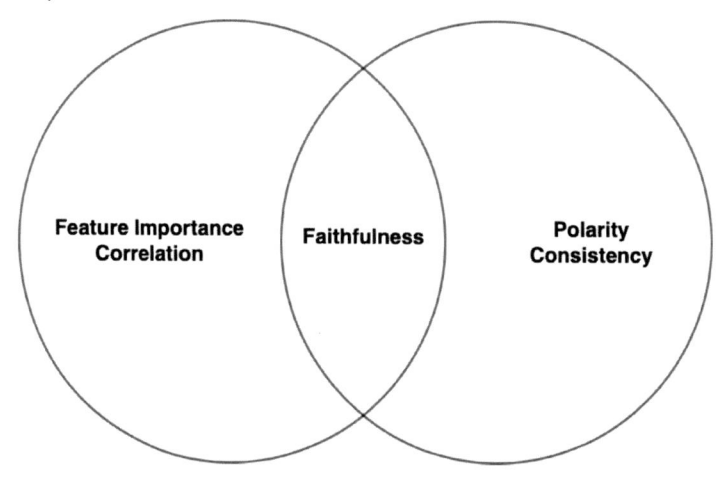

Figure 9.3 – Faithfulness Venn diagram

In contrast, **monotonicity** in XAI evaluates feature attribution by adding pre-defined important features incrementally to validate feature relevance. The expectation is that model performance should increase gradually as important features are added incrementally. *Figure 9.4* compares faithfulness versus monotonicity in XAI evaluation:

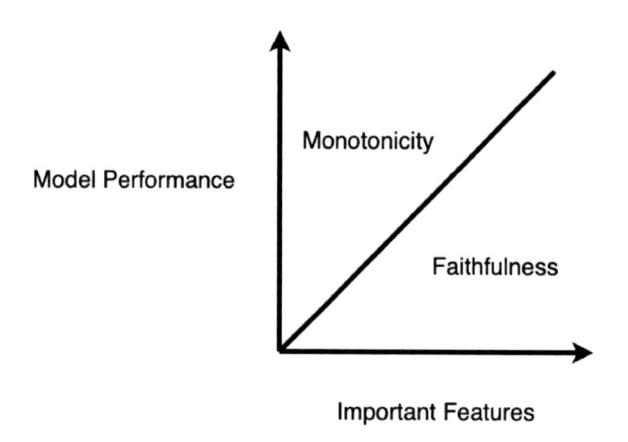

Figure 9.4 - Faithfulness versus monotonicity

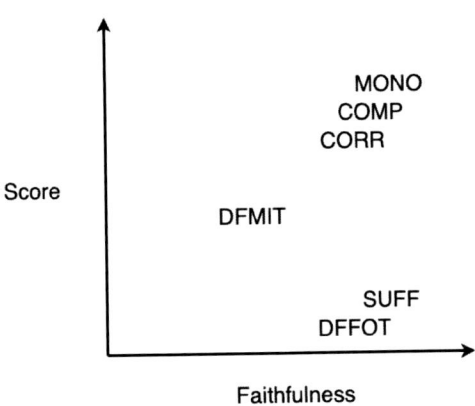

Figure 9.5 shows a plot for visualizing various metrics in quantifying the extent of faithfulness for an explanation:

Figure 9.5 – Faithfulness metrics

Let's understand what each faithfulness metric represents and its scale in quantifying faithfulness:

- **Decision Flip – Most Informative Token (DFMIT)**: This measures faithfulness between 0 and 1. A score of 1 means the explanation is faithful. An explanation is faithful if it demonstrates valid reasoning for a model's prediction. For example, measuring faithfulness in **natural language processing** (NLP) using DFMIT is done by observing the average percentage in a model's decision flips after removing the highly important token from the test dataset.

- **Decision Flip – Fraction of Tokens (DFFOT)**: Here, the lower the DFFOT value, the more faithful it is to an explanation. Like DFMIT, instead of removing the highly important token as a whole, DFFOT observes the percentage of decision flips by measuring the minimum fraction or threshold of important features to be removed that causes a change in the model's predictions.

- **Comprehensiveness (COMP)**: This measures an explanation's faithfulness based on the representation and distribution of important features. A COMP score is calculated based on the change in output probability due to important feature removal. To test an explanation's comprehensiveness, create a contrasting example and remove the predicted rationale or known important feature. The new predicted probability should decrease since the known rationale has been removed. The difference between the original and new predicted probability yields the COMP score. The higher the COMP score, the more faithful it is to an explanation.

- **Sufficiency (SUFF)**: This measures faithfulness by evaluating whether important features contain sufficient information to retain the original prediction. SUFF augments COMP by assessing the continuous importance of a feature to the model. For example, removing a subset of known influential tokens or phrases from an NLP classifier should cause a change in the new predicted probability. SUFF measures the average percentage change in this classifier, starting with retaining the top 5% of known important features, then incrementally until there is a change in the model's prediction. A lower SUFF score indicates a more faithful explanation.

- **Correlation between Importance and Output Probability (CORR)**: Here, an explanation is considered faithful if the feature importance and predicted probability are positively correlated as the important features are incrementally removed. A higher correlation value indicates a more faithful explanation.

- **Monotonicity (MONO)**: Starting with an empty vector, observe the change in classification probability after adding features incrementally. An explanation is faithful whether the probability of the predicted class increases monotonically with the feature addition. A higher monotonicity value indicates a more faithful explanation.

We have covered several XAI metrics to evaluate the faithfulness of explanations by isolating the impacts of model features and observing model simulatability. These XAI metrics help capture intuition on how explanations can improve model interpretability and a user's understanding of the model's behavior. However, choosing the appropriate XAI metrics is crucial to ensure a model's trustworthiness with justifiable rationale.

The following section explores how the human-grounded evaluation framework enables quantitative analysis of human reasoning in ML-generated explanations.

Human-grounded evaluation framework

Explanations are practical and helpful when they enable the target audience to build a mental representation of model behavior and grasp the inferential process. The target audience encompasses end users without domain knowledge and expert users who can provide informed feedback.

Measuring human simulatability is essential to evaluate the extent of a person's understanding of an ML model behavior. There are two types of human simulatability:

- **Forward simulation**: A human predicts a model's output based on a given input. For example, ask a user to estimate house prices given a specific zip code.

- **Counterfactual simulation**: Given an input and output, a human predicts a model's output or makes a causal judgment if the input is different. For example, ask a user to predict if they will miss a flight if they arrive 20 minutes earlier at the airport.

Simulating model prediction from end users provides insights into inaccurate model predictions based on unusual or irrelevant features. Alternatively, users can interact with XAI systems and provide feedback through survey mechanisms such as the SCS Likert scale questionnaire on whether they gain any insights from the XAI system by the end of the trial period.

Accurate and meaningful XAI explanations should support model debugging. Expert users, such as data scientists, can provide feedback on whether machine-generated explanations help identify gaps and improve model performance.

The human-grounded evaluation benchmark, `https://doi.org/10.48550/arXiv.1801.05075`, evaluates local explainability by asking human annotators to annotate images and manually capture salient features for specific classes. This approach summarizes an average human representation or interpretation of an explanation using a weighted explanation map by comparing human subjective ratings to ground-truth single-layer segmentation masks. Although the human-grounded evaluation benchmark provides a more granular evaluation of salient features, the result shows limitations due to inherent bias in human attention to certain features.

Summary

After reviewing XAI evaluation schemes and benchmarking metrics in this chapter, you now understand how to analyze qualities of explanations based on NIST's fundamental XAI principles.

This chapter brings us to the end of the book. Thank you for staying with me through the journey to explore various XAI topics. We studied XAI's challenges, opportunities, and significance in deep learning anomaly detection. You learned about building explainable deep learning models in detecting anomalies in NLP, time series, and computer vision by integrating theory and practice throughout the book. You now understand how to quantify and assess model explainability to meet regulatory compliance and mitigate bias to ensure fairness and ethical analysis.

As we often hear, correlation does not imply causation. It is challenging to identify causality based on observations without performing controlled experiments. XAI systems aim to facilitate reasoning in ML algorithms and hold organizations accountable for AI-assisted high-stakes decision-making such as medical diagnosis, credit applications, and criminal justice.

With competing priorities in a multidisciplinary XAI field, domain experts must choose appropriate evaluation schemes using mathematical or human-subject evaluations based on different requirements. For example, the computer vision community is interested in visualizing the inner workings of complex models, while **human-computer interaction** (HCI) researchers focus on user trust and interpretability.

Earning trust takes thought, dedication, and time. Trust is also easy to lose and difficult to re-establish. Firms must carefully analyze data sources, proactively identify outliers, provide traceability, and communicate and manage algorithmic limitations to ensure diversity and inclusiveness when defining their AI governance model.

I hope you can apply what you have learned to achieve a balance between model accuracy and interpretability. It is still day 1 in this emerging field. All the best in your future learning about XAI.

Index

A

adaptive path method (APM) 172
advanced persistent threat (APT) 22
Amazon SageMaker Clarify 172
anomalies
  collective anomaly 4
  contextual anomaly 5
  point anomaly 4
  types 4-12
anomaly detection problem 81
  solution 81
anomaly detection techniques
  semi-supervised anomaly detection 24
  supervised anomaly detection 24
  unsupervised anomaly detection 24
Article 12 37
  reference link 37
Article 15 37
  reference link 37
Article 22 37
  reference link 37
Artificial Intelligence (AI) 123, 181
AutoEncoder architecture
  code 14
  decoder 14
  encoder 14

AutoGluon 44, 154, 155
  overview 45-56
  reference link 45
  with Kernel SHAP 155-171
automated machine learning (AutoML) 44
automated teller machine (ATM) 79

B

backpropagation 136
backpropagation explainability
  reviewing 136
  saliency maps 137-141
backpropagation XAI
  versus perturbation XAI 151
BAM feature attribution methods
  input dependence rate (IDR) 185
  input independence rate (IIR) 185
  model contrast score (MCS) 185
Benchmarking Attribution Methods (BAM)
  exploring 183, 184
bidirectional encoder representations
  from transformers (BERT) 56

C

CAM
   reference link 102
Cleanlab 44
CNN architecture
   convolutional layer 102
   fully-connected layer 102
   pooling layer 102
collective anomaly 4
computer vision anomaly explainability
   problem 104
   requisites 103
   solution 104-119
contextual anomaly 5
convolutional neural networks (CNNs) 125, 135
counterfactual simulation 188

D

DeepExplain
   reference link 151
deep learning 23-25
   architecture 24
deep learning anomaly detection
   challenges and opportunities 25, 26
   forecasting-based models 80
   for time series 79, 80
   hybrid models 80
   reconstruction-based models 80
deep learning anomaly detection life cycle 34
   business problem phase 34
   data preparation phase 34
   explainability phase 35
   feature engineering phase 34
   model deployment phase 35
   model development phase 34
deep learning model
   sliding window 80
   timestep 80
deep neural network (DNN) 126
deep visual anomaly detection
   integrating, with XAI 102

E

electrocardiogram (ECG) 5, 79
explainability 31
   versus interpretability 31
Explainable AI Toolkit (XAITK) 29
   URL 29
Explainable AI (XAI) systems 181
Explainable Artificial Intelligence (XAI) 22
   as multidisciplinary field 29
   basics 28
   deep explanation 29
   evaluating 29
   explainability, versus interpretability 31
   future state 33
   implementing 33-36
   interpretable models 29
   model induction 29
   motivations 29, 30
   significance, reviewing 36
   stakeholder needs, contextualizing 32, 33
explainable artificial intelligence (XAI) methods
   selecting 178, 179
explainable artificial intelligence (XAI) techniques 136

F

faithfulness 185, 186
faithfulness metric
  comprehensiveness (COMP) 187
  Correlation between Importance and Output Probability (CORR) 188
  Decision Flip - Fraction of Tokens (DFFOT) 187
  Decision Flip - Most Informative Token (DFMIT) 187
  monotonicity (MONO) 188
  sufficiency (SUFF) 187
forecasting-based models 80
forward simulation 188

G

GDPR articles examples, XAI
  Article 12 37
  Article 15 37
  Article 22 37
General Data Protection Regulation (GDPR) 26
generalized linear models (GLMs) 125
global explainability 30
gradient-weighted Class Activation Mapping (Grad-CAM) 185
  reference link 103
graphics processing units (GPUs) 25
guided backpropagation 185
  using 137
Guided Integrated Gradients (Guided IG) 172
  saliency, interpreting with 173-178

H

human-grounded evaluation framework 188, 189
  reference link 189
hybrid models 80

I

image-level visual anomaly detection
  examples 100, 101
  reviewing 100, 101
in-processing XAI techniques 36
input dependence rate (IDR) 185
input independence rate (IIR) 185
Internet of Things (IoT) 21
interpretability 31
  versus explainability 31
Interpretable ML 123
intrinsic global explainability 125
intrinsic explainability 123, 125
  versus post hoc explainability 133
intrinsic local explainability 125, 126
intrusion detection systems (IDSs) 22

K

Keras 154
Kernel SHAP 155, 172
k-nearest neighbors (KNN) 8, 100
knowledge distillation 125

L

Least Absolute Shrinkage and Selection Operator (LASSO) 125
local explainability 30

local interpretable model-agnostic
    explanations (LIME) 141-155
  LimeImageExplainer 141
  LimeTabularExplainer 141
  LimeTextExplainer 142
LSTM model
  creating, for anomaly detection in
    time series dataset 81-96

M

machine learning (ML) 13
  approaches 100
  models 123
magnetic resonance imaging (MRI) 22
Matplotlib 154
Mean Absolute Error (MAE) 87
ML model
  accuracy, versus interpretability 30
  fully interpretable models 30
  partially interpretable models 30
model-agnostic explainability
  reviewing 154, 155
model-agnostic XAI methods 154
model contrast score (MCS) 185
model-specific explainability
  reviewing 172
model-specific XAI methods 172
monotonicity 186
MoveColumn 154
multilingual natural language
    understanding (NLU) 73
multivariate time series 78
MXNet 154

N

National Institute of Standards and
    Technology (NIST) 181
National Oceanic Atmospheric
    Administration (NOAA) 23
Natural Language Processing
    (NLP) 30, 43 45, 187
  Venn diagram 44
neural machine translation (NMT) 125
neural network 23
New York Stock Exchange (NYSE) 23
NLP anomaly explainability
  problem 56
  solution 57-72
Numenta Anomaly Benchmark (NAB)
  reference link 96
NumPy 154

O

one-class classification (OCC) 101
One-Class Convolutional Neural
    Network (OC-CNN) 101

P

pandas 154
perturbation explainability
  LIME 141-150
  reviewing 141
perturbation XAI
  versus backpropagation XAI 151
Pillow 154
pixel-level visual anomaly detection
  reviewing 101
point anomaly 4
polarity 185

Index

post hoc global explainability 126
post hoc explainability 123, 126
  versus intrinsic explainability 133
post hoc local explainability 126-133
post-processing XAI techniques 36
pre-processing XAI techniques 36
PyOD
  reference link 5

R

real-world use cases
  cybersecurity threats, monitoring 22
  discovering 12
  environmental impact, reducing 23
  financial strategies, recommending 23
  fraud detection 13-21
  industrial maintenance prediction 21
  medical conditions, diagnosing 22
reconstruction-based models 80
region of interest (ROI) 133, 140
Return on Investment (ROI) 39

S

saliency 154
  interpreting, with guided integrated gradients 173-178
saliency maps 137-141
Scikit-learn 154
semantic monotonicity constraints 125
semi-supervised anomaly detection 24
SHapley Additive exPlanations (SHAP) 44, 154
Shapley values 155
sparsity 125
stakeholder
  needs, contextualizing 32

supervised anomaly detection 24
System Causability Scale (SCS)
  reviewing 182, 183
System Usability Scale (SUS) 182

T

t-distributed stochastic neighbor embedding (t-SNE) 55
TensorFlow 154
text classification 45
TextPredictor 46
time series 77, 78
  anomaly detection problem 81
  components 79
  cyclical fluctuation 79
  deep learning anomaly detection 79, 80
  irregular variation 79
  LSTM model, creating for anomaly detection 81-96
  measurements 78
  multivariate time series 78
  seasonal variation 79
  secular trend 79
  univariate time series 78

U

univariate time series 78
unsupervised anomaly detection 24
unsupervised pixel-level approaches
  feature modeling 101
  image reconstruction 101

V

vanilla gradient descent 185
visual anomalies assessment
  image-level 100
  pixel-level 100
visual anomaly detection
  image-level visual anomaly detection, reviewing 100
  pixel-level visual anomaly detection, reviewing 101
  reviewing 100

W

World Economic Forum
  reference link 38

X

XAI. *See* **Explainable Artificial Intelligence (XAI)**
  deep visual anomaly detection, integrating with 102
XAI approaches, for ML model building
  examples 35, 36
  in-processing XAI techniques 36
  post-processing XAI techniques 36
  pre-processing XAI techniques 36
XAI motivations
  business interests 29
  model debugging 29
  regulatory compliance 29
  social trust 29
  user interests 29
XAI significance
  business risks, mitigating 39
  reviewing 36
  right to explanation, considering 36, 37
  social impacts 37, 38
XAI stakeholder personas
  auditors 32
  data scientists 32
  end users 32
  industry experts 32
  research scientists 32
XAI techniques
  data modalities, identifying 39
  scope of explainability, analyzing 39
  selecting 39, 40
  stakeholders, analyzing 39
  success criteria, determining 40
  XAI algorithms, selecting 40

‹packt›

www.packtpub.com

Subscribe to our online digital library for full access to over 7,000 books and videos, as well as industry leading tools to help you plan your personal development and advance your career. For more information, please visit our website.

Why subscribe?

- Spend less time learning and more time coding with practical eBooks and Videos from over 4,000 industry professionals
- Improve your learning with Skill Plans built especially for you
- Get a free eBook or video every month
- Fully searchable for easy access to vital information
- Copy and paste, print, and bookmark content

Did you know that Packt offers eBook versions of every book published, with PDF and ePub files available? You can upgrade to the eBook version at www.packtpub.com and as a print book customer, you are entitled to a discount on the eBook copy. Get in touch with us at customercare@packtpub.com for more details.

At www.packtpub.com, you can also read a collection of free technical articles, sign up for a range of free newsletters, and receive exclusive discounts and offers on Packt books and eBooks.

Other Books You May Enjoy

If you enjoyed this book, you may be interested in these other books by Packt:

Modern Time Series Forecasting with Python

Manu Joseph

ISBN: 978-1-80324-680-2

- Find out how to manipulate and visualize time series data like a pro
- Set strong baselines with popular models such as ARIMA
- Discover how time series forecasting can be cast as regression
- Engineer features for machine learning models for forecasting
- Explore the exciting world of ensembling and stacking models
- Get to grips with the global forecasting paradigm
- Understand and apply state-of-the-art DL models such as N-BEATS and Autoformer
- Explore multi-step forecasting and cross-validation strategies

Production-Ready Applied Deep Learning

Tomasz Palczewski, Jaejun (Brandon) Lee, Lenin Mookiah

ISBN: 978-1-80324-366-5

- Understand how to develop a deep learning model using PyTorch and TensorFlow
- Convert a proof-of-concept model into a production-ready application
- Discover how to set up a deep learning pipeline in an efficient way using AWS
- Explore different ways to compress a model for various deployment requirements
- Develop Android and iOS applications that run deep learning on mobile devices
- Monitor a system with a deep learning model in production
- Choose the right system architecture for developing and deploying a model

Packt is searching for authors like you

If you're interested in becoming an author for Packt, please visit `authors.packtpub.com` and apply today. We have worked with thousands of developers and tech professionals, just like you, to help them share their insight with the global tech community. You can make a general application, apply for a specific hot topic that we are recruiting an author for, or submit your own idea.

Share Your Thoughts

Now you've finished *Deep Learning and XAI Techniques for Anomaly Detection*, we'd love to hear your thoughts! Scan the QR code below to go straight to the Amazon review page for this book and share your feedback or leave a review on the site that you purchased it from.

`https://packt.link/r/1-804-61775-X`

Your review is important to us and the tech community and will help us make sure we're delivering excellent quality content.

Download a free PDF copy of this book

Thanks for purchasing this book!

Do you like to read on the go but are unable to carry your print books everywhere? Is your eBook purchase not compatible with the device of your choice?

Don't worry, now with every Packt book you get a DRM-free PDF version of that book at no cost.

Read anywhere, any place, on any device. Search, copy, and paste code from your favorite technical books directly into your application.

The perks don't stop there, you can get exclusive access to discounts, newsletters, and great free content in your inbox daily

Follow these simple steps to get the benefits:

1. Scan the QR code or visit the link below

    `https://packt.link/free-ebook/9781804617755`

2. Submit your proof of purchase.
3. That's it! We'll send your free PDF and other benefits to your email directly

Made in the USA
Middletown, DE
04 April 2023